THE VONNE at VIVONNE

Susan B. Chaffee
3343 Monterey Avenue
Davis, CA 95616

D1602047

FRENCH LEAVE Favourites

Richard Binns

Drawings & maps by the author
Watercolours by Denis Pannett

CHILTERN HOUSE

For
my readers
in appreciation of their unflagging interest,
constructive criticism and endless support.

Like its predecessor, *Hidden France*, sales of this first Chiltern House edition of *French Leave Favourites* will be limited. Total sales in this case however will be restricted to less than 20,000 copies.

Watercolours by Denis Pannett. *Honfleur* is reproduced with the permission of Dr and Mrs P. B. Capstick.

If you would like a set of Denis Pannett's eight watercolours (same size but unbacked and printed on heavy white card) send £3.95 ($9) to him at his home: 'Heathers', 1 Woodlands Drive, Beaconsfield, Bucks HP9 1JY. Please make cheques payable to D. Pannett.

Also published at the same time as this new book is my *En Route: The French Autoroute Guide*, a Corgi Original. It's a unique guide with over 300 maps, showing facilities available at nearly 400 autoroute exits. See page 15 for further details.

Copies of *Bon Voyage* – French Menus Made Easy – are available from Chiltern House Publishers Ltd., Chiltern House, Amersham Road, Amersham, Bucks HP6 5PE, at the special price of £1.25 or $5 (normally £1.95) per copy – post and packing free of charge. *Bon Voyage*, a 96-page pocket book, is an extract of all the culinary information from the *French Leave* series and is an excellent complement to this new title.

Any reader wishing to have advance information of my further publishing ventures – including perhaps, sometime in the near future, a periodical 'mapoholics' newsletter – should send their name and address to me at Chiltern House Publishers Ltd., as above.

© Richard Binns 1986 (Text, Maps and Pencil and Ink Drawings)
Published by Chiltern House Publishers Limited, Chiltern House, Amersham Road, Amersham, Bucks HP6 5PE
ISBN 0 9507224 9 9
All rights reserved. No part of this publication may be reproduced, stored in a retrieval system, or transmitted, in any form or by any means, electronic, mechanical, photocopying, recording or otherwise, without the prior permission of the copyright owner.

Editing assistance: Jane Watson
Cover design by Frank and Shirley Clancy, Clan Creative Limited, 22 Hollow Way Lane, Chesham Bois, Amersham, Bucks HP6 6DP
Typeset in Korinna by Art Photoset Limited, 64 London End, Beaconsfield, Bucks HP9 2JD
Printed by Butler & Tanner Limited, Frome, Somerset BA11 1NF

ABBREVIATIONS

category	see notes on right-hand side of this page
menus	range of cost of fixed-price menus or, if these are not available, the minimum cost of three courses from the à la carte menu
rooms	number of bedrooms and price band range (inclusive price for **the room** but breakfast not included). Establishments are obliged by law to offer bedrooms without demanding that clients dine in their restaurants
cards	accepted: A – Access (Eurocard); AE – American Express; DC – Diners Club; V – Visa. Check ahead
closed	annual and weekly dates of closing. Check ahead
post	local post code, village or town name, *département*
phone	telephone number (area codes of the past are now incorporated in all French telephone numbers)
Mich	Michelin '200' series map number on which recommendation is located. These maps are strongly recommended
map	numbered location of recommendation on either of the two maps of France on pages 4 and 6 – followed by the distance to the nearest big town

PRICE BANDS

A	50 to 100 Francs	**C**	200 to 350 Francs
B	100 to 200 Francs	**D**	Over 350 Francs

D2 & **D3** – multiply **D** by figure indicated. All price bands include service charges and taxes; wine is not included in meal price bands, nor are breakfasts included in room price bands. For *pension* terms write direct to establishment.

CATEGORIES

Please read the following notes carefully

For ease of reference *French Leave Favourites* is set out in the same regional order as *French Leave 3*.

Within each regional text recommendations are listed alphabetically by town or village names. Example:

Name of town/village   Name of hotel/restaurant

PEGOMAS   Le Bosquet

At the end of each entry, following the abbreviation *category*, readers will notice one of four different numbered classifications: **1**, **2(S)**, **2** and **3**. I used this form of classification for the first time in *Best of Britain* and I found it an extremely accurate method of categorising standards of cooking.

Category 1 These are 'base' hotels – nearly always *sans restaurant* (no restaurant) and invariably in a quiet location. Some may offer light evening meals but these are **not** recommended.

Category 2(S) Cooking will be simple and straightforward: **do not** expect marvels from the chef. The entry is a favourite for other reasons: often it is value-for-money; perhaps the site or attractive local terrain; or particularly friendly hosts.

Category 2 Cooking will range from an above-average level to an often excellent standard.

Category 3 These are recommendations where, in my opinion, cuisine is of the very **highest** standard; they include simple and luxury establishments and some chefs who have yet to win a Michelin star. Nine entries are particularly recommended – the homes of some of Europe's most talented chefs. These are highlighted by a ★ placed immediately after the figure **3**: in addition, the index on pages 5 and 7 also shows the ★ by the establishment's name.

3

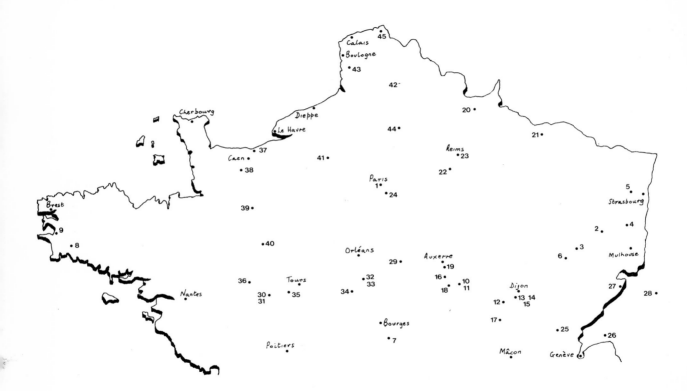

Calais •45
• Boulogne
•43
42
20 •
Cherbourg
Dieppe
Le Havre
44 •
21 •
Reims
Caen •37
41 • •23
22 • 5 •
38 • Paris Strasbourg
1•
•24 2 • •4
39 • •3
Brest 6 •
•9 Mulhouse
•8 •40
Orléans Auxerre
29 • •19
36 • 32 16 • 10 Dijon 27 •
Tours 33 18 • 11 •13 14 28 •
30 • •35 34 • 12 • 15
31 17 •
• Bourges •25
•7 •26
Poitiers Mâcon Genève •

4

CONTENTS

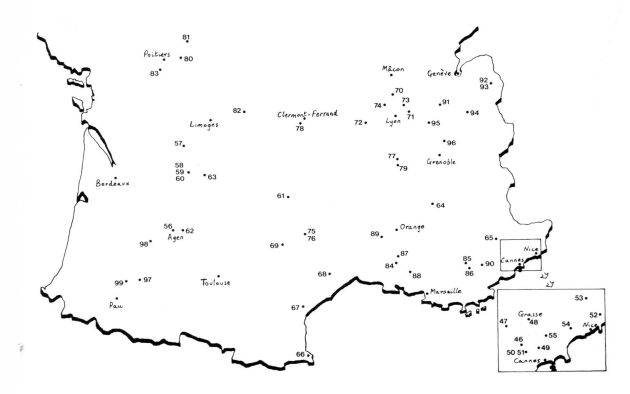

ODDS AND ENDS

Tim Heald, in his *Daily Telegraph* column, stressed how encouraging it is for any author to know 'that one is not always writing to an empty house.' Like all authors, Tim Heald is grateful to readers who take the time and trouble to write and share their numerous and varied memories with him.

How fortunate I have been in that respect. My annual postbag of readers' letters is close to one thousand and I calculate that, since I started my do-it-yourself publishing venture in 1980, nearly five thousand envelopes have dropped through the letterbox at Chiltern House, our Amersham home. What a pleasure it has been to get them all – and I think I can safely say that every reader who has written has had a reply from me.

Letters have been complimentary, constructive, critical and cynical! 'Feedback' has been amazingly varied – covering every subject under the sun: about the writers themselves; about France and Britain; about the French and the British; about people readers have met; about places – especially out-of-the-way spots – they have visited; and, above all, about the hotels and restaurants that readers have used. Every one of the 600 or more recommendations made in the three editions of *French Leave* has been the subject of some sort of feedback.

French Leave Favourites

This book is based upon those thousands of readers' letters. I estimate that each letter, on average, has contained reports on three or four hotel and restaurant visits. *French Leave Favourites* is a detailed account of readers' one hundred most liked hotels and restaurants – from the simplest to the greatest.

Every favourite has been revisited anew by me; not to review it critically but to establish why the hotel or restaurant has been so appreciated by readers. The common thread running through all favourites, from humble to great, lies in the personalities behind the establishments; a revelation that came as no surprise whatsoever to me. This book is about **people**.

I have never made any claim to be a skilful writer; my objective is to try to be accurate, enthusiastic and unflinchingly honest. (I have little time or respect for acerbic writers – by far the easiest form of writing I know. My 'sharp' contributions to this book come at the very end!) *French Leave Favourites* is the first book I have written where I would recommend readers to read all of it, or most of it, from cover to cover. I realise of course that no-one is likely to visit every single one of the hotels and restaurants listed within these pages. But the book covers far more ground than just reporting on bricks and mortar and on the owners of the various hotels and restaurants. I have included many different subjects – in the reports on the favourites themselves and in a score of additional chapters, written both by me and a handful of friends. The topics range from a visit to a typical French market to the story of one of the most poignant cemeteries in France; people, places, drives, regional wines, cheeses and specialities, Nature's delights, man-made treasures – from organs to quarries – and a great deal more; all find a place within the pages of this new book.

I have set out *French Leave Favourites* in the same regional order as *French Leave 3*. This will help those of you who have the latter book – the vast majority I would hope – and who wish to refer to the corresponding regional chapters within it. Even if you visit only one favourite in any one region, do try to read the other regional entries – as very often information included under one recommendation applies also to its near neighbours. For example, few of you may be able to visit the luxury Auberge des Templiers at Les Bézards in the Loire Valley — but all of you who travel that way should read the final paragraphs for the entry and then seek out the Maquis de Lorris memorial, deep in the Forêt d'Orléans; it's an inspiring spot.

In addition, do please read all the other chapters included within the regional sections and at the start and end of this book to discover all sorts of snippets of information.

Contributors

Like its predecessors, this new book is highly idiosyncratic. For the first time I have included several dozen of my own modest attempts at pencil (and in one case ink) drawings; earlier books had some tiny ink sketches. The extra glitter on the illustration front comes from the eight watercolours painted by my good friend and neighbour Denis Pannett. Other friends, too, have made their own personal contributions to *French Leave Favourites*; you can read about them in the chapter called *Contributors* at the start of this book (see page 20).

Feedback on hotels and restaurants

Readers' feedback falls into four categories: the first is where comment is 90 per cent or more complimentary — though it's true to say that every favourite, even the greatest, has been the subject of at least one serious unfavourable report; then there's a mass of establishments where letters bring a very mixed response — generally favourable but more than a few complaints as well; the third and largest category involves a relatively small number of readers' letters — recommendations making little impact one way or the other; and, finally, a very small number of hotels and restaurants where feedback is

On the D17, west of Châtillon – Lyonnais

9

mainly critical – including one three-star restaurant on the Côte d'Azur which I've yet to get a complimentary report about!

All the favourites within this book are members of the first type though one major surprise for me has been how few of Brittany's hotels are members of that special 'club'.

Do-it-yourself publishing

It's a high-risk business – particularly when your entire annual income comes from just one book each year. Any of you who bought the hardback edition of *Best of Britain* during the last two years will know that our 'samizdat' came desperately close to disaster in 1984. The *French Leave 3* Profit & Loss Account included in *Best of Britain* highlighted the numerous financial pitfalls lurking in the self-publishing jungle. We survived the setback and lived to fight another day; but, surprisingly, for the most ironical of reasons.

In the critical year that followed our setback, 1985, over 50 per cent of the books we sold (both *FL3* and *BofB*) were to 'non-book trade' outlets: buyers included tour and ferry companies, drug manufacturers, garage groups, hotels, restaurants and many others; most bought for promotional purposes. It's true to say that these sales were 'lifesavers'.

In 1986 additional financial help came from the publication by Corgi Books of high-quality paperback versions of *French Leave 3*, *France à la carte*, *Hidden France* and *Best of Britain*. Just as large publishers of hardback books sell 'rights' to paperback publishers, so Chiltern House did the same for the very first time; later I tell you why I made that decision. This proved to be an important step in our publishing story.

I'm told regularly, by both publishers and The Society of Authors, that I'm possibly the only person in the UK who researches, writes, finances, markets and distributes his own work – and depends on those activities for 100 per cent of his annual income! It never ceases to amaze me that this could be true; it really should not be so rare an achievement. The reasons are complex and this is not the place to analyse why our do-it-yourself venture is so unusual in British publishing. About 50 or so likely do-it-yourself authors have come out to Amersham over the years to quiz me on the pitfalls; perhaps about ten or so took the plunge and published their own work.

GB-plate ghettoes

In my travels around France, visiting every one of the *French Leave* favourites, I was pleasantly surprised how few of my readers I met. It was this that persuaded me to give Corgi Books the go ahead to publish their versions of my earlier books.

From time to time one reads in books and the press of places supposedly being 'GB-plate ghettoes'. I can understand any hotel situated along the Channel coast being occupied on any given night by predominantly British clients – particularly in the Pas-de-Calais. In the latter area the French or other Europeans are unlikely to be passing that way. But what I cannot understand is why critics can be so selfish in claiming that guidebooks to France are to blame for the gradual destruction of the charm and character of much that was sought after by the British on holiday.

One writer had this to say: 'The problem is clear. You find a quiet, attractive, uncrowded hotel – you praise it to the skies, and then it's no longer quiet and uncrowded.'

I don't agree. Hoteliers, everywhere, work like Trojans and if some do a really sterling job they deserve to be successful and to have their hotels **full**; (later on I write about some of the present-day pressures on French family hotels). If, as hoteliers or *cuisiniers*, they are exceptionally good they'll be known by the French, Germans, Dutch, Belgians, Americans – and the British! Consider a favourite hotel with say 15 bedrooms: when full it's likely to be occupied by a mixture of nationalities – with, at the most, four or five Anglo-Saxon couples. Are these critics saying that we, the visiting British, really only wish hotels to be half full – the owners surviving on severely depressed, or minimal profits?

Why should they? Businessmen readers will realise that any successful business (and why shouldn't hotels be included in that description) should run at, or near, full capacity. Why should hoteliers be thought of as 'different'? Are Anglo-Saxons the only nationality that hate seeing their fellows on holiday? One writer moaned: 'The last thing you want on the next table is an enthusiastic English francophile.'

Until the late summer of 1985 I had not received a single letter from any reader complaining about places I had recommended being full of Anglo-Saxons. Then several arrived. And, without exception, they complained about a handful of *FL3* hotels – all of which had been included in a newly-published book, hyped unmercifully by TV, where 100,000-plus copies were subsequently sold. That book, believe it or not, contained only 50 hotel recommendations – and 30 per cent of them were already *French Leave 3* entries. Considering the tens of thousands of alternative hotels and restaurants available in France it's statistically staggering to think that 15 of the 50 had been *FL3* entries!

All this leads me to another quite separate problem: how many copies of a book like *French Leave Favourites* should a publisher sell? You really are treating your readers with contempt if you give them no chance to book in at your recommendations. Bearing in mind what I said earlier I know that 100,000 copies and 50 recommendations do not make sense – and I'm not going to be guilty of such contempt.

Critics

Readers are my toughest critics. 'Abominable', 'hype', 'awful' and 'con' have been some of the more colourful descriptions applied to my books! However, 99 per cent of readers' criticisms are always constructive; in fact I've incorporated many of their best ideas within my various books.

Rarely has professional criticism been anything but constructive though occasionally one does get the rough end of the stick. In one case I discovered more about the critic himself than the subjects criticised. Paul Levy of *The Observer* reckons 'I can see no value in any of them' (my books). 'Nothing in them convinces me that he has the education, taste or judgement to set himself up as a critic. He is completely self-appointed and I can see no reason to take him seriously.'

Levy is a delicate soul with sensitive flesh; a twist of lemon juice sprinkled on his tail makes him snap. One lesson you learn early in life is that bully-boys can't take a dose of their own medicine: Levy's 'bite' came after I had a go at him about one of his regular 'deflating digs' at the British Michelin Guide. His hatred of the tyre men ('Fat Mich') is monumental: 'pig-headed silliness', 'bad judgement', 'best left in the car's glove box', 'abysmal', 'not even reliable as a guide to addresses and telephone numbers' (tinkle-tinkle – I hear breaking glass!) and 'worst of the lot' are typical of the barbs he has stuck into the backs of the Michelin inspectorate. Yet the UK catering trade considers it the best of the British guides!

Levy turns fact into fiction to justify his Michelin baiting. An example follows: 'John Burton-Race deserves his star even though Michelin boobed by giving it to him a week or so after he had moved from Summertown to his new conservatory premises' (Le Petit Blanc, Oxford) – described four months earlier as 'a vast conservatory that seats several times the number of guests they could formerly serve.' In fact numbers rose from 40 to 70 and the Michelin Guide went to press long before the contract for the new premises was signed! (By the time *FLF* is published John and Christine Burton-Race will have moved to a new base in the Chilterns.)

Cuisine moderne

That, conveniently, leads me on to the 'foodies' of this world. I hope you are not one of that precious breed who look for 'messages' and pretty 'pictures' on plates, 'themes' running through their meals; who dissect tastes like forensic scientists and who need to know the precise minutiae of just how a speciality is produced, second by second and step by step.

The great joy of *cuisine moderne* is its refreshing simplicity; common sense usually prevails though you still find many examples of what I call 'padded-cell' or 'punk' cooking. A great chef is both artist and scientist: long years of experience eventually qualify him or her to create work where simplicity and confidence are the keys but built on an essential base of skill. 'Enquire, encourage, enthuse and enjoy' should be the philosophy of all my readers. People matter most in 'common sense' cooking: a chef's personality influences his cuisine more than any other facet. (For years I've been grumbling about some aspects of modern cooking: baby food mush,

CHÂTEAU DU VAL

Château du Val, alongside one of many man-made Dordogne 'lakes' – Auvergne compulsive decorative 'additions' and idiotic marriages of ingredients are certain signs of 'padded-cell' cooking.)

I spent 25 years dealing with the complexities of, first, accounting and then, later, computing systems. The most joyful aspect of modern cooking is its simplicity: may *faites simple* long be the most important motto of all *cuisiniers*.

Self-taught chefs

Frédy Girardet in Switzerland, Raymond Blanc and Nico Ladenis in England, and Michel Bras and Michel Trama in France are among the world's most talented chefs. They have two things in common: all are self-taught and all of them have one hand in the cooking pot and the other hand in the ground!

The five are intelligent individuals – unable to accept any culinary practice just because it has always been so. They share the essential requirements for any great modern chef: enthusiasm, flair, hard work, a scientist's eye for detail and an inquisitive passion to find out how produce is cultivated. Despite their intuitive need to question every culinary tenet all five are loyal to the prime rules of common sense and good taste. There are scores of chefs who follow the same path; those who scorn modern-day ways have really failed to grasp why the culinary scene has dramatically changed.

Michelin 1934 and 50 years on

One of my most prized possessions is a copy of the 1934 Michelin Red Guide for France. What intriguing reading it makes – and how the culinary world has changed in 50 years. Did you know that three stars were awarded in 1934 to the simplest of hotels and restaurants? Barattéro at the Midi in Lamastre (one 'roof' for the hotel); Madame Bourgeois at her bistro in Priay (great news – the restaurant re-opened in '86:

pâté chaud, omble chevalier and loup braisé au Chablis – all can be savoured again); and André Pic at his Le Pin restaurant (two 'knives and forks') were just three examples.

Alas, Michelin's requirements have since changed – dramatically. Three stars today require luxury fittings, numerous staff and all the glamour that supposedly goes with so-called progress. How I wish 1934 attitudes still applied 50 years on. Consider Michel Trama at Puymirol as an example: he's one of France's most creative chefs – as talented as any three-star *cuisinier* – yet it's doubtful whether Michelin will award him a third rosette at his present restaurant. Why? Read the Puymirol entry; I think it's a great shame that 'trappings' should have anything to do with culinary accolades.

If you want to spot how culinary trends have changed, all you need do is to flick through the pages of both the 1934 edition and today's version: *truites, gratin de queues d'écrevisses, coq au vin, escargots, grenouilles, quenelles, poulets, volailles, filets de sole* and a dozen or so other classics pepper the pages of the '34 edition. *Cuisine moderne*, based on scores of different raw materials, has thousands of interpretations; the Michelin inspectors of the '30s must have had ox-like constitutions to cope with all that flour, butter and cream.

Readers will be interested to know how severely Michelin used their guillotine in 1985/86 on two-star restaurants. If you read the entries in *FL3* for the Paris at Moulins, the Poste at Avallon, L'Escale at Varces, La Bonne Etape at Château-Arnoux, Meissonnier at Les Angles, Host. du Château at Fère-en-Tardenois, Aub. de Noves at Noves and Aub. Bressane at Bourg-en-Bresse you'll not be surprised to hear that all of them lost their second stars. Chapon Fin, at Thoissey, lost its second star a year earlier – as did Les Santons at Grimaud (both entries were dropped from *FL3*) and the Manoir d'Hastings at Bénouville, too.

France's hotels: love them or hate them

There's a special appeal about France's simpler hotels which is sometimes hard to put one's finger on. For me, like the majority of readers, there's a willing acceptance of anything that is a little decrepit, of down-at-heel fittings, or horrendously-styled wallpapers and decorations, of cheap, tatty plumbing and lighting, of threadbare carpets and spongy beds. That's part of the fun at simpler French hotels. Remember, above all, what value for money they provide. But, for some readers, it's all too much to swallow – for them it's much too difficult to come to terms with such down-to-earth appeal. What a shame.

French 'privies' are an especially enjoyable subject – guaranteed to give you a laugh whenever you get off the beaten track. Toilets where it's impossible to sit down and close the door at the same time; bathrooms where tubs are shoehorned into unbelievably small spaces – one I know of fits a tunnel-like space, five feet by two feet, with the taps at the far end; washbasins so tiny that you flood the floor when you wash in them; jammed 'snorkel' taps where you're liable to break your nose as you bend over; electrical plugs of every permutation imaginable; towels the size of teacloths; and showers which either scald or freeze. I've had some marvellous laughs at the expense of French 'privies' over the years.

I hope readers realise the tremendous pressures that French family hoteliers have to endure these days. Price freezes and Government-imposed price rise restrictions have been two common hazards; an ever-decreasing French clientele is another – austerity has seen to that; but the worst menace is the mushrooming growth of newly-built, 'budget' hotels sprouting up everywhere – owned by the likes of Ibis, Climat de France, Campanile, Fimotel, Balladins and other chains. The resulting pressure on already non-existent profits makes it all but impossible to refurbish old buildings and facilities.

Brickbats and Boos

Smoking in French restaurants is a national scandal. I've yet to meet a chef in France who has the courage to ban smoking completely in his dining rooms. It's quite unbelievable that restaurateurs and chefs, who spend so much energy on creating superb specialities, should then allow clients to spoil it for others by letting them indulge in non-stop smoking orgies.

Breakfasts are now more often than not a joke in France. It's by far the most common grumble from readers – and it applies to many of the favourites, too. The quality of bread is often an insult; 'toast' is the norm – served to hide the fact that bread is stale. And why have vegetables disappeared from French restaurants? This is the land where the range and quality of vegetables is legendary – yet you see few of them in many restaurants. The potato is all but dead, too. Yes, plenty of *pommes frites* in cafés – but regularly one sees no spuds at all, and perhaps only one veg, in most restaurants.

Soups seem to have gone out of fashion; French lamb and desserts too, are often an insult. Food out of bags, *pâtés* out of tins and commercial sweets are regularly served at even the simplest restaurants. Wines are murdered – most drunk too young or served too cold; or, alternatively, white wines that come with no means of keeping them cool! And how I wish hotels would keep to the new French law which requires them to offer accommodation without the need for the occupants to eat in the restaurant – many of you have complained about this: the Blots at Fère-en-Tardenois are the worst culprits – adding more 'inkstains' to their already poor record.

Other boos include the disgraceful habit of selling hard-porn books at French autoroute service stations; the early-morning antics of refuse collectors emptying dustbins; lorry drivers who refuse to wave one on when the coast is clear – compare them with their British cousins; the racket created by church clocks during the night; and the annual slaughter of birds during the winter months; all are just a few examples of personal hates.

I made a habit during my travels in France of asking French hoteliers which nationality they disliked most amongst their clients. The unanimous answer? Their own countrymen!

Other books

Appearing at the same time as this book is my *En Route: The French Autoroute Guide* – published by Corgi. It's a unique, inexpensive guide, invaluable for any motorist travelling in France. It has nearly 400 French autoroute exits, personally researched and mapped by me, displayed on 300 maps: each one of which identifies a **selection** of the nearest hotels, restaurants, garages, banks, supermarkets, camping sites, chemists, petrol stations, public telephones, post offices, car parks, police stations, hospitals, tourist information offices and general shopping areas. The research for the autoroute guide and this new book was done at the same time – over an eighteen-month period. I completed the entire project right up to the 'camera-ready copy' stage; it proved to be a mind-boggling exercise – a clear case of a masochist mapoholic madman at work!

Bits and pieces

There should have been two additional entries in this book: Guy Tricon and Jean André at Tours (they moved there after their spell at Mouans-Sartoux); and Bernard and Martine Morillon at Montmerle-sur-Saône. Both were huge favourites. I visited the two restaurants in 1985 but shortly before I went to press I discovered they had sold their establishments to new owners and were uncertain of their future plans.

What of other places that came close to being included? Firmin Arrambide, an old favourite of mine, was a possible candidate but, alas, a few too many complaints ruined his chances of being included. Michel Guérard was a favourite; but he failed to answer no less than three of my letters in which I set out what my plans and requests were. I can only assume he has so much business these days that being included in this new book was of no interest to him whatsoever.

Of the smaller, more modest hotels and restaurants several are worth mentioning: the remote Auberge des Montagnes at Pailherols, the pretty Relais Fleuri at Molles, the Parc 'base' hotel at Sancoins, Les Grillons at Talloires, the Relais de l'Armagnac at Luppé-Violles; and many others came close to being included. Use *FL3* to complement this new guide.

I'm often asked about my Paris favourites. For 'base' hotels I use Regent's Garden (17e) and the Résidence du Bois (16e and expensive) on the right bank; the Suède and De Varenne (both 7e) on the left bank. Restaurants? Try not to miss the incomparable Robuchon at Jamin, the young stars of the future – Guy Savoy and Michel Rostang – and Le Divellec, a favourite of readers in his La Rochelle days.

Bon Voyage! Happy motoring and enjoy France.

ODETTE

Many readers will already know the 'Odette' story; they may have read the book, *Odette – The Story of a British Agent*, by Jerrard Tickell (Chivers Press), or, perhaps more likely, they will have seen the film in which the late Anna Neagle played the part of Odette Sansom (later Mrs Peter Churchill).

Within this book I make many references to the work of the French Resistance during the Second World War: the tragic story of the Vercors, the Maquis Bernard in the Morvan and the redoubtable patriots of the Sologne are three examples. But what should never be forgotten is the heroic work of the special agents who were sent to France during the dark days of 1941–45; those agents, British, French and others, men and women, linked up with the *maquis* and carried out the most hazardous of tasks (the Resistance patriots, fighting in the 'underground', took their name from the French word for 'scrub'). All of them were members of the French section of the Special Operations Executive (SOE) – led by the legendary Maurice Buckmaster.

Odette Sansom was born in Picardy in northern France and, of all the special agents, her story is perhaps the most famous. She landed at Cassis, east of Marseille, in October 1942 and, during the next six months, was involved in a number of operations with her Commanding Officer, 'Raoul' (Peter Churchill). Her initial activity was in a western suburb of Cannes – at La Bocca on the road to Pégomas. In early 1943 she and Raoul, together with 'Arnaud' (Captain Alec Rabinovitch), did some of their most important work in the Lake Annecy area.

Their base was at St-Jorioz, and Arnaud, the radio operator (a 'pianist'), did all his transmitting from the tiny hamlet of Les Tissots, in the hills above Faverges (see Faverges – Savoie). Before heading north for Lake Annecy, Raoul made one unsuccessful effort, in February 1943, to return by Lysander to London; this attempt, from an airfield near Périgueux (more of that later) nearly ended in disaster. In March he made it to London – returning by Lysander from a field near Compiègne, north of Paris. Flying to France by the same plane was a newcomer, 'Roger' (Francis Cammaerts), who immediately headed south for St-Jorioz; for the next 18 months this exceptionally brave Lieutenant-Colonel was to cause the Germans an immense number of problems.

Raoul returned to Annecy on April 15th, parachuting from a Halifax and landing on top of the Semnoz (see *Seductive Savoie*) where Odette and Arnaud, with the help of the *maquis*, had prepared the bonfires needed to identify the 6000-ft-high makeshift landing ground. Within hours both Odette and Raoul were captured by the Germans at St-Jorioz.

From mid April 1943 until early May 1945 Odette was imprisoned at Fresnes, south of Paris, and later at the horrific Ravensbrück Concentration Camp for Women in Germany. She was tortured brutally at Fresnes. She managed to persuade the Gestapo that she and Raoul were married and that he had come to France only because of her insistence; her charade was successful. She managed, too, to avoid giving the Gestapo the whereabouts of both Arnaud and· Roger. Her silence not only saved the officers' lives but, because of her bravery, both agents were able to continue their vital work. Her courage earned Odette the George Cross.

Denis Pannett, like myself, has a great interest in the work of the Resistance and the SOE. *Les femmes sont parfois volages*

Denis Parnett

Denis Parnett

is a brilliant attempt by Denis to capture the events of a bitterly freezing February night in 1943 when Raoul, Odette, Henri Frager ('Paul', a heroic and legendary Resistance leader), and his lieutenant Jacques Latour, were nearly captured by the Germans, near Périgueux in the Dordogne.

Maurice Buckmaster had instructed Raoul and Paul to return to London. The RAF identified a disused airfield ten kilometres east of Périgueux, near a village called Bassilac, where a Lysander could land and pick the two men up. (It amazes me, knowing the area well, that the field chosen should have been so close to such a large town.) The party of four accepted the instructions, reconnoitred the field and waited for the BBC call-sign, *les femmes sont parfois volages* (women are sometimes fickle), on their hastily set up radio. Even that simple action was fraught with danger as the 'listening' had to be done in an attic room of a hotel in the centre of Périgueux.

It turned out the field was not disused. As the Lysander was preparing to land, and only seconds before Raoul gave the plane the all-clear with his torch, an Aldis lamp flashed from the otherwise dark outbuildings on the southern edge of the supposedly deserted airfield. The buildings burst into life. A trap had been set – but it was sprung too early; if the Germans had waited one minute longer it would have spelt disaster for all concerned. As it was the Lysander didn't land and all four members of the group managed to escape back to Périgueux.

Francis Cammaerts built up a network of over 200 agents in south-east France. He played a part in the Vercors story (see *Vive le Vercors*) and made his escape from the plateau in July 1944 by wading across the Drôme – the river depicted in another of Denis' watercolours (opposite page 145).

A sleepy village near Arles – Provence

THE BOURNEMOUTH STORY

If any of you asked me what has given me most satisfaction since I started my do-it-yourself publishing venture, my answer would be: "The Bournemouth Story."

"What on earth is Binns on about," I can hear you impatiently grunt to yourself. I'll get on with the tale.

In *Best of Britain* I described in some detail the dramatic improvement in British culinary standards; in 1984 nothing gave me more pleasure than sampling the Renaissance for myself as I travelled around Britain. The British culinary 'sapling' is flourishing. Though it cannot be compared with the size of the French 'tree', nevertheless, its rapidly increasing strength and growth is going to be of vital importance to the country's finances when our disappearing oil revenues ensure that we will have a weaker sterling exchange rate and when the UK's balance of payments turns red in the years to come.

Our currently thriving tourist industry will become not only the nation's biggest but also our most profitable currency earner. Alas, today, many French people, and other Europeans, reckon British cooking to be a great joke; on my travels in France I spend a lot of time defending our culinary reputation. But one day the tables will be turned: it will be Britons who'll find France more expensive and the French will get the benefit of a weaker pound. (At the moment for every ten Britons crossing the Channel only one French citizen visits our islands.) Will our culinary standards be put to the test by the year 2000 and stand the critical attitudes of the French?

Surprising as it may seem there are dozens of top chefs in France who already know of our culinary Renaissance; indeed those very same *cuisiniers* are playing a significant part in nurturing the British culinary sapling and they're making sure that at least one branch of the young tree is going to grow into a really healthy limb. Let me explain.

Five years ago I provided, unwittingly, the catalyst for what is, today, a remarkable British culinary story. It's an amazing tale – a vivid demonstration of just what initiative, enthusiasm and determination can achieve.

On January 17, 1982, a feature I prepared called 'Three star eating at one star prices' appeared in a national magazine. For three lecturers at the Department of Catering at Bournemouth and Poole College of Further Education – Peter Taylor, David Boland and Tony Baylis – the article was a spark. Using a copy of *French Leave 1982/83*, which they bought in the week after the article appeared, they immediately set about contacting many of the chefs I had written about. What a bright fire burns today – ignited by that first spark five years ago.

Since that tentative start the Bournemouth College has built up a network of more than 40 French chefs, all of them willing to take young students for five months of industrial release training and also 'pay' them a sensible wage at the same time. The benefits of this building of culinary bridges are staggering: well over 200 students have now crossed the Channel since the three lecturers started to put in numerous hours of effort organising it all every year. Each chef is visited beforehand and every student is seen, *in situ*, during their training stints; in addition the youngsters' hosts send the college detailed performance reviews at the end of each course. 1986 saw 60 boys and girls off to France; the college now has more places available in French restaurants than students to fill them!

The youngsters return from France full of enthusiasm, innovative ideas and sound working habits – and all who stay the course (the failure rate has been very small) have had the priceless good fortune of being exposed at an early age to strict discipline, grinding hard work and superb skills. All but one or two of the students lose weight during their five-month stints and all of them most certainly grow up very fast indeed. Ninety per cent of the students who complete their courses are still working in catering two years later – as against the norm of 70 per cent who leave the industry in the same period.

It wasn't until the end of 1983 that I was told about the efforts of the college lecturers; naturally I was tickled pink to discover that I had played an indirect part in the setting up of this culinary network. During the last two years I have met many of the students, all teenagers by the way, and I've done my bit to ensure that even more French chefs join the 'operation'. I've been thrilled to meet the boys and girls in France. The students are dropped very much in the deep end; initially homesick, rarely knowing more than a few words of kitchen French, they are expected to work excruciatingly hard for very long hours. What has been so encouraging, too, is to hear their hosts' praise: the young Britons have been A1 ambassadors.

The youngsters return to Bournemouth after their five month training spells full of ideas: the results of their efforts are seen in the marvellous meals served in the college's two restaurants, particularly the evening *menu dégustation* dinners which are representative of what the students' hosts would serve in France. (It gave me great delight to include the restaurants in my *Best of Britain* guide published at the end of 1984.) It's a revelation, too, to see how the students have sharpened up the talents of their Bournemouth college tutors!

The boys and girls return home with amusing stories to tell: one for example who now knows how many times a copper pan can ricochet off kitchen walls when thrown at a speed of 60 m.p.h. by an irate chef; another discovered that suitcases float when flung into a nearby stream — again by a tempestuous hotel owner (not the student's case, I hasten to add); and others found that they had a talent for rowing when the Rhône burst its banks — it became their job to ferry clients from annexe to hotel. All of them have done sterling work in persuading French chefs that the staple UK diet is not just eating 'Big Macs' — a common belief in the French culinary trade.

Why did it become necessary for the college to seek out those additional new training grounds? Since 1976 — when the college courses started — many British-based chefs have made superhuman efforts to help Bournemouth students (and other colleges, too). Brian Turner, Richard Shepherd, Michel Bourdin, Anton Mosimann, Peter Kromberg and the Roux brothers are just a few who help as much as they can. But far too many hotel and restaurant chefs say "No." Why?

The latter are mortgaging the future of British culinary standards by accepting too readily YTS students (along with financial aid from the Government) before taking college students (who have to be paid over £70 a week); shame on them, especially some of the fancy up-market London hotels which are long on self-promoting chat and stuffing their tills with American dollars but short on practical support.

By the end of this century well over 1,000 students will have had a long training spell in French kitchens. Marry that with all the other changes taking place on the British culinary scene

RESTAURANT GIRARDET — CRISSIER

and we may yet see the day when our French neighbours start to do their bit to strengthen the *entente cordiale* here in Britain — and to give our cooks a chance to show off their skills.

It's not possible to list all the many *French Leave* recommended chefs who have helped the Bournemouth College — though I am anxious to identify those establishments within the pages of this book who have given of their time: Alain Rayé in Paris; Madame Le Coz at Ste-Anne-la-Palud; Solange Gardillou at Champagnac-de-Belair; Roland Mazère at Les Eyzies-de-Tayac; Michel Bras at Laguiole; Gilbert Laurent at Loué; Michel Trama at Puymirol; Didier Clément at Romorantin; Michel Chabran at Pont-de-l'Isère; Jerôme and Susan Bansard at Javron; Christian Germain at Montreuil; Pierre Carrier at Chamonix; Maurice Coscuella at Plaisance; and, finally, Jean-Pierre Capelle at Segos.

19

CONTRIBUTORS

There's one feature of *French Leave Favourites* that gives me great personal pleasure: the chance to include 'contributions' from several good friends of mine. Two of them live in France and the rest are neighbours; all have an interesting, different 'story' to tell. Five of the contributions appear in written form. The sixth takes the form of eight evocative Denis Pannett watercolours; specially commissioned, they provide a 'visual' story of the fascinating magic of France that appeals so much to all of us who live on this side of the Channel. Let me tell you a little about the various contributors.

Denis Pannett

Anne and I first fell in love with Denis' work over ten years ago when he lived a mile down the road at nearby Chesham and had just started to paint in his spare time, initially exhibiting his work both locally and in London. In those days he worked for De Beers in the City but his painting 'hobby' became so successful that he was soon able to become a full-time professional; in 1982 he took the plunge and started working for himself. What a risk he took but his brilliant talent has ensured that the fateful decision, made five years ago, proved to be a wise one. Like all of us who become self-employed he has had loyal support from his wife, Valerie — an essential prerequisite.

The Pannett family is an artistic one: both Valerie and Belinda, the couple's 13-year-old daughter, are skilful painters; Juliet, Denis' mother, is famous for her portrait paintings; Phoebe, Juliet's sister, is well known in the Sussex area for her watercolours and collages; and Elizabeth, Denis' sister, exhibits her modern art creations in the London area.

Denis' work is now regularly exhibited in the south-east of England. If any of you would like details or other information about his work, contact him at 'Heathers', 1 Woodlands Drive, Beaconsfield, Bucks HP9 1JY. Also see page 2.

R.H.N. Hardy

Richard has had a lifelong passion for trains. But in his case, unlike all of us who had childhood dreams of being train drivers (me included), he turned that fascination into reality. Now retired, Richard spent 42 years of his life working with trains, starting as an LNER apprentice fitter and finishing as a Divisional Manager, no less, with British Rail.

Richard is one of the most charismatic men I know. Apart from always being pleased to hear him talk of his great love, railways, I know of no other man who has such an instinctive feel for 'management'; he must have been a supreme manager — the epitome of just what is needed to motivate men through respect, enthusiasm, knowledge and, above all, fair play.

If any reader wants to know more about my good friend they can do no better than to read his two autobiographical books: *Steam in the Blood* and a second, *Railways in the Blood* — both published by Ian Allan. Richard and Gwenda are neighbours; retired or not, the couple are extremely active and Richard still keeps in touch with the numerous friends he made in France — all of whom have steam and railways in their blood, too!

Christine Starmer

Some readers will recognise Christine's name immediately: it appeared on the 'credits' page of *French Leave 3*. Christine has helped me with some of my books — ensuring that my French was accurate. She and David, her husband, are neighbours of ours and both teach at the local grammar school, Dr.

Challoner's. Christine was born in Brittany and is fluent in French, German and English; after living so many years here in England she now feels as much British as French!

Christine's contribution provides an insight into the sort of busy activity that goes on all the time in the background; it's this unseen effort at improving relationships between the French and British that, at the end of the day, does more than anything else to improve the *entente cordiale.*

Ray Hewinson & Peter Trotter
Ray and Peter are two members of the tiny Lacey Green (Bucks) community who have made such a success of the village's 'twinning' with Hambye in Normandy. Readers perhaps will not realise what hard work and effort is needed at local level to make twinning work; after all it's a voluntary exercise and, human nature being what it is, it's not always easy to get enough backing from a sufficient number of villagers, or townspeople in the case of bigger twinning ventures, to make it work. You'll find their contribution in the Normandy section.

Owen Watson
Every reader who visits the Loire Valley should ensure they seek out this contented, charming man – a publisher and lexicographer turned potter; his splendid contribution is a revealing, happy one. Let me explain how to find him: midway between Blois and Amboise, on the northern or right bank of the Loire, you'll find Mesland. Half a kilometre south of the village, on the D65 and on the western side of the road, you'll pass Owen's *'poterie'*, a cottage called Les Fraisiers.

What innovative work he produces: a combination of wood-firing using oak and silver birch from the Forêt d'Amboise, clay from St-Amand-en-Puisaye (west of Vézelay in Burgundy), ash from vine and apple tree trimmings, and talented skills. I defy anyone to leave Owen's small 'showroom' without buying something from his stunning display. See the Loire section.

Selwyn Powell
A delightful bit of writing graces the Southwest section of this book. Selwyn, now 74, is one of my most loyal readers and, on several occasions, I've had the pleasure of meeting him and his wife, Rosemary, deep in the heart of Gascony. I'm not surprised for a moment that they've made so many friends in their corner of France – they are the perfect example of just what makes many British people so respected the world over.

Selwyn's life has been an eventful one. The '30s saw him working for a spell as an assistant to Richard de la Mare at Faber & Faber followed, in 1937, by a short but memorable few months as Art Editor of *Night and Day*. Selwyn, together with Graham Greene and John Marks, was one of the founder members of that legendary weekly magazine. Have any of you seen the anthology published by Chatto & Windus?

In the '50s and '60s Selwyn was first the Executive Editor, under Michael Huxley (its founder), of *The Geographical Magazine* and later he succeeded him as editor. What an ironic twist of fate to think that *The Geographical Magazine* article I refer to in *Elephants, Mapoholics and Enthusiasms* should have been commissioned by Selwyn!

Finally, may I say a word about two friends and neighbours who have helped me right from the start: Jane Watson, a mother of four young children, has worked hard to make certain I don't make too many English 'howlers' and Frank Clancy, another francophile, has ensured that all my book 'covers' have had a professional look about them.

VAPORISTE ET TECHNICIEN   Richard Hardy

It is a warm summer evening in 1961 at Aulnoye in Northern France. Steam traction has nearly done on this section but tonight, André, René and I are going to draw wonderful work from our old locomotive, the S2, which has but a month to go before she is laid aside for ever. André, the *mécanicien*, is five foot tall, a little gold-toothed, pink-faced ball of fire of 48 who knew all about the Railway Resistance in the War, a marvellous driver, artistic in his use of the brake; René is one of the best of firemen, tall, strong, quiet and immensely experienced. *L'Equipe* Duteil/de Jongh come from the historic depot of La Chapelle, under the shadow of Montmartre.

I know the road so André motions me to take charge of the locomotive. It is hot in the cab but when we are moving the wind will freshen us up although the fire will become blindingly white, requiring constant attention over the enormous grate; our faces will soon be black with coal dust and certainly the bucket of water containing bottles of *citron* will be needed for we shall have to work very hard tonight.

We are away with a huge, packed train of 780 tonnes and the S2 soon gets into her stride. One does not need to press her with that load, but nevertheless, because we are late and time must be regained, we are going to reach our maximum permitted speed of 120 k.p.h. quickly and then hold it, uphill and downdale. This will need constant and careful adjustment of the controls and speed of firing, an intimate knowledge of the route, gradients and position of the signals, for in the left-hand corner of the cab, under my only lookout window, lies the speed recorder which tells me everything I want to know but

also charts our speed: *L'Espion* – the spy!

And now the light has gone, a wall of blackness lies ahead of the long boiler for no headlights probe the darkness: stations flash by, Le Cateau, Busigny, one's head outside in the wind to pick up, as soon as they appear, the green signals that beckon us on, our old engine tearing into it, René in his element, for we are living parts of our machine which depends on the skill and courage of its crew. We are in a world of our own, cut off from authority, from our passengers, from every living soul except those in distant places who control the signals.

We stop only once, at St-Quentin, running up the long platform as fast as possible to save a few seconds, for every little counts. On again into the night, Tergnier, Noyon, Compiègne and then, as we approach the great junction near Creil, first yellow, then red lights bar the way but the road clears as we pass slowly through the station. We have lost some of the time we regained from Aulnoye, so now the S2 is opened out to shoulder her load, thundering up the long rise, spitting sparks of defiance high into the sky. On through Chantilly, over the viaducts, she gradually accelerates to 100 k.p.h. before we reach the summit near Survilliers, passing under 'le pont de soupirs', momentarily illuminated by the open fire door. And now our work is done and we can spin silently, but ever vigilantly, down to Paris.

As we climbed through Chantilly, André had served a good Bordeaux, brought specially for the occasion. Having uncorked, tasted and approved the wine, very much at room temperature, we drank to the great days of steam and to our own good fortune. At length, we drew quietly to a stand in the Gare du Nord. We have covered 134 miles in 132 minutes and, as we looked down at the passing throng, we knew we had reached the end of an era.

And what lay ahead? 21 years later, we are in the Gare de Lyon with Roger, our *conducteur*, a man who knew not steam traction but who is dedicated to the TGV with which he will travel at up to 260 k.p.h. Whereas André stood at his work, in overalls, cap and scarf, Roger sits comfortably at his controls, brake to his left hand, power regulator in the centre, vigilance devices to his right. He wears a blue smock over smart but casual clothes. Whereas André and René looked outside their cab to sight signals in fog, wind or rain, Roger works in an air-conditioned silence, his vision unencumbered, each signal repeated on the panel in front of him, with an automatic power device to ensure speed limits are not exceeded. He can telephone the *poste de commandement* in Paris to report an incident at a speed of 260 k.p.h. and the *poste* can contact him at will. How utterly different this new world is: clinical, regulated, incredible, exciting – and fast! André was a *vaporiste* – Roger is very much a *technicien*.

By 1982, a TGV railway had been cut across France, a country where the railways are regarded as a national asset and treated accordingly: the new line was not completed until 1983, so our speed was limited to a mere 160 k.p.h. over the old line to St-Florentin. Roger had started quietly, almost imperceptably until the motion had become discernible, so different from the sonorous exhaust, the rotating parts and the hiss of steam. But once on the new line, he wound on the power, notch by notch, and one experienced the fantastic surge as speed mounted rapidly to 260 k.p.h., to be held effortlessly uphill and downdale. Gone was the anticipation needed to face an adverse gradient for the power is always there for the asking, drawn from overhead wires at 25,000 volts, enabling us to·climb gradients of 1 in 28 at about 200 k.p.h. – banks which would have reduced the S2 to a crawl. For this railway has been built as no other in the world – straight, long banked curves, sweeping gradients and but two stations between the Gare de Lyon in Paris and the city of Lyon itself.

The ride is perfect, conversation a simple matter, cab cool and clear, no draughts, no vibration, almost tame until one looks down or one passes another TGV at a combined speed of 520 k.p.h. But never for a moment does Roger's concentration waver: he may sit relaxed, calm, hand on the controller but, every 50 seconds, he must make a movement of some sort to defeat the ever watchful vigilance devices which, along with the 'deadman's' control, have the power to apply the brakes if he fails, momentarily, to acknowledge their existence. This is no place for a good Bordeaux!

Le Creusot, Mâcon, the only stations on the line, the latter passed at a full 260 and, at last, Lyon lies ahead. The air brake is applied inaudibly, almost invisibly, by two fingers of Roger's left hand and we come gently to a stand. We have come like a bat out of hell but you would never have believed it. By 1983 the new line was complete – 267 miles in two hours; a new world and, for the passengers, comfort, silence and freedom from the stress of high speed driving on France's A6 autoroute.

Roger will step down on arrival, clean and smart, will hang his smock in the locker and drive home to lunch but, on that night in 1961, it took André half an hour to wash and change before going home by train, tired and hungry. But he loved his work and he was proud to be known as a *gueule noire*.

23

BECASSINE EN GRANDE-BRETAGNE

Christine Starmer

When I arrived in England, at Christmas in 1968, it was the time when the Beatles were still very much at their peak, when enterprising young people were starting businesses and when qualifications didn't seem to matter too much as long as you were enthusiastic about what you were doing. Coming from France and having studied in Germany for two years, I was surprised to see the country run by all those long-haired youngsters. It was at the same time encouraging and worrying, but altogether it seemed a happy, trendy place.

I had problems getting a work permit because I had come as a 'tourist' but, once I had obtained it, and because there was a shortage of teachers, I was offered several posts straight away. When I went for my first interview at Burnham Grammar School I was so nervous that I arrived outside the school exactly an hour too early. Not wanting to venture too far out of the village I went to the nearest pub where I ordered a cup of tea. The lady laughed and said that tea wasn't served in pubs, but that I could try ginger beer. I loved it so much that a week later I got myself a ginger beer plant and started brewing it on a large scale, with cider bottles all over my kitchen and the corks popping up in the middle of the night — to my flatmate's great annoyance. By the way, I got the job.

Pupils regarded me as a curiosity, being French and teaching German, and I had extreme difficulty in pronouncing their names properly which caused great hilarity. After all the time it had taken me to master the English 'h' I noticed that Buckinghamshire children didn't bother with them and at times I couldn't understand them at all. *C'est la vie!*

At that time people seemed to know a lot about India and Australia, but thought Cherbourg was in Brittany and asked me if I had been to a town whose name sounded like 'Reemes' and which I, to their amazement, had never heard of. Those who had been to France, had invariably been to the Dordogne: being *bretonne* myself I couldn't imagine why people should want to spend their holidays so far from the seaside! I came to the conclusion that the Dordogne represented an ideal England, lovely and green with lots of rivers and woods, but with the bonus of sunshine, good wines and fine food.

Something I found hard to accept was the fact that being French, I was expected to 'act' French. Since I didn't look *petite* and *coquette*, didn't drink much, and didn't cook like a chef, a lot of people didn't think I was a very interesting sample of the French nation. They would not listen to what I was painstakingly trying to say, but would mimic my accent and pull my leg with very straight faces, leaving me wondering what they were all laughing about. When you don't master a language very well, there is a trend in every country you visit for people to start speaking louder — rather than choosing simple words to talk to you. But on the whole most people were incredibly patient and took the trouble of correcting my mistakes and explaining them to me.

In spite of my linguistic problems, I found England fantastically interesting and above all 'different'. I loved the red double-decker buses, the fish and chip shops, the threepenny bits, the walnut whips and the numerous jumble sales. I find it disappointing nowadays, when you travel through Europe, wherever you go, you begin to find the same things: Mars bars, Sinclair computers, *courgettes* and silvery telephone kiosks.

When I first arrived, people thought they were terribly continental when they drank real coffee or French wine, and ate *coq au vin* or fennel. And there I was, waiting to be invited to a dinner party where Lancashire hot pot and home-made Bakewell tart would be served. Talking of dinner parties, why did my English friends try to introduce me at all costs to other French people living in England? I was in England to speak English and discover the country and wasn't particularly interested in meeting Madeleine from Marseille or Martine from Metz. I suppose they thought I might be feeling homesick at times and would enjoy having a little chat in French.

Oddly enough, after 18 years in England, it is now that I sometimes have the urge to have a good chat with French friends. There are in fact a lot of French women in my area who are married to English men and also a few French men married to English women. Some have started twinning associations with French towns and a lot of them, like me, teach French in schools.

In the secondary schools things are changing and the examination boards are putting more emphasis on listening and reading comprehension as well as oral work. The juniors are taught how to cope when going to France, rather than given lists of verbs to learn by heart. Grammar is not forgotten but taught in a more practical way. Pupils are going on exchanges rather than 'school trips'. They stay with French families and often form lasting friendships.

There are also exchanges between teachers, organised by the Central Bureau. A colleague of mine is spending one year in the Grande Chartreuse not far from Grenoble, enjoying a much lighter timetable (Wednesday off plus one afternoon) while his French counterpart is with us, still recovering from the shock of having to face eight different classes each day and, on top of all that, coping with extra duties as well!

With people going to France more and more, they realise that their school French is a little rusty and the adults, young and old, attend day and evening classes at adult education centres where they have a chance to brush up their spoken French. At the Missenden Summer School, near Amersham, they can speak it every day for a whole week.

The French 'circles' run by the Alliance Française are flourishing. People come and enjoy an evening listening to a speaker, watching slides, learning about France and above all speaking French. More and more people go abroad for their holidays and those who go to France tell me of their marvellous stays in camp sites, hotels and *gîtes*. Some have the same linguistic problems as I had, like the friend who ran down to the reception of her hotel asking for a doctor to come and have a look at her husband who had broken a few ribs after falling in the shower . . . and was sent a plumber!

A lot of francophiles ask me if I wouldn't prefer to go back to live in France. If I did, I would probably introduce jumble sales, Oxfam shops and baby-sitting circles there. I would miss the long weekends, the daffodils at Easter, Wimbledon and cream teas. France is only a few hours away and will appear even closer when the Channel Tunnel is finished in a few years time; so it is up to me and the English people who have chosen to live in France to help break down all the barriers.

(*Bécassine en Grande-Bretagne?* Readers may have seen in France the children's books that relate the adventures of a young lady from 'backward' Brittany in Paris and elsewhere. RAB.)

PARIS   Alain Rayé

Comfortable restaurant

How is it that there's a Paris entry in *French Leave Favourites*? Well, like most things in life, it's necessary sometimes to compromise; there are good reasons why the entry should be included and, what is more, it is entirely appropriate for the Rayé entry to be the very first in this new book.

1986 saw Alain Rayé make a move from his previous base in Albertville to Paris. Alain and Frédy Girardet share one singular honour among readers: they have been by far the most appreciated favourites. Alain should be as proud as punch that readers have voted him the 'tops'.

Nicole, his sparkling, English-speaking wife, deservedly shared that honour though, alas, the couple have now gone their separate ways. I know of no chef in France who has such passionate ambition as Alain. He intends one day to be a 'great' chef; and I guarantee he will make it. Never has he taken short cuts; that's his great forte. But that 'strength' was also his 'weakness' at his French Alps base. He employed numerous staff to ensure perfection; he never compromised on standards and he never used anything but the best produce. But making ends meet in Savoie eventually proved impossible. All was fine at the height of the winter and summer seasons – but not so good in the many quiet months of the year when Albertville was hardly on any tourist's 'I must go there' list!

Alain has impressed so many of you. Not just for his brilliant, innovative cooking – more of that later – but also because he has helped many readers in other ways: on one occasion he opened up specially for a client who had inadvertently turned up with a reservation without realising he had arrived on the wrong (closing) day; and he has been a great supporter of the Bournemouth College – taking many students over the years.

In *French Leave 3* I detailed just what 'not cutting corners' means in culinary terms. In Alain's case it means a magnificent assortment of home-made breads, succulent *petits fours*, a long list of wines – with a huge choice of half-bottles (Chapel and Bocuse don't know the meaning of the word 'half') – and he never stints on helpings. Every 'favourite' in this book has had at least one serious complaint made about it: in Alain's case he holds the unique record that no less than half a dozen of you complained that he served too much food! That's probably his reaction to the more general criticism that 'too little' is served in the great *cuisine moderne* restaurants.

My last meal at Albertville, just before Alain left the town, was studded with masterpieces. One was a rare jewel; tiny bits of pigeon and sweetbreads, accompanied by a compote of green *lentilles* in a reduction of *foie gras* and lentils. Another delight was a *filet de rouget poêlés en bouillabaisse*; the latter being three small dishes of moussaka, *courgettes* in the finest of olive oil, and tomatoes in basil and *ail rosé*.

During 1986 several readers told me about their visits to Alain's new home. It's evident he has yet to match the same standards he set in Savoie – and I'm sorry to have to report that Nicole is sadly missed. What a difference she made!
category **3** *menus* **B**(lunch)-**D**(dinner) *cards* V
closed Mid July-mid Aug. Xmas-New Year. Sun. Public hols.
post 48 rue du Colisée, 75008 Paris. (Previously La Dariole)
phone (1) 42 25 66 76 *Mich* Atlas (11); 17-F9/F10 *map* 1

BAS-RUPTS

Host. Bas-Rupts

Comfortable hotel
Quiet/Tennis

I'm writing these words with a heavy heart – a few days before the manuscript for *French Leave Favourites* is due to be handed over for typesetting. The postman brought an unwelcome letter this morning: the tragic news of the death, in a motorcyle accident, of 25-year-old Thierry Philippe.

Only a few months ago I revisited the much appreciated Hostellerie in its isolated 800-metre-high site, surrounded by forests and pastures. I've known Michel and Marie-Louise Philippe for a long time and, on my last visit, I was delighted to see *les enfants* working alongside the couple; the future seemed to hold so much promise for the likeable family.

The most important change I noted was that Thierry had taken over from his father the major task of running the kitchen. He had had a thorough training – at the local hotel school and in the kitchens of famous chefs. In September 1985 the young chef had married Marie Hélène Chardigny, a lovely girl whose parents own La Sablière – a Michelin one-star restaurant at Etuz, near Besançon. She, too, had worked in many fine restaurants including a long stint with Marc and Françoise Meneau at St-Père; her greatest pals are the Martins who help to run the three-star shrine so efficiently.

In the summer of 1985 Roger and Denise Chardigny, Marie Hélène's parents, were asked to cook a special meal for the Queen Mother who visited Franche-Comté on a trip to France. Thierry assisted his father-in-law in the kitchen and Marie

Hélène helped her mother with the welcome and service. The couple were thrilled to show me a photograph of the family together with our incomparable Queen 'Mum'.

The third and youngest memeber of the Philippe family that I met on my last visit was Sylvie – a happy, well-travelled girl who speaks fluent English. No wonder, as she has worked in London for the Roux brothers and also in the States.

Now Michel will once again have to return to the responsibilities of *la cuisine*. Helped by the young ladies, Marie Hélène and Sylvia, I have no doubt that the Philippes will continue to please all those who visit Bas-Rupts in the years to come. Meanwhile our heartfelt sympathies, prayers and thoughts go out to the family during these sad, sorrowful days.

Don't have any fixed ideas of the best season in the Vosges: Bas-Rupts is open most of the year so take advantage of the seasonal benefits awaiting you. In the winter you can ski on the high slopes of the Vosges; but, better still, why not try your hand at *ski de fond* – cross-country skiing? There are many trails starting near the hotel and the surrounding terrain is considered some of the finest in France.

Spring ensures the numerous streams are at their best – and the high meadows are blanketed with wild flowers. Even casual reference to the yellow Michelin map 242 will identify many cascades and *sauts*; when the rivers are full they really are worth seeing. It goes without saying that summer is idyllic: there are plenty of lakes with all forms of water sport, endless walks and, at the hotel, there's a tennis court and, hopefully by 1987, a swimming pool to entice you to stay put. Autumn is my favourite season. The crowds have gone, the air is fresh and clear, the early morning mists add a mysterious shroud over the black pine-forested hills and there are many deciduous woods where dying autumn leaves add a rich splash of colour to the landscape. It's a spellbinding time of the year.

Mapoholics know full well that to absorb the best of Nature's creative art you need large-scale maps. So put 242 on a table, and with the help of the accompanying map, let me guide you to some of the best of the nearby scenic highlights.

Start by navigating yourself along the forestry roads (RF on the map) to the immediate north-east of Bas-Rupts. These narrow tracks slice through dense woods with many a 'surprise' view and eventually bring you to the Lac de Longemer (on clear autumn days the reflections on the surface are sharp and intense) and the tiny Lac de Retournemer. Other equally small lakes are to the north of the Col de la Schlucht: Lac Vert, Lac Noir and Lac Blanc. Take your car to the summit of the Hohneck. Like the Grand Ballon peak, further south, both are almost 5000 ft above sea-level and, on clear days, you can spot all the high summits of central Switzerland very easily indeed.

Use as many of the 'white' and 'yellow' roads as you can. One site you must on no account miss is the haunting hillside of Le Linge, north of Munster. Hidden in the pine woods is a museum telling the story of the First World War battlefield – but it's the remnants left on the neighbouring slopes that so graphically illustrate the horror and futility of the thousands of similar sites, throughout France, that claimed so many lives seven decades ago. The trenches and rusty barbed wire are still there – a grisly reminder of the tragic waste of so many lives, all lost for the sake of gaining no more than a yard at a time.

As further evidence of the high price that was paid in human sacrifice during that War, combine your drive along the Route des Crêtes, which takes you past the Hohneck and the Grand Ballon, with a visit to the National Cemetery at Vieil Armand, at the southern end of the mountain-top run. The road was built during the Great War for strategic purposes.

On either side of the high road are endless opportunities to use minor tracks to 'dive' down into quiet, isolated valleys. Man, too, has created his own charms to the east: seek out the many picturesque Alsace villages, all of which are associated in one form or another with the heady delights of the wines of the region. But I implore you to visit Mulhouse for three very good reasons: first the French Railway Museum – a must for all railway 'buffs'; then the unique Schlumpf Motor Museum where no less than 150 Bugatti cars alone are housed under one roof; and, finally, the zoo – one of the best in the world.

Back at the Hostellerie your days will end on a pretty sound culinary note. The above average Philippe style is a sensible, modern one: examples are a fillet of *rouget* with a hint of thyme, small *noisettes de chevreuil* served with *pommes fruits au safran* and *céleris au cumin*, and tiny portions of *caille* accompanied by a tasty *gratin dauphinois*. Complementing the wide range of menus (all pockets are accommodated) is a formidable wine list: ranging in cost from 20 to 900 francs, you can choose from 80 half-bottles, 200 others and a small select list of rarer wines. The Alsace section includes all my favourites – inexpensive Faller wines and others like Kientzler, Bayer, Dopf, Hugel and the expensive Clos Ste-Hunne.
category **3** *menus* **B-C** *rooms* 32**C** *cards* AE DC V
closed Dec (first 3 weeks). Please check in view of the above.
post Bas-Rupts, 88400 Gérardmer, Vosges. (S of Gérardmer)
phone 29 63 09 25 *Mich* 242 *map* 2 Gérardmer 4 km.

FOUGEROLLES

Au Père Rota

Simple restaurant with rooms
Good value (rooms)

Little seems to have changed at Fougerolles in the 25 years since Anne and I first visited the small town. Today it sports a welcome bypass and the surrounding terrain is still a mass of orchards, primarily cherry trees, for which the unpretentious town is nationally famous; or should I say for the heady products that emerge after the townspeople have weaved their magic on the annual harvests of fruit. Those skills were born three centuries ago when fruit trees were imported from Italy; the first commercial distillery opened during the last century.

Don't miss the many distilleries in Fougerolles. I suggest you call on Roger and Agnes Coulin – their warehouse and office is just 50 metres from the restaurant. Have a look at the myriad delights on their shelves: *kirsch* (cherry) – the most famous of all the colourless liqueurs distilled from fermented fruit and berry juices; but also a dozen or more other *eaux-de-vie – framboise sauvage, abricot, quetsche, prune, mirabelle, reine-Claude, poire William* and rarer ones like *myrtille, fraise, gentiane, coing* and *mûre*. Marvel at a 'pear in a bottle' and take pleasure from the many colourful fruits bottled in *eaux-de-vie*. Inexpensive miniatures are also available.

On the face of it not much appears to have changed at Au Père Rota either. Joseph Rota, decades ago, put his humble bistro very firmly on the French culinary map – he was known throughout the land for his *écrevisses* and *poulet aux morilles*. Anne and I still have happy memories of the very basic

29

bedrooms and the classic fare served by the old chef.

But today, there's a younger, modern master working in the tiny kitchen – Jean-Pierre Kuentz. Both he and his wife, Chantal, are locals – they were born and bred in nearby Plombières-les-Bains. Jean-Pierre makes considerable use of *vin jaune* from the hills to the south in Jura country: his own home-made *foie gras d'oie* is presented sitting on a *gelée au vin jaune* and a *petite nage de turbot* is also served in a masterly sauce of *vin jaune et gingembre*. Though one is so far from the sea, nevertheless tuck in to the surprisingly welcome taste of *crevettes grises* and *huîtres* served as an appetiser. Other treats are a variety of *chanterelles, champignons des bois, cèpes* and, of course, the local cherries (try *griottes* for dessert). Though it's unlikely you'll visit Fougerolles at the end of May, when the blossom is at its best, you'll get a feel for the scene from the bright menu cover – painted by Chantal's father.

The Vosges lie to the east and the Jura hills to the south, but don't ignore the immediate vicinity. Have a look at the nearby spa towns: small Bains-les-Bains, Plombières-les-Bains and the bigger Luxeuil-les-Bains. Drive south-east from Fougerolles through a wooded landscape – dotted with *étangs* (pools) – to Ronchamp where Le Corbusier's highly distinctive and ultra-modern Chapel of Notre Dame du Haut sits atop a hillside. Built three decades ago, every visitor should see the unusual concave roof and the interior with its novel use of natural wall lighting.

category **3** *menus* **B** *rooms* 5**A-B** *cards* AE DC V
closed 2 wks Feb. 1st wk July. Mid nov-mid Dec. Sun evg. Mon.
post 70220 Fougerolles, Haute-Saône. (NW of Belfort)
phone 84 49 12 11 *Mich* 242 *map* 3 Belfort 59 km.

KAYSERSBERG   Remparts

Comfortable hotel
Quiet/Gardens

Those simple descriptive words above cannot do justice to this much appreciated readers' favourite; after all they could be used to describe many hotels in France. What makes the modern Remparts 'different' is Madame Christiane Keller, the English-speaking owner; she's a lively, intelligent woman who takes great care of her clients and who will do everything possible to make your stay both enjoyable and rewarding.

Of the *FL3* restaurants in the area only the Couronne at Baldenheim and the modest du Faudé at Lapoutroie (a real Baldinger family enterprise) get consistently good reports. Many of you visited the Château restaurant, in the old village and a short walk from the Remparts. Extra pleasure there comes from the attention you get from Denis and Christine Kohler: Denis is Christiane's brother and Christine, who was born in the States, speaks fluent English. Basic menus give you the chance to try a wide range of Alsace specialities.

Don't leave Kaysersberg without paying charming Colette Faller a call – Christiane will make the introduction. I'm particularly fond of Alsace wines and the Faller varieties are among the region's best – especially the *vendanges tardives* (late vintage), truly deserving their *cuvée exceptionelle* labels.

category **1** *menus* No rest. *rooms* 30**B-C** *cards* A AE Visa
closed Open all the year.
post 68240 Kaysersberg, Haut-Rhin. (N of Colmar)
phone 89 47 12 12 *Mich* 242 *map* 4 Colmar 11 km.

COLMAR

MARLENHEIM

Host. du Cerf

Comfortable restaurant with rooms
Gardens

Your letters gave the clue during 1985: the Cerf was rewarding lucky visitors with cooking far and away above normal Michelin one-star standards – and at prices which make their UK equivalents look like blackmail. The predictable happened: in March 1986 the Husser family won their second Michelin star! It seemed just that the honoured accolade arrived on chef Robert Husser's 50th birthday – he's the father of the family. It's hard to believe but, on the same day, his son Michel, now 27, and his daughter-in-law, Catherine, celebrated their own special arrival – the birth of their second daughter, Mélina. Michel, a talented young chef, has worked hard alongside his father; how appropriate that so much pleasure should come to the family on one happy day!

My last visit, in the spring of '86, confirmed why such a lot of you have been so enthusiastic: an enterprising selection of specialities, marrying both old traditions and the modern ways of today, was more than sufficient proof, if it was needed, of why the culinary duo have won so many hearts.

Let me give you a taste of the evidence – a 'Menu Printemps' offered for the miserly sum of £20, service and taxes included. While you wait for the first of your four courses, a succession of hot appetisers arrive one by one – served as accompaniments to your *apéritif*; the latter perhaps the 'Clara' variety, named after Michel's oldest daughter. The first course could be a *salade de Presskopf du grand-père Wagner aux cébettes*

31

et œuf poché aux lardons – a dish similar to one that Robert's grandfather, Paul, served decades ago.

A *suprême de sandre au pinot noir sur lit de pâtes fraîches* followed – a tasty, light dish made even better by the home-made 'spinach' noodles. Next, a *rognons de veau à la crème d'échalotes* – the ideal meat course for the local village *pinot noir*, a light and delightful red-hued wine. Dessert was a masterpiece – *crêpes chaudes farcies aux griottes au kirsch Mélina*; you'll notice it was named in honour of baby Mélina who arrived a few weeks earlier. With your coffee you'll relish
· home-made *petits fours*.

Ask to meet Robert and Michel – both speak English. You'll certainly be greeted by Marcelle, Robert's wife, and more than likely you'll have your letter of reservation confirmed by Catherine. The 60-seater dining room is in the capable hands of Daniel Krier, an efficient English-speaking *maître d'hôtel*. Breakfast, which you should take in the dining room, will be the chance for you to 'natter' to Irmgard, Robert's mother; she's as proud as punch of her violets. Ask her to show you her other pride and joy – the key word is 'Clementine'. Look, too, at the entry dated May 8, 1940 – a remarkably cool tune!

I'm sure Robert and Michel will be happy to present you with a set of eight recipe cards – just ask; they're beautifully printed by the way. At least one of the recipes is super: small slices of salmon (larded with smoked bacon in the preparation) and served with green Le Puy lentils and a light horseradish sauce.
category **3** *menus* **C** *rooms* 19**B-C** *cards* AE DC V
closed Jan. Mon. Tues.
post 67520 Marlenheim, Bas-Rhin. (W of Strasbourg – on N4)
phone 88 87 73 73 *Mich* 242 *map* 5 Strasbourg 20 km.
32

PORT-SUR-SAONE   **Château de Vauchoux**

Very comfortable restaurant with rooms (see text)
Secluded/Gardens/Swimming pool/Tennis

Not every French chef wants to win fame and a trio of Michelin stars: Georges Berger, in his days at Priay, was a classic example. At his best there was no finer *cuisinier* on the face of this earth. Yet Georges and his delectable wife, Jannie, had simple tastes and both were quite content to live their busy lives in the most humble of restaurants.

Jean-Michel Turin, a 42-year-old talented chef, is another excellent example. But there are some striking differences between the Turins and the Bergers. Jean-Michel and his gentle, attractive wife, Franceline, own a small, handsome château, set in a wooded park with a swimming pool and tennis court hidden in a corner of the grounds. In commercial terms the only snags are that the hamlet of Vauchoux is off the beaten track and the couple have, as yet, no bedrooms.

The restaurant 'business' therefore is never exactly brisk – other than at Sunday lunchtime and on Saturday evening. The couple, who opened the restaurant 12 years ago, have always been very much in love with their home and their *pays* – and there's nothing that Jean-Michel adores more than to be able to work at his craft in his modern kitchen. The problem facing the Turins some years ago was a stark one: to retain their way of life something had to be found to subsidise the modest returns from the restaurant business. Jean-Michel came up with a most unusual and clever solution – a financial 'glove' that fits his culinary fingers to sheer perfection.

You'll see the first 'other business' clue in the garage next door to the château where you'll spot an immaculate, modern refrigerated lorry. On its side is a large sign saying 'Vauchouxfrais'. Basically the idea is a simple one: once a week, during the two days the restaurant is closed, Jean-Michel and another driver head for the Rungis market to the south of Paris. There, in the early hours of the morning, he first inspects and then buys a kaleidoscope of fresh produce: fish, shellfish, meat, vegetables, fruit, cheeses, flowers, *foie gras*, fungi and endless other delights. The Mercedes lorry is then driven back to the château where the driver and another colleague start a delivery cycle to 50 or so local clients – using both the lorry and a smaller refrigerated van.

"Where to?" you ask. The 50 'clients' are other hotel and restaurants in southern Alsace and the neighbouring Jura. Many of them are *French Leave 3* recommendations; some, like Goumois and Bas-Rupts, are included in this book. All his clients put their complete trust in Jean-Michel's ability to buy the best and freshest of fine produce. The buying business works like a dream: happy clients, all-important extra revenue, the weekly Rungis visit does not compromise his restaurant work, and, best of all, it means that Jean-Michel can use superb produce to complement his brilliant cooking ability.

You'll be seduced in all sorts of ways by his talent: by quails eggs, offered as an appetiser; or perhaps by magnificent oysters, served on a bed of seaweed, still with its Atlantic aroma, and with limes as an accompaniment, or by a fillet of fresh *bar poché à la vapeur beurre blanc* with fresh *girolles* encircling the fish. The chef keeps things simple – tastes count more than anything else: for example a *rosace gourmande de*

pigeonneau rôti rosé couldn't be more basic yet it's unlikely you'll savour a better *pigeonneau* anywhere else in France. Sorbets are smooth and authentic – a sorbet *menthe fraîche* is a classic. Desserts could include a brilliant *profiteroles amandines glacées* – ten tiny 'mushrooms' of ice cream, topped with 'hats' of crushed almonds and served in a chocolate sauce – and a featherlight *gâteau Opéra, arôme café*. You can also order, if a *grand dessert* is to your liking, *la dînette – l'assiette plaisir des gâtines*; a dozen or so mouthfuls of differing sweets served in small glass 'vases'.

Cheeses are another highlight – particularly the large and unusual variety of *chèvre* alternatives from all parts of France. By now you'll realise just how the weekly buying expedition to Rungis pays off – for Jean-Michel and his clients.

To their great disappointment the couple cannot yet offer you rooms – though by 1987 that may have changed as their financial situation improves. What I suggest is that you ask them if bedrooms are available; if not use the Hôtel Lion at nearby Vesoul. Alternatively why not give the Turins and the local terrain a day of your time; enjoy a lunch, the wooded park, the swimming pool and the tennis court. Ask Jean-Michel to show you his 'cellar'; in it are some 15,000 bottles (400 varieties), ranging from a first-class selection of Champagne, clarets and Burgundies to a surprisingly good *vins de pays* white from Champlitte – a village to the west of Vauchoux.

There's plenty locally to interest you. You could walk across the fields from the restaurant to the nearby Saône but I suggest instead you use your car and drive south, following the river and criss-crossing from bank to bank through a series of unspoilt, quiet villages.

At Chemilly, two km. south of the restaurant, stop on the small bridge where, unusually, a statue of St-Jean Népomucêne stands on the parapet. At Pontcey there's a cheese co-operative where huge disks of Emmental Français are made – it takes four months to complete the production cycle. The riverside views at Scey-s-Saône are most attractive and the villages of Rupt-s-Saône and Ray-s-Saône are both dominated by handsome châteaux with imposing towers. From Rupt use the minor D8E south-east to the point it crosses a canal; within walking distance in one direction is a lock and, to the east, a canal tunnel.

category **3** *menus* **B-D***rooms* See text *cards* A AE DC V
closed Mid Jan-Feb. Mon. Tues. (W of Vesoul)
post Vauchoux, 70170 Port-sur-Saône, H.-Saône.
phone 84 91 53 55 *Mich* 242 *map* 6 Vesoul 12 km.

CHÂTEAU DE RAY

BANNEGON   Auberge Moulin de Chaméron

Comfortable restaurant with rooms
Secluded/Terrace/Gardens/Swimming pool

There are a host of good reasons why you are bound to feel at home here: there is the secluded site for a start; the ancient mill – now a cosy restaurant with old beams, character and a warm feel to it; a high standard of cooking; a terrace, informal garden and swimming pool; but, above all, the friendly welcome from the owners – Jacques and Annie Candoré – both of whom speak excellent fluent English.

These two have an interesting background which is worth a brief explanation. They converted the water mill into a restaurant in 1972 – the bedrooms came later when a small, wooden block was built on the far side of the garden. Jacques was born in Bannegon – and the strange twist of fate is that his great-grandfather was once employed at the mill when the wheels actually produced flour; the *moulin* closed in 1880. Jacques has opened a small museum above the restaurant which explains the history of the mill; the photographs showing the various stages of restoration, starting from a scene of utter dereliction, are amazing.

Jacques had a whole series of jobs after school: he worked in a number of hotels; for three years he was employed by the French Line on the *Liberté*; he had a spell as a chauffeur in Paris – driving for Hollywood 'names' like Alfred Hitchcock, Gary Cooper and Grace Kelly; and, in the eight years before returning to France, he and Annie lived in California. Their son, Patrick, was born there; now 20, he works in Paris and frequently helps his parents during weekends at the mill. Patrick, in fact, has kept his American citizenship.

The family connections continue because the chef is their son-in-law, 34-year-old Jean Merilleau. He has a sure, capable touch – mixing classical, regional and modern styles in a most effective way. Alternatives on the menus could include specialities like *soupe de langoustines et les feuilletés au poivre doux* or a *pavé de faux-filet à la moelle, sauce au Sancerre* (red wine); certainly the latter was one of the best cuts of Charollais beef I've ever enjoyed in France. A chocolate gâteau was in fact an illusion – in reality a light-as-air mousse that was a pleasure to eat. All in all the high standard of cuisine comes as a welcome bonus to the other pleasures at the *moulin*.

There's plenty to see in the vicinity. There's Bourges – one of my own favourite French towns where you'll find many medieval architectural jewels. Then, just to the west, is the handsome château at Meillant; before you visit the interior be sure to walk a complete circuit of the grounds – the only sure way of appreciating the attractive exterior of the building. Near Meillant is the Cistercian abbey at Noirlac – founded by St-Bernard in the 12th century. To the south of Bannegon is the Forêt de Tronçais – a treasure-chest of ancient oak trees.

The *moulin* is three kilometres to the south-east of Bannegon; follow the signs from the village.

For details of 23 similar *moulins* in France write to Annie for a copy of an excellently produced booklet.

category **2** *menus* **B-C** *rooms* 10**B-C** *cards* V
closed Nov-mid Mar. Thurs (out of season). (S of Bourges)
post Bannegon, 18210 Charenton-du-Cher, Cher.
phone 48 60 75 80 *Mich* 238 *map* 7 Bourges 42 km.

ROSPORDEN   Bourhis

Very comfortable hotel
Lift

Justice has been done: and, in this particular example, it could not have come at a more crucial time for 36-year-old Marcel Bourhis – the Michelin star I've been predicting for six long years shone for the first time over Rosporden in 1986. Over the years I've correctly predicted scores of rising stars (from one to three) – and those falling fast the other way – but not one of the other predictions gave me such pleasure. Why?

Well, on the night of May 26/27, 1982, disaster struck the young chef: the family hotel caught fire and, hours later, stood a lifeless, blackened shell. Marcel's grandmother, Marie, started the enterprise in 1936 as a humble café; in 1946 his father, Marcel, took over and began the job of turning it into a serious restaurant. After graduating from the Clermont-Ferrand Hotel School in 1970, followed by a long apprenticeship at his father's side, Marcel was handed the reins in 1978. I first visited him two years later and was immediately impressed.

The fire was a hammer blow. Anne and I well remember the sad hour or two we spent in 1983 with Marcel and his pretty wife, Maryvonne, at their rented two-room flat above a garage next door to the burnt out wreck of the hotel. They had suffered and it took over two years to resolve all the insurance problems, re-building and additional financing worries of creating from scratch, and in a difficult site, a new modern hotel.

All that's now behind Marcel: Kipling's words 'And so hold on when there is nothing in you – Except the will which says to them "Hold on"' could have been written for him. He 'held on' and has started his working life again with a triumphant fanfare. You'll notice he's one of only nine chefs I've given my special ★ award. (I know Anne Manning agrees!)

What a stunning meal I had in the late spring of 1986. Of several audacious and inventive creations (attention to detail is Marcel's forte) I recall with pleasure the following: three original, hot appetisers accompanying the *apéritif*; a *terrine d'artichaut* served *tiède*; a *tian de lotte au beurre de ciboulette* – the fish resting on a small, round bed of *courgettes*; a *tourte de lapereau et son jus* – mouthwateringly light and scrumptious; and a tiny, tiny *crépinette de ris de veau au foie gras* – a perfect example of Marcel's finely-tuned taste buds.

Alas, there's one sad bit of news to report after Marcel's return from disaster: he and Maryvonne went their separate ways in 1986. Marcel's mother, Sidonie, has returned to add her captivating charm to her son's culinary skills. Father, too, can be seen about the hotel doing all sorts of odd jobs. (So many culinary marriages seem to suffer these days: I know of at least six casualties among friends of mine who are chefs.)

Don't bypass Marcel's rebuilt home (once called the Gare); the ultra-modern design works well and has welcome benefits for the disabled. Two final comments: the first a blast fired at Christian Millau – shame on you for totally ignoring one of Brittany's best chefs; and to Michelin – how long will it be before the second star rises above Rosporden station?
category 3 ★ *menus* B-C *rooms* 27C *cards* A AE DC V
closed Mid Feb-mid Mar. 2nd half Nov. Sun evg/Mon (Oct-mid June).
post pl. Gare, 29140 Rosporden, Finistère. (SE Quimper)
phone 98 59 23 89 *Mich* 230 *map* 8 Quimper 22 km.

STE-ANNE-LA-PALUD   Plage

Very comfortable hotel
Secluded/Gardens/Swimming pool/Tennis/Lift

Anne and I first fell in love with the idyllic Hôtel de la Plage over two decades ago. Today our great enthusiasm and affection for this most captivating of favourites remains undiminished. Any reader who makes Brittany a port of call should seek it out: the fortunate among you may well be able to stay a few days, but even those with the smallest of budgets should try the marvellous value-for-money menu; recently introduced, it's available at both lunch and dinner but not at Sunday midday.

The Plage is a place to escape to when you need to celebrate something special: on retirement perhaps, when a cash sum allows a couple to treat themselves to a luxury holiday; or for an anniversary when ten, twenty or thirty years of marriage earn a well-deserved 'reward'; or maybe a break from the kids – or even take them if you feel 'Mum' needs an expensive 'thank-you' present; so the list goes on. Why is it the ideal hotel?

First the setting: totally isolated, it's at the end of a dead-end lane, the only difference with this road that goes nowhere is that it finishes literally on the sands of the Baie de Douarnenez. Stretching for over two kilometres to the north, the golden sands are completely free of all those man-made horrors that spoil so many beaches. To the immediate left of the hotel a small headland (a splash of dazzling hues in June when a tide of azaleas and rhododendrons flood the hillside) protects the site from the occasional south-westerly gales; but it does not prevent you from having extensive views of the northern half of

Douarnenez Bay – right across to Morgat.

The second benefit comes in the amenities on hand: swimming and tennis; walks on beaches and headlands or further afield on moors, hills and high cliffs; drives that take you to ports, old inland villages, nature reserves, forests, streams and rivers; and boat excursions of various sorts – one based at Morgat allows you the unusual treat of the Grandes Grottes.

Then there's the Le Coz family. Manick, the 'Mum', is as indefatigable as ever: at 63 she's been 'involved' in the business for 48 years though for a decade now she's not done any cooking. (Her mother started it all as a simple *auberge* just after the First World War; you'll spot her portrait as you enter through the main door.) You'll also meet Manick's son, Jean-Milliau, and Marie, the friendly receptionist; both speak English.

For ten years the kitchen has been in the capable hands of Breton-born, 35-year-old Jean-Pierre Le Goloanec; he's a third-generation *cuisinier* – his father was a *traiteur* and his grandfather a chef. Fresh fish, of all types, comes daily from the port at Douarnenez (though in rough weather supplies can dry up). You can enjoy sea food served in its simplest, most natural form or, instead, try some of Jean-Pierre's modern, light inventions; he's fond of very brief cooking and he hates using cream, butter and flour. In 1986 a bargain menu cost 140 francs; a small price to pay for sharing in the long list of Plage pleasures. (See *FL3* for the nearby 'base' hotel at Plomodiern; alternative cheaper overnight accommodation.)
category **3** *menus* **B-C** *rooms* 30**D-D3** *cards* A AE DC V
closed Mid Oct-Mar. (NW of Quimper)
post Ste-Anne-la-Palud, 29127 Plomodiern, Finistère.
phone 98 92 50 12 *Mich* 230 *map* 9 Quimper 25 km.

AVALLON

Morvan

Comfortable restaurant
Terrace/Gardens

Let me start this appreciative review with a strong caveat. If your culinary tastes are exclusively influenced by the world of modern cooking – all lightness and brightness, served on black octagonal plates and with the seal of approval of Gault Millau and their band of 'foodie' followers – then don't, under any circumstances, pay Jean and Marinette Breton a call. Jean, a *maître cuisinier de France*, is a loyal disciple of classical and traditional skills; he has never been moved to turn the page of culinary history. Bravo for that!

Mind you, he has had many a sleepless night worrying and fussing about whether he should change his ways; because culinary fashion has meant that, by and large, he has been shunned, even ridiculed, by trendy Parisians. However, he made the decision years ago to stick to what he does best and thank heavens for it. 'Old-fashioned' standards have an important part to play in present-day French cooking styles; you'll not be disappointed by your visit.

Marinette Breton welcomes you with a happy, genuine smile and offers you a choice of two fixed-price menus and a selection of à la carte dishes. By the time this book is published the menus should be available in both French and English – the translation work being done by an English friend of the Bretons. Choose one of the menus if you want to, although I think this is a restaurant where you should not worry too much about quantity; instead, choose two or three dishes, depending on your budget, from Jean's à la carte specialities.

His 'creations' are excellent and deserve your support. Consider first the national reputation he has for a range of *terrines* and *pâtés*. You'll not taste better. Normally the à la carte description of *les terrines du chef* includes three of his most popular varieties – *lapin*, *canard* and *foies de volaille*. But, from time to time, Jean makes others, too: *terrine de campagne* and *terrine de canard sauvage fumé*; a *pâté au crevettes et curry* and *pâté aux fruits de mer*; or perhaps a *mousseline de grenouilles*. I bet you'll be tempted after your meal to buy some of the home-made bottled *terrines* and *pâtés*; I can vouch that they travel well.

An alternative starter could be a dish created by Jean in 1970. Described simply as *le rougeot*, it is in fact a plate of paper-thin slices of smoked duck *filet* – served on its own with bread and butter. The latter incidentally is a football-sized mound placed on the table. Whatever your first choice, I would certainly follow it with a *timbale d'escargots au Chablis*. This is no more than a small bowl of *escargots* with chopped nuts, mushrooms and capers in what I can only describe as a Chablis 'soup'. The aroma and taste of the 'soup' is memorable – a local Chablis white is the obvious accompaniment.

To follow, choose from a variety of different dishes: *truite farci 'Mode d'Icy'* (ask for the recipe); *rognons de veau Bourguignonne*; *noisettes d'agneau*; or *suprême de canard sauvage* (in season). Cheeses are fresh and include local and national varieties – and there's a wide choice of desserts.

Just to show that Jean can produce some little touches that equal the efforts of the modern greats, savour the four or five delightful appetisers served with the *apéritifs* including: thin slices of what looks like a sausage roll – the filling in this case being a *terrine de lapin*; marinated sliced cucumber, laced with chives, on a bread base; or, similarly, little florets of crunchy cauliflower prepared in the same way.

Stay a day or two in north Burgundy – don't just rush through. I suggest many sights that you can seek out in each of the recommendations for the area; here are some others.

East of Avallon is the Serein Valley. Enjoy its tranquil, natural beauty and appreciate too, the medieval gem of Noyers – a tiny town with narrow streets and 500-year-old buildings, contained within a fortified wall with 16 towers. Montréal is further upstream; just as old and a perched site gives it added interest. You'll see few tourists hereabouts.

Further east still is the Armançon Valley. Downstream, to the north, are the famous châteaux of Tanlay and Ancy-le-Franc, but I would prefer to give my time to Fontenay, lost in the woods to the east of Montbard. Founded in 1118 – though greatly restored in later centuries – it's a perfect example of the hugely important Cistercian influence on Burgundy many centuries ago. In addition, include Semur-en-Auxois on your travels. The river loops in a circle around the town's massive walls – the combination of the latter, many narrow streets and absorbing views is hard to resist. Finally, call on the Taylor-Whiteheads at Buffon, north-west of Montbard; the family have worked like Trojans to restore the old forge (open afternoons only – June to September).

category 2 *menus* **B** *cards* A AE DC V *closed* Jan. Mid-end Nov. Evgs (out of season – but not Sat). Sun evg. Mon.
post 7 rte Paris, 89200 Avallon, Yonne.
phone 86 34 18 20 *Mich* 238 *map* 10

AVALLON

Moulin des Templiers

Comfortable hotel
Secluded/Gardens/Terrace

The Moulin has been the cause of a flood of appreciative letters
– from readers on both sides of the Atlantic. Yet, on my last visit
to this seductively-sited 'base', I was brought down to earth by a
Texan who, on being told that it was one of my favourite
recommendations, then asked me: "Why do you recommend
it? It's not a Holiday Inn, is it?"

It most certainly is not that and, come to think of it, that
omission in itself would be cause enough for me to
recommend the Moulin des Templiers! But, joking apart, there
are a score of reasons for its universal appeal. The old mill is
well clear of Avallon and sits alluringly alongside the tree-lined
Cousin – one of many small wooded river valleys in north
Burgundy. A long terrace – shaded by high trees on the edge of
the stream's bank – is the ideal place for an early-evening drink
or breakfast on a sparkling, sunny morning. Just sit and relax:
you may be lucky enough to watch red squirrels high above
you – scurrying busily about in the branches; or you can hold
your breath as passing canoeists negotiate the metre-high 'fall'
in the river alongside the terrace. It's that drop in the river bed
that provides the constant background sound of rushing water
– a soothing, natural sound if ever there was one.

The bedrooms of the converted mill are certainly not on the
large side – in fact they couldn't be smaller. However they're
comfortable and quiet – and prices, too, are modest.
Youngsters will love the animals in the field above the car park.

Madame Hilmoine is proud of her immaculate *moulin* and,
in spite of many difficulties, has not let her high standards fall.
It's possible you may meet her daughter, Catherine, who
speaks excellent English. Catherine has written a most
interesting guide to the best of the numerous Far Eastern
restaurants in Paris: Chinese, Vietnamese, Japanese, Indian
and others. I saw part of her manuscript and, by the time this
book is published, her efforts should be out in printed form. I
hope her mother makes sure the book is on sale at the hotel;
Catherine really is an expert on Eastern cooking.

I mentioned earlier that north Burgundy – much of which lies
in the peaceful hills of the Morvan Regional Park – has many
pleasing small rivers. Explore the Cousin for a start – making
sure you see it from Avallon's south gate, high above the river.
(Behind you is the old walled part of Avallon with splendid
medieval houses and the Church of St-Lazare.) Take in, too, as
much of the Cure Valley as you can. All sorts of treats await you:
the *grottes* at Arcy – downstream towards the Yonne; the
handsome château at Chastellux (the final drawing in this
book); the cascade at Gouloux; and the one-way drive through
the Forêt Au Duc. Be sure to desert your car at the foot of the
Rocher de la Pérouse and make the not-too-steep and not-too-
long climb to the observation table at the summit of the rocks.
Below you is a typical Morvan panorama.

There's much to see and do to the east of Avallon too; read
the other Avallon entry for details.
category 1 *menus* No rest. *rooms* 14**B-C**
closed Nov-Mar. Sat.
post 89200 Avallon, Yonne. (On D427 in vallée du Cousin)
phone 86 34 10 80 *Mich* 238 *map* 11

BOUILLAND

Host. du Vieux Moulin

Very comfortable restaurant with rooms
Secluded/Gardens

I'll make a cast-iron prediction immediately: many more readers are going to make the detour up the Rhoin Valley once they know the treats that are awaiting them. For a start it's a hugely satisfying scenic drive from Beaune; just 16 km. along a wooded valley which, for all the world, could be part of the Jura hills that lie to the east on the Franco-Swiss border. Trees, green meadows, modest-sized hills – some with rock faces – and a 'bubbling' stream (Bouilland is derived from the word *bouillant* – boiling) are a world apart from the horrendous A6 autoroute to the west. In the pastures adjacent to the Moulin, cows with clanging bells around their necks make it seem even more like the Jura country to the east.

All that is reason enough for staying overnight at the old mill which straddles the small gurgling stream. But there's an even better dividend to come – in the shape of 30-year-old Jean-Pierre Silva. Make no mistake about it: he's going to be one of the great chefs of the future. Michelin have only just 'discovered' him – but my Anglo-Saxon readers have a 'nose' for young, budding talent and, for years now, they have appreciated this young magician's brilliant efforts.

My last meal was one of the very best I had in France during the many research trips I made preparing this book. I'll describe it in detail – but first some background information.

Jean-Pierre hails from Lyon. Basically self-taught, his kitchen training consisted mainly of the year he spent with Jean

André and Guy Tricon at Mouans-Sartoux in the hills below Grasse. But he travels widely, too; witness the dozens of menus from some of the great French restaurants that take pride of place on a stand in the reception area. He learns fast – and he puts his memory and eye for detail to much good use. Jean-Pierre and his dark-haired wife, Isabelle, bought the *moulin* in 1981 from Raymond Hériot who had made such a reputation for himself over the years, before he called it a day in his early seventies. (The Queen Mother was perhaps the most famous person to eat at Bouilland – a visit made a decade or so ago.)

Why I feel certain Jean-Pierre Silva will make his mark in the future is that, even as young as he is, he has an intuitive feel for simplicity, natural flavours and letting things taste of what they are. I had his *menu surprise* – a Swiss custom of offering six or seven small servings; you take the meal as it comes. I assure you it was no hardship to take what did come!

First some *asperges et foie gras chaud à l'huile de truffes*; don't, for heaven's sake, leave the truffle oil that remains – use a morsel of *pain* to soak it up and surprise yourself by bread that never tasted quite like that before. Next *pigeonneau de Cussigny* (a hamlet south of Nuits-St-Georges) *rôti dans son jus*: quite superb and simplicity itself – repeat the bread 'dip' once more. Then wild asparagus with a thin slice of salmon, cooked for just a few seconds, served simply with some *huile d'olives citronné*. Why over-complicate perfection?

Then followed yet another magnificent dish: *estouffade de jeunes poireaux jambonette de grenouilles en meurette de lie de vin* – three tiny frogs' legs on a bed of leeks with a mouthwatering red wine reduction. Use your bread again. At this stage you worry about coping with any more food – but it's not a problem. The lack of cream, butter and flour leaves you eager for more. Small helpings make a difference, too. To refresh the palate Jean-Pierre serves a cold *consommé de bœuf à la coriandre*.

A small *ris d'agneau rôti* in a *vinaigrette* of herbs and accompanied by minute roast potatoes and a mixture of *girolles*, *pleurotes* and *mousserons* followed the *consommé*. Wow – absolutely amazing! There was still room for some cheese – the tray included regional treats such as Cîteaux, Epoisses, Chaource and a Bouilland *chèvre*. Sweets, too, were of a very high standard – with a choice of about 17.

It was all really quite special. I was well and truly bowled over by the prodigious efforts the young man is so obviously making. Until 1986 Michelin ignored him. Why? I have not received a single letter of praise for the three-star Lameloise at nearby Chagny; yet Jean-Pierre has been the reason for many appreciative letters – and he has only just won his first star!

Jean-Pierre has a go at all sorts of different dishes; not just his own creations but traditional classics like a *daube de cochon confite aux pommes de terre* and, for those who want some cream, a *cassolette de morilles fraîches à la crème*. And to add to all the culinary wizardry the formidable wine list of over 400 vintages includes more than 80 half-bottles.

By the time this book is published five additional, really excellent bedrooms, in a new building, should be available – to add to the eight modest ones currently in the *moulin* itself.

There are other good reasons for staying a night or two – and I don't mean the obvious attractions of the wine villages to the east. Instead head north – up the valley.

Follow the D2, initially climbing through wooded hills. About four km. from Bouilland turn right on to the D115 for Antheuil. You'll get your first views of the Ouche Valley as you descend. When you reach the D33 turn right and in three km. stop at the point the road crosses the Canal de Bourgogne. You have the chance to picnic here or to walk the tree-lined towpath of the attractive canal; if you're feeling lazy why not watch a boat or two through the lock? You may be asked to give a hand!

Nearby is Bussière-sur-Ouche with its abbey in landscaped grounds. Head west on the D33 and then on the narrow C2 to Châteauneuf – you'll have the road to yourself. The village has been saved from dereliction not by the State but by private individuals who were appalled by the thought that the ancient village could die. The views are extensive and the narrow streets and old houses are absorbing pleasures.

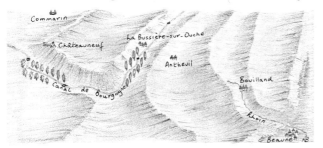

category 3★ *menus* B-C *rooms* 8B-C *cards* A AE DC V
closed Mid Dec-Jan. Wed. Thurs midday. (NW of Beaune)
post Bouilland, 21420 Savigny-lès-Beaune, Côte-d'Or.
phone 80 21 51 16 *Mich* 243 *map* 12 Beaune 16 km.

GEVREY-CHAMBERTIN

Grands Crus

Comfortable hotel
Quiet/Gardens

The vast majority of Anglo-Saxon visitors to France seem to insist that they must eat where they sleep. For them the special attractions of my 'base' hotels are an unknown treat. What a pity – they know not what they miss! Here is one of the best.

The smart, flower-bedecked building was erected 10 years ago; it's on the northern outskirts of the village – near the château. The large entrance hall/breakfast room has the air of a much older, authentic Burgundian house; that's no accident as the owners, Pierre and Simone Mortet, made sure that the beamed ceiling and the warm tiled floors were incorporated into the design. The site is quiet, parking is easy and you're free to eat wherever you want to – or not at all.

Another reason why visitors will like Les Grands Crus is the charming, young manageress, Geneviève Méry. She has worked hard, very hard, at improving her English and now it's getting quite fluent. Geny, as she likes to be called, is an attractive, helpful girl; long is the list of clients who have had help from her – help going well beyond the normal call of duty.

Don't rush through this famous part of Burgundy. Certainly wine buffs will give the series of neighbouring villages their undivided attention – it's all hallowed ground for them. Some tourists will seek out, inevitably, both Dijon and Beaune – others will not even bother to do that. But 'mapoholics' look for quieter byways, too: why miss some of life's best pleasures? Try the following trip as an example of what I mean.

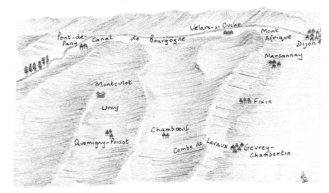

Use map 243. Head west from the village, along the Combe de Lavaux and climb through woods to Quemigny-Poisot. Then north through Urcy and past the château at Montculot; these are quiet, green parts. Descend to Pont-de-Pany where you'll see the Canal de Bourgogne for the first time. Walk its banks, help at the locks – and ignore the A38 autoroute. At Velars-sur-Ouche drive south-east to the top of Mont Afrique (fine views east over the Saône Valley) and then descend to Marsannay, following the Route des Grands Crus to Fixin. West of the latter is the Parc Noisot – in the park is a small museum with Napoléon associations.

category 1 *menus* No rest. *rooms* 24**C**
closed Dec-3rd week Feb.
post 21220 Gevrey-Chambertin, Côte-d'Or. (S of Dijon)
phone 80 34 34 15 *Mich* 243 *map* 13 Dijon 12 km.

GEVREY-CHAMBERTIN   Les Millésimes

Very comfortable restaurant

French Leave readers will know this restaurant was not a main entry in the last edition. At that time I had not been able to try it; but many of you recommended it and, without any doubt, it's a favourite of readers – hence its inclusion.

What a sophisticated restaurant the Sangoy family have made of it in the four years since they returned from Argentina. Like La Rôtisserie, it's set in old wine cellars and it's very expensively furnished: Limoges crockery, crystal glasses, candelabra, an exceedingly handsome wine list and menu – both printed on heavy, rich paper – attractive small flower arrangements on the tables, lots of greenery and the family dressed in a manner that complements the serious Michelin one-star restaurant that it now undoubtedly is.

What a family enterprise it is. Father Jean is the chef and he's helped by sons Denis and Laurent in the spotless, modern underground kitchen. Monique, the mother, runs the front-of-the-house and she's assisted by Didier and Sophie. Cooking is very much in the classical style – following safe, traditional paths: *gratin de queues d'écrevisses, carré d'agneau rôti* and *ris de veau braisé* are typical. Cheeses are impressive – 30 of them, including Cîteaux and l'ami du Chambertin (you can buy the latter at Brochon, north of Gevrey).
category **3** *menus* **B-C** *cards* A AE DC V
closed Jan-mid Feb. Tues. Wed midday. (S of Dijon)
post 25 r. Eglise, 21220 Gevrey-Chambertin, Côte-d'Or.
phone 80 51 84 24 *Mich* 243 *map* 14 Dijon 12 km.

GEVREY-CHAMBERTIN   La Rôtisserie du Chambertin

Very comfortable restaurant

Any of you who visited La Rôtisserie in 1983 or 1984 will know that Céline Menneveau – such a talented *cuisinière* – was working under the immense strain of ill-health. Alas, Céline died at the end of May 1985, just a few months after the arrival of a new 30-year-old chef, Serge Lanoix, in her small, modern kitchen. Céline will be greatly missed by all her friends.

Her influence is still felt however: Céline took a considerable interest in the development of her able young chef and he had in fact worked at her side for two years a decade earlier, after his initial training at the Plaza-Athenée in Paris. From Gevry Serge went on to two spells at the Troisgros home in Roanne and, sandwiched between them, a two-year stint in Brazil. He's a great friend of Michel, Pierre Troisgros' son; they collaborate regularly in developing new culinary tricks.

La Rôtisserie's menu is one of the most balanced you'll see anywhere: some famous Burgundian specialities like *œufs en meurette* and *le vrai coq au vin comme autrefois*; some classical dishes such as *filet de bœuf en tournedos aux trois sauces* (*morilles, Bordelais and Béarnais* with *cresson* added); and many modern-style interpretations. Representative of the latter is *assiette de soupe Bretonne au safran* – a mixture of fish but served in a light sauce with a distinctly Provençal kick to it. Other treats are Serge's home-made *foie gras de canard des Landes* – as good as any; a *foie de canard poêlé chaud* served in a *bigarade* sauce; and a clever dish of *gigot de grenouilles fraîches au coulis de persil et mousseline d'aïl* – six tiny legs

43

encircling a green sauce and a mousseline with the bonus that no garlic taste remains in the mouth.

Two of Céline's memorable specialities continue – both are among my own great personal favourites. One is *les ravioli aux truffes* – crushed truffles and wood mushrooms in the thinnest possible covering and served in a reduction of mushrooms, tarragon, lemon and cream. Another is the *assiette des trois saveurs* – some raw salmon with a mousse of smoked haddock and a minute serving of caviar; be certain to try the three ingredients together – rather than one at a time.

Céline worked hard to win her nationwide reputation – anyone who knew her would say much too hard. She and Pierre opened La Rôtisserie in 1969 – more about the unusual restaurant later; they had met in Paris where Céline had originally trained as a lawyer. An American admirer, a lawyer himself, put it so succinctly in a 'thank you' letter: 'one always feels poorer after paying a lawyer, but one always feels richer paying for a meal prepared by a fine *cuisinière*.'

Pierre, who speaks fluent English, has had a life-long interest in Gevrey-Chambertin and its wines. The majority of the vintages offered at the restaurant carry his own Le petit fils de Charles Marchand label. (Charles was his grandfather on his mother's side.) Pierre still owns some vineyards in the village – but he buys, too, from other producers and neighbours. His list is a roll call of Chambertin magic: over 50 superb Chapelle-Chambertin, Gevrey-Chambertin, Latricières-Chambertin and Chambertin alternatives. They cover the years from 1962 to 1980; you'll be a lucky man if you can persuade Pierre to part with the few remaining precious bottles of even older vintages – ones safely hidden away in his cellars. Worthy of note is that prices are nothing like as high as all the best Burgundian wines seem to be these days in the great French restaurants.

One notable aspect of the many letters I have received commending La Rôtisserie is how much Pierre will put himself out to help his clients; there doesn't seem much he wouldn't do to promote his village, its memorable wines, and, best of all, the greatly appreciated restaurant that his dear wife slaved so energetically to establish over 16 years.

I'm sure, too, he would be happy to let you have a taste of his *'porto'* experiment – grenache grapes from Roussillon, bought in 1970, put in casks for four years and then bottled.

The restaurant is underground – in old wine cellars; many readers have been fooled because when they drive into the courtyard they fail to find the door that leads downstairs. (Pierre: please display a menu!) Behind the door, and at the foot of the stairs, are rooms with plaster figures, dressed authentically, carrying out various tasks associated with wine making; each scene is full of detail, matched by clever lighting and taped background Burgundian drinking songs. The restaurant itself is also cleverly lit and the air-conditioning does an effective job. If Pierre has time ask him to show you some of the larger rooms in the house above the cellar; what magnificent Burgundian treasures they are. It seems highly likely that part of the house will soon be used as a shop; what good news – those delectable wines can then be bought by happy restaurant clients.

category **3** *menus* **C**
closed Feb. 2 weeks beginning Aug. Sun evg. Mon.
post 21220 Gevrey-Chambertin, Côte-d'Or. (S of Dijon)
phone 80 34 33 20 *Mich* 243 *map* 15 Dijon 12 km.

MAILLY-LE-CHATEAU   Le Castel

Comfortable hotel
Quiet/Gardens/Good value (meals)

I have good news to report for all those readers who, in the past, have appreciated the many benefits of Le Castel – except for just one! The noisy Town Hall clock (Belinda: was 'Trumpton's' a copy of this one?) now rings at 10.00 p.m. and then, like all good clocks should do, it shuts up and goes to bed itself. At 7.00 a.m. it starts the daily clanging once more and, would you believe, does the job not once but twice every hour. I lost count of the letters that grumbled about the wretched bell. Now, at last, this quiet, restful *Logis de France* lives up to its otherwise absolutely correct *Relais du Silence* tag.

Of the many modestly-priced recommendations I made in *Hidden France*, back in 1982, Le Castel has proved to be as popular as any. There are many good reasons for that popularity but the one that counts most is the friendliness of the owners – Michel and Janet Breerette.

Michel was born 50 years ago at St-Nazaire. After studying at the Toulouse Hotel School he applied to join the French Line, owners of many legendary ocean liners – the France and Liberté among them. "Fine," they said; "but go and learn some English first." He did just that: at Gleneagles Hotel in Scotland and then at the Queen's Hotel (sadly now demolished) in Snow Hill, Birmingham; both were then owned by British Railways.

His 15 years with the French Line polished up his English no end and it also did wonders for his cooking skills. But a life on the ocean waves hardly suits a married man. In 1975 Michel called it a day and, with Janet, managed the Castel Marie-Louise at La Baule. Their first child, Alexandre, arrived soon after. In 1979 they bought Le Castel – its reputation, locally, in tatters. They borrowed a small fortune, crossed their fingers, and after three tough years, have never looked back.

Michel's cooking is loyal to classical traditions. One speciality he's proud of is his award-winning *escalopes de saumon frais à la crème de cresson* (Marc Meneau, no less, was on the judging panel). Just as nice is another fish speciality – *medaillons de lotte à la fondue d'oseille*; fresh and hugely enjoyable. Starters can include a regional *jambon persillé de Bourgogne*, *jambon de Morvan* from the hills to the south, *escargots aux noisettes* – appreciated by readers, and various fish and meat *terrines*. There's always a home-made soup, too.

For the main dish of your meal you can choose from alternatives such as *pièce de bœuf à la moutarde à l'ancienne*, *côtes d'agneau poêlées au basilic*, *bœuf Bourguignon* or a relatively simple *jambon à la Chablisienne*. If you like trout do try the *truite de Prégilbert aux amandes*; these farm fish, together with salmon trout, come from a little hamlet just to the north of Mailly. Pay the farm a visit – it's an interesting site.

Like all good chefs who have worked on ocean liners, Michel serves up many good desserts – a *coupe de fraises Chantilly* is one prime example. Yumm – just great!

Rather than choose some of the more famous Burgundy wines from Michel's list why not try a local variety instead? Perhaps an Epineuil red or *rosé* (the village is a northern neighbour of Tonnerre, east of Chablis); or the very good Irancy vintages – Palotte is a wine from the best slopes above the village. Be sure to pay a call on both Irancy and St-Bris.

45

Briefly, let me return to the subject of the clock again. You would be amazed – though possibly not when you account for the contrariness of human nature – by the fuss the local community made when they heard the council had decided to agree to Michel's request to gag the bell at night. The peels of outrage even rang out in the regional newspaper. So sensitive is the Mayor about it all that he insists the council vote on this 'political' issue every year! I was introduced to the kindly Mayor and I told him what my readers thought of Mailly's midnight, ding-dong gong. Let's hope they keep it gagged.

What is there to see and do? In the other Burgundy entries I suggest many ideas but here are a few more. Across the road from the hotel is a medieval church (it's a protected monument – as is the 400-year-old lime tree between it and Le Castel); and around the corner is a terrace from which there is an eye-catching view. Tree-lined arms of the River Yonne, a canal (these days very popular with Britons), distant wooded hills and the lower half of Mailly lie below you. The view is particularly pleasing in the evening when mist occasionally rises in soft white eiderdown clouds from the water below.

Not far to the east are the *Grottes d'Arcy* – 500 metres of underground caves carved out millions of years ago by the River Cure. They are full of all sorts of stalagmites and stalactites and, at the end of the caves, the floor surface looks as if a tiny part of the surface of the moon has been transported back to earth. Mother Nature, as always, has the last word.
category 2 *menus* **A-B** *rooms* 12**B-C** *cards* A V
closed Mid Nov-Feb.Rest.Wed.Tu evg(10-3).Hot.Tu evg&Wed(10-3).
post pl. Eglise, 89660 Mailly-le-Château, Yonne. (S of Auxerre)
phone 86 40 43 06 *Mich* 238 *map* 16 Auxerre 30 km.

46

MERCUREY   Hôtellerie du Val d'Or

Comfortable restaurant with rooms
Gardens/Good value (meals)

Thousands of French hotelier families are dedicated, hard-working marvels: you meet them throughout France at every level of establishment. Here at Mercurey is a family that epitomises them all; described by a *French Leave* reader who has lived for a long time in Paris as 'in every way typical of the very best of the breed'. I agree wholeheartedly.

First there's Jeanne, the 'mother' of the house. In her seventies, she's still determined to do her bit; you'll see her sitting quietly at the reception desk – always ready to smile and always willing to attend to any request. Her late husband, Jean Cogny, achieved wonders at this modest Burgundy restaurant: in 1952 he won the much coveted *Meilleur Ouvrier de France* competition – for the best chef in France. That honour has been won over the years by many famous chefs.

It's her son, Jean-Claude Cogny, who is now at the heart of this happy home. Unpretentious, always ready to smile and to help and to give a bit of himself to all his clients. His wife, Monique, together with the friendly *sommelier*, Roger, who has been at Mercurey seven years, look after the small, cosy dining room. Monique's daughters, growing up quickly now but still at school, are more than likely to appear on the scene during your stay. (Years ago Roger was based at Les Gentianes in Les Rousses on the Franco-Swiss border – in lovely Jura country.)

There are so many good reasons for visiting Mercurey. Jean-Claude's *plats* are a joy – full of Burgundian gems: *jambon persillé de l'hôtellerie* – quite perfect; a *persillé de lapin aux herbes* is an equally interesting alternative; *œufs en meurette au vin rouge* – another ideal starter; *escargots*, of course – served with *leur sorbet au crémant* (using the final local 'sparkler'); *le vrai coq au vin de Bourgogne* – inevitably; and a wide choice of other modern and classical specialities.

Then there are the local wines – from the vineyards of the Côte Chalonnaise: the *appellation* villages are Rully, Mercurey, Givry and Montagny (the latter includes Buxy). The general standard of so many of the 'lesser' wines of France has risen enormously over the last decade. Here in the Côte Chalonnaise is an area which is as good an example as any.

Further north are the great wine villages of Burgundy – making wines at prices that make hearts miss a beat or two. Ouch – they hurt: don't they? But lose no sleep my friends: consider the bargains on hand in Rully and Mercurey.

Seek out, in Rully, the Domaine de la Renarde of Jean-François Delorme. He's a knowledgeable man who, since his training some 25 years ago as an oenologist at Dijon University, has transformed his vineyard of 60 hectacres – mainly in Rully but with other parcels of land in nearby villages. His grandfather started the business in 1900; today, Jean-François has developed its reputation considerably.

The reds are perfumed delights – with no bitterness. His whites – a Bourgogne Aligoté (from vineyards at Bouzeron) and a Crémant de Bourgogne – are light and fruity. Jean-François bottles his whites in late spring – the reds during the summer. All visitors to this part of the world should include a buying expedition to his office and warehouse in Rully – where, incidentally he is mayor.

MERCUREY

Alternatively, call on the one-man business of Michel Juillot in Mercurey – Jean-Claude will make the introductions for you. His reds are from the Clos des Barraults – super harvests have come over the years from his vineyards. I've enjoyed 71 and 78 reds and have always relished his Chante Fluté whites – a 1976 example was delicious on a visit in 1982.

Try to head south for a few hours to two sites with ancient and modern ecclesiastical links. Cluny was once the spiritual hub of the Christian world. Little remains of Cluny Abbey, which, until St-Peter's was built in Rome, was the largest Christian church in Europe. But Cluny continues to merit every visitor's attention – apply your imagination as you tour the grounds. Its influence, centuries ago, was enormous; it radiated from Burgundy, throughout France and Europe. Its hundreds of 'children' (dependent abbeys and priories) kept alive the Christian faith when it came close to dying.

On your way there stop at Taizé – with its world-famous community, founded by Brother Roger in 1940; each year over 70,000 young people, of all nationalities and denominations, spend time at the tented village camp. At first glance the 'church' resembles a concrete bunker; but what a transformation takes place when you enter the dark interior. Peace and an overwhelming feeling of faith grips your heart. Short services of song and prayer are at 8.00, 12.20 and 20.30 on weekdays; 10.00, 17.30 and 20.30 on Sundays. I never miss the chance to attend a service at Taizé.

category 3 *menus* A-C *rooms* 12B-C *cards* V *closed* Last wk Aug. 1st wk Sept.Dec.Mon.Sun evg(Nov-Mar).Tues midday(Mar-Nov). *post* Mercurey, 71640 Givry, Saône-et-Loire. (S of Beaune) *phone* 85 47 13 70 *Mich* 243 *map* 17 Beaune 27 km.

ST-PERE   Espérance

Very comfortable hotel
Gardens

For ten years it was a sure-fire prediction: the day would come when Marc Meneau would win three Michelin stars. The question was – when? Anne and I were first stunned by the *cuisinier* genius in 1974 – shortly after Marc and his wife, Françoise, had moved into their newly-acquired St-Père property. He was 30 then – a smouldering volcano of talent biding its time to explode forth. But Michelin require other elements of the three-star set of rules to be met before the accolade is begrudgingly given. In 1984 the honour came. It makes interesting reading to study the history of the couple who have given everything to achieve their objective.

Marc was born a few steps away from the present Espérance – above the family restaurant in the main street of the village. After hotel school training and a stint at a restaurant in Charleville-Mézières on the Belgian border, the couple took over the family business in 1968. Françoise comes from a village near St-Fargeau, between Auxerre and Gien. (The St-Fargeau château is well known but now it's making a bigger name for itself each year when, during the end of July and the month of August, a *Grande Spectacle Historique* is organised: 600 actors, 3,000 costumes and 50 horses are involved.)

Marc's first star came quickly – in 1970. Four years later, when a big privately-owned village house with an idyllic garden – especially the huge trees – came on the market, the couple snapped it up, sinking all their savings in the property. And, of

Denis Parrett

Denis Pannett

course, they borrowed their first rather large lump of capital. In 1975 the second star arrived – it took another nine years to win number three. Marc was as good a chef during those nine years as he is now at 42 – but the 'requirements' insisted upon by Michelin before awarding the third star took all the couple's profits, huge further borrowings, and a lot of courage and belief in their own skills. It really is a frightening financial gamble for a couple determined one day to own a three-star Michelin hotel.

First, the small dining room had to be changed; so a clever 'glass' dining room was added. Next the bedrooms desperately needed renovation; at huge cost each one, in turn, has been modernised in the old building. Then extra staff had to be employed – an expensive business. This step caused problems in the early 80s as readers quickly pointed out. Today service is all but perfect – principally because Philippe Martin is such a superb young *maître d'hôtel*; his wife, Dominique, looks after the reception desk. (I witnessed a split-second reaction by Philippe who spotted a guest's obvious discomfort from a neighbour's newly-lit pipe. Within seconds a tactful request saw the offending odious menace extinguished.) A dozen staff look after the restaurant's 60-odd diners and another 15 work in the kitchen.

Three years ago the couple bought a nearby *moulin* – where, 300 metres from the main hotel building, eight additional bedrooms have been expensively fitted out. Marc's kitchen has not changed one iota in 12 years – that's the next project needing a hunk of extra capital.

Frankly you wonder how Marc has maintained his culinary talents at all. Well, he most certainly has. Big, friendly and a man of his *pays*, he's full of innovative thinking and capable of turning those thoughts into practical reality. Consider one example where a 19th-century Polish recipe is adapted to suit one of his own creations using, in the main, French ingredients. It's called *cromesquis de foie gras en serviette*. Hiding between the folds of a serviette are four hot, dice-sized cubes. The waiter will suggest you eat them whole: do so – unless, like me, you want to spot mark the tablecloth and your clothes. The *chapelure* covered 'kromesky' (using the finest of fine-grained breadcrumbs) is deep fried for a brief period; the browned cube hides a teaspoon or so of liquid *foie gras*, granules of truffle and port wine. One word describes the dish accurately: Wow!

Another culinary surprise is *asperges à la brioche*. This time a potato-based 'egg' is served – again in a *chapelure* covering: break the top, like you would a soft-boiled egg, and, inside, is a hot 'dip' of butter, parsley, tarragon and garlic for your asparagus. Eat the lot! A treat for me was a *turbot rôti au four*: straight from the oven, in its cooking dish, came a perfect fillet of turbot with *champignons*, onions burnt brown (a favourite of mine) and all of it served with a *jus de viande*.

Volaille chevalière en deux services means two servings of chicken: the white meat comes first – a bit over-elaborate, honestly, with slices of truffle embedded deep in the chicken breast; but the small leg served in the heady aroma of a *consommé* is simplicity itself. Always leave room for one of Marc's hot cheese specialities: this could be a *feuilleté de Roquefort chaud* or a *feuilleté de fromages* (using Roquefort, Reblochon, Emmenthal and a local *chèvre*).

There's no point in carrying on torturing you. Save your francs and, if the rooms are too expensive, use the Moulin des

VÉZELAY

Templiers 'base' down the road at Avallon. You'll not regret the financial sacrifice; and, hopefully, you'll not curse me for being so dogmatic when I say simply – Go!

Go, too, to the heights of Vézelay, overlooking the village of St-Père – to the inspiring Basilica of Ste-Madeleine. Whether you stand and admire the tympanum sculpture, the glorious rounded arches of the interior, or the view from the tree-shaded terrace, you'll most certainly be filled with an overpowering sense of history past: this is where St-Bernard preached the Second Crusade; where Richard the Lionheart and Philippe-Auguste, arch-enemies, undertook jointly the Third Crusade; and where, in 1166, Thomas à Becket took refuge and pronounced the excommunication of Henry II of England. I was fortunate enough, on my last visit, to hear an impromptu recital by a group of Germans; singing from the steps of the choir, the touring choral society's joyful singing showed off the Basilica's stunning acoustics. It was an all too-brief few minutes of magical sound.

category **3**★ *menus* **C**(lun:Mon-Sat)-**D** *rooms* 17**D-D3** *cards* AE DC V
closed Jan. Last wk June. Rest: Tues. Wed midday.
post St-Père, 89450 Vézelay, Yonne. (W of Avallon)
phone 86 33 20 45 *Mich* 238 *map* 18 Avallon 12 km.

50

MAQUIS BERNARD

During April 1982 I spent two days in the Morvan, busily exploring the wooded hills of the Regional Park for my book *Hidden France*. On the second of two sunny days I made a 'discovery' which, in the years since, has taken me back to one specific corner of the Park three times – and has been the cause of probably hundreds of Anglo-Saxons seeking out an inspiring spot hidden within the secretive Morvan woods.

I was heading south-west from Montsauche on the D977. As I crossed the stream called Le Chalaux I spotted on my left a sign saying 'Maquis Bernard Cimetière Franco-Anglais'. I braked. "What can that be?" I said quietly to myself. I had certainly never seen reference to it in any guide book.

I turned left – following the tarmac road southwards. After half a mile a second sign, at Savelot, took me from the metalled road onto an unmade track. The stony lane climbed steeply and was somewhat rough but, with care, was driveable. I began to think I was on a wild goose chase as no further signs encouraged me onwards (today, years later, there are); but dead-end roads and Binns go together like hand and glove – so on I went. (Michelin map 65 showed no trace of any lane though the new 238 does identify track and cemetery.)

Just over 1½ miles after leaving the D977 the lane flattened out and entered the Bois de Montsauche. Very soon, on the right, a tiny cemetery appeared, shrouded by a curtain of dense trees. I had never seen such a natural setting for a simple cemetery; the dignity and poignancy of the sacred spot made an instantaneous and dramatic impact on me.

I moved slowly among the white wooden crosses, shaded by overhanging branches. There wasn't a cross for every grave which themselves were no more than moss-covered stones set in the leaf-strewn soil. There was a flagpole flying the tricolour and a handsome stone monument with the modest dedication 'Maquis Bernard A Nos Morts'. Immediately I resolved to find out more about the isolated cemetery and the 26 graves.

The task has proved very difficult. Who was I to ask? It took three further trips to get satisfactory, non-contradictory evidence – and then only after I set aside the best part of a day to do so. I did this because, ever since I first wrote about the cemetery, an astonishing number of letters has arrived at Chiltern House from readers who tracked down the postage stamp-sized bit of ground. I got phone calls, too, and local readers have told me personally about their visits.

No other place I have written about has attracted such an overwhelming response. One lady walked the last mile from Savelot; alas, I didn't intend her to do that. An American couple hired a car in Dijon and managed to find the spot; they left some carnations at the foot of the monument. A letter and some colour photographs arrived from Gus Ide who had made that unscheduled trip: 'I have witnessed many simple burials at sea and I have seen many glorious cemeteries in Europe, but the poignancy and the aura of sacrifice at this small burial ground was greater than I have ever experienced.'

Some of you felt an overpowering feel of a 'presence': one of you said that 'souls were still there'. Another witnessed a mysterious movement among the branches; as if a whirlwind had suddenly descended from an otherwise still, blue sky on a heat-wave day in July. The cemetery has been the cause of much heart-stirring: it's an inspiring, overwhelming place.

What then is the story behind that modest sign on the D977? First it's important to know that the Morvan was one of the main strongholds of the French Resistance (the *maquis*) during the Second World War. Groups of men and women took responsibility for underground resistance to the Germans throughout the Morvan; each group covered an area of perhaps 400 square kilometres and adopted the name of their leader. In this case it was 'Bernard' – a pseudonym for Louis Aubin, who, before the outbreak of hostilities, had been a gendarme. For obvious reasons most members of French Resistance groups were known by pseudonyms.

The 'Maquis Bernard' started operations at the end of 1942 – centered on Montsauche. Their 'camp' was deep in the Bois de Montsauche, not far from the present-day site of the cemetery. The group's activities continued throughout 1943 and during the first few months of 1944. The D-Day landings in June 1944 triggered off a huge increase in Resistance work – not just in the Morvan but throughout France. In the days following the establishment of the Normandy beachhead, activity rose dramatically in the Morvan when ten officers of The Special Air Services (SAS) parachuted into the wooded hills: two on the 6th of June; two on the 11th and a further six on the 22nd.

Attacks on the Germans commenced immediately. In some cases retaliation was horrific. On the evening of June 24 the Maquis Bernard, together with members of the SAS (their base was also in the Bois de Montsauche, just a few hundred metres from the 'Bernard' camp), attacked two German lorries at La Verrerie – about four km. south of Montsauche on the D37 (near a present-day monument). 25 Germans were killed.

On the next day, the 25th, the Germans took savage revenge; 131 homes were put to the torch at Montsauche. On the 27th June, in another horrendous reprisal, the Germans murdered 17 inhabitants of Dun-les-Places, including the mayor and *curé* (the village is nine km. north of Montsauche). Houses were burnt and women raped. This sadistic retaliation followed the 'Battle of Vermot', a hamlet north-west of Dun-les-Places, on the 26/27th June; it, too, was destroyed. This was the pattern throughout France: in the Vercors, in the Morvan, and worst of all, the unspeakable outrage on the 10th of June at Oradour-sur-Glane (north-west of Limoges) where 650 men, women and children were butchered.

The story of the Morvan Resistance is told at a newly-created museum based at the Maison du Parc du Morvan at St-Brisson (14 km. north-east of Montsauche) and open from June-Sept.

And what of the graves at the cemetery? 19 of them were members of the Maquis Bernard – but only one grave is identified by name. The others are seven named British airmen who died when their Halifax crashed in flames near St-Brisson in the early hours of August 12, 1944 – returning from a raid on Dijon. Each year the townspeople of all the nearby communities make a pilgrimage to the cemetery and, in June 1985, the first emotional reunion took place at Montsauche between old comrades of the Maquis and the SAS. There was a simple, moving ceremony of remembrance at the *cimetière* where, during the service, a Union Jack joined the tricolour already flying on the flagpole at the cemetery.

Please, one day, try to make your own personal pilgrimage to this unforgettable piece of Burgundian soil: pay silent homage to just a few of the millions who died fighting for the freedom all of us still enjoy today, over 40 years later.

VAUX

La Petite Auberge

Comfortable restaurant

Many of you will read *The Sunday Times*. Do you remember the major feature I prepared for the colour magazine in January 1982? I identified about a dozen young up-and-coming French chefs: people like Marc Meneau – who went on to win his third star; and others who have since gone on to star number two – Gardillou, Chabran and Arrambide. Tessa Traeger – so talented with her cameras – did the photographic work for the article. The magazine cover and the first two pages of the story featured a broad-smiling chef, Jean-Luc Barnabet, and his then pregnant wife, Marie: Jean-Luc, who comes from Limoges, is now 35; Marie, a *Parisienne*, had a safe delivery not long after the photograph was taken – her daughter, Julie, is five. How times have moved on for the couple.

It's always a joy to see dedicated married couples progress in the culinary world; I can think of scores of examples over the years. The Barnabets are yet another husband and wife team who continue to improve and polish both their personal skills and the bricks and mortar that they sink all their profits into. The bedroom section of the *auberge* stays closed – and will continue to do so. But what a change has come about in the kitchen; a brand new modern affair is Jean-Luc's pride and joy. The tidied-up courtyard, the freshly-decorated façade, smart new toilets above the restaurant, a second dining room (the two rooms seat about 50 diners) and a word processor – all represent evidence of the Barnabets' success.

Thankfully, too, Jean-Luc has developed as a *cuisinier*. What has clearly emerged is his instinctive feel for keeping to the *faites simple* road. You see it in various ways: a *daurade rôtie au vin rouge* – simplicity itself with a fillet of sea-bream resting on a bed of onions and accompanied by the lightest of red-wine reductions; or, alternatively, a *pigeonneau rôti tout simplement* – honestly and accurately described on the menu. With the latter is served a plate of young vegetables. Hurrah!

Another excellent speciality sounds a bit rich – but it's not so in the tasting: *langoustines au Sauternes 'Château Le Mayne 1978'* is presented in a Sauternes-based reduction – together with matchstick strips of not-too-sharp-tasting ginger and some bright-coloured *airelles*. A starter makes refreshing use of grapefruit and melon – *salade de melon et de pomelos glacés au Ratafia* (the local Burgundian version). A sweet is equally refreshing – slices of orange, mango, strawberries and a mint sorbet served in a Crémant de Bourgogne base.

Marie has skilled professional help in the dining rooms these days – in the handsome form of her *maître d'hôtel*, Jean-Claude Mourguiart. Not surprisingly he speaks English fluently – he worked many years ago as a *sommelier* for Raymond Blanc at his restaurant in Oxford. It was a happy surprise for me to see such a familiar face again. Jean-Claude has settled in Auxerre and it is to be hoped that he will become a permanent member of the Barnabet establishment.

Jean-Claude and his boss, Jean-Luc, know their wines; the much improved current list – not exceedingly long as that expensive restaurant overhead needs costly financing – includes many fine Burgundies. But due respect is also paid to the local north Burgundy vintages: the whites of St-Bris – two varieties made from Sauvignon and Aligoté grapes; the rosés

and reds from Irancy; the reds of Coulanges; and the less-expensive whites and reds from Vaux itself. The small vineyards are on the hill above the village and the wines from them are marketed under the cooperative name of Les Nantelles.

Put aside some time to visit the villages of St-Bris and Irancy – both completely ignored by tourists. At St-Bris head south-east on the minor road that takes you to the viewpoint immediately to the east and high above Irancy. Enjoy a scene dominated by cherry orchards and vineyards – in early May a picturesque, colourful sight. Two proprietors are well worth calling on in Irancy: the down-to-earth, larger-than-life Colinot family – their basement *cave* is opposite the town hall; and the modern premises of Bernard Cantin, in the northern shadow of the handsome village church. Incidentally, his little 'bar' is a picture – literally: a wall painting of the church, splendid wood sculptures and some amazing fossil finds from his vineyards add extra appeal to your *dégustation* of his many wines.

La Petite Auberge has no bedrooms – but that's not a problem with Auxerre just four miles to the north. Use the very comfortable Le Maxime overlooking the Yonne in the town or, alternatively, to the north of Auxerre, the modern Les Clairions. It's a pity La Petite Auberge doesn't have bedrooms as the site is perfection – overlooking the calm Yonne in a green, wooded valley. On cool summer evenings many a craft goes chugging by and I gather, increasingly, more and more restaurant business is coming from that passing trade.

category **3** *menus* **B-C** *cards* V
closed 1st 2 wks July. Xmas-mid Jan. Sun evg. Mon. Pub hols.
post Vaux, 89290 Champs-sur-Yonne, Yonne. (S of Auxerre)
phone 86 53 80 08 *Mich* 238 *map* 19 Auxerre 6 km.

AUVILLERS-LES-FORGES
Host. Lenoir

Comfortable restaurant with rooms
Quiet/Gardens/Lift

Jean Lenoir is as good an example as any of just what can be achieved in France by a chef who, against all the odds is prepared to work grindingly hard, year in, year out, for decade after decade. Consider the evidence.

Jean has lived all his life in the tiny, sleepy hamlet of Auvillers, just a mile or two south of the main road from Cambrai to Charleville-Mézières. He's as proud as punch to tell you he was born in the room above the bar at his famous restaurant. In those days it was called La Paix – a modest café, no more no less. It was still that when he went off to the hotel school in nearby Namur in Belgium; on his return, aged 21, he took over the running of the simple bistro from his parents. A year later he married Maryse who, like him, was born and bred in Auvillers.

Three decades later, you would think that Jean could now take it easy: after all his first Michelin star arrived in 1957 and his second in 1975. My first visit was 20 years ago and I've seen all sorts of material improvements over the decades: a three-storey modern bedroom block at the rear and comfortable dining rooms among them.

But don't be misled. He toils away six days a week in the large kitchen – helped by a team of four and his elder sister, Ginette, who has been at his culinary side for all those 31 years. The restaurant closes in January and February but that does not mean Jean puts his feet up: far from it. Instead he uses those tired but strong legs to take him all over the world – to earn additional income and to put Auvillers on the culinary map. Each year sees him travel to the Far East – to Osaka perhaps, or Manila, or Bangkok and Hong Kong. These winter visits are supplemented by working stints in European cities: 1986 saw Jean take over the Mayfair kitchens in London for two weeks.

He's proud of his success: you'll understand why when you realise how exceptionally hard it has been to achieve it off the beaten track. There'll never be a third Michelin star shining overhead here – Jean knows that. He will have to graft away exceptionally hard just to retain his second star. His standards are high and his culinary philosophy is a straightforward one: use the best produce, make it simple, keep it light, provide generous helpings and give value for money. Examples of this logic can be seen in dishes like poached egg, topped with dill-marinated salmon; steamed fillets of sole served with crispy vegetables, 'lemon grass' (bean sprouts) and soya sauce – with a hint of ginger and local *pleurotes* as an accompaniment; or scallops cooked in a Champagne Bouzy red wine.

Stay a night or two: there's glorious river and wooded hill country to the north-east and a dozen or so interesting fortified churches to the west of Auvillers (see pages 30/31 in *France à la carte*). For those of you prepared to stay three nights, the Lenoirs offer very attractive 'package' terms – making a long weekend break a real bargain. With the new A26 autoroute open to St-Quentin it's now only a short drive from the Channel ports to the gentle country of La Thiérache.

category **3** menus **B** rooms 18**B-C** cards A AE DC V
closed Jan. Feb. Fri. (Site: see text)
post Auvillers-les-Forges, 08260 Maubert-Fontaine, Ardennes.
phone 24 54 30 11 *Mich* 241 *map* 20 Charleville-Mézières 31 km.

LONGUYON   **Lorraine**

Comfortable restaurant with rooms

Where would you, a reader, choose as the perfect choice to site your own hotel or restaurant in France? It's likely you would select an attractive spot in one of thousands of different locations but I'll wager any sum you like that not one of you would elect to risk your all in Longuyon. "Where?" you ask. In a small town on the road to nowhere and in a region of France, Lorraine, where the rate of unemployment is notoriously high and where the old traditional industries of steel and coal have taken such a hammering in recent years.

Somehow Gérard and Viviane Tisserant have overcome all the pitfalls they've faced in the 15 years since they took over the family business. To succeed in Longuyon you need three essential personal characteristics: ability, a talent for prodigious hard work and an Everest-sized sense of humour. You'll not find receptionists welcoming you – nor will you see high-salaried chefs helping Gérard in his kitchen; expensive overheads like those are a luxury hereabouts. Let me tell you their story in a paragraph or two; it's a revealing tale.

Gérard went to the hotel school at Colmar where he completed a management training course. After a spell in Germany he then worked for the American Forces in France (before de Gaulle said "Yanks – go home!") and later for various organisations in Paris. Not surprisingly Gérard speaks good English. In 1971 he took over the family business.

Gérard taught himself the finer points of cooking – so well that a dozen years later he won a Michelin star. Like Solange Gardillou and Jean Pierre Capelle he soon got fed up with 'employing' a chef with all the trials and tribulations that can bring. By 1978 the couple had completed a major refurbishing of the building: modern bathrooms were added, the old *garage de hotel* was converted into a restaurant (called Le Mas) and the whole place got a general facelift. Three weeks after they opened the 'new' business the town's biggest employer shut its huge works! See what I mean by a sense of humour?

Well Gérard and Viviane have that for sure. It does one a power of good to hear how they've battled on as the local unemployment situation went from bad to worse during the 80s. Inevitably the couple depend a lot on visitors. The season is desperately short and often on winter nights they are left looking at blank walls in an empty restaurant.

So, my friends, why not make a detour and give them a helping hand to ease their tough financial plight? But be sure to 'natter' with them – though that can only be before or after meal times as Gérard, for example, does everything in the kitchen himself. He works like a Trojan and reckons the only advantage Longuyon offers him is that freshly-landed fish at Boulogne is with him within hours – the town is on the main Calais-Metz railway line. We often take high culinary standards for granted in Michelin-starred restaurants but here it means real graft. Bear all that in mind in the Le Mas restaurant.

Gérard's cooking style is a modern, no nonsense one: fresh produce and a simple technique results in food tasting of what it is. Fish, as I said earlier, comes directly from Boulogne and the choice could be alternatives such as *bar*, lobster, sole, *rouget* and turbot. Vegetables, invariably, come from the garden at the rear of the building – lovingly looked after by

56

Gérard's father, Maurice: marvellous beans and *courgettes* are representative examples of the huge assortment available in that profitable plot behind the kitchen. *Viandes* include *pigeonneau*, *rognons de veau* and *noisettes d'agneau* and other conventional alternatives. Cheeses are particularly well represented in the *chèvre* section and sweets are served from a trolley. The latter confirm Gérard's light touch and, by the way, his culinary sense of humour can be enjoyed with an appetiser consisting of a tiny *millefeuille* with equally minuscule 'cherry' tomatoes. There's a choice of over 150 wines — one of Gérard's passions in life — ranging in cost from 40 to 700 francs.

As with any of the favourites within this book it would be a mistake to stay just one night and hurriedly pass on. Allow some minutes to talk to Gérard and then put aside a few hours to have a taste of history — a salutary reminder of tragic days in 1940. Seek out the fort at Fermont, a few miles south-east of Longuyon, which was part of the formidable Maginot Line. One's instant reaction is to scoff and say what a 'folly' it was. Amazingly the Germans were unable to overcome Fermont — the fort was still battling away when Hitler signed the Armistice in Compiègne Forest on June 25, 1940. You'll soon grasp why the French were able to bloody the Germans' noses when you descend into the underground 'town' with its electric train, lifts and tunnels. The fort is open during afternoons every day from April to September, Saturday and Sunday in October, and Saturday from November to March.

category 3 *menus* A-C *rooms* 15A-C *cards* A AE DC V
closed Jan. Rest only: Mon (not July-Sept).
post face gare, 54260 Longuyon, Meurthe-et-M.
phone 82 39 50 07 *Mich* 241 *map* 21 Verdun 48 km.

MONTMORT   Cheval Blanc

Simple restaurant with rooms
Good value

Try to approach the tiny hamlet of Montmort from the northwest, using the minor roads that run alongside the Surmelin stream from the point it joins the Marne, east of Château-Thierry: in the process you'll pass through three villages all incorporating the word Brie in their names — Condé-en-Brie, Baulne-en-Brie and Mareuil-en-Brie. Shortly before the latter, stop at the fine church in Orbais. The navigational effort will reward you richly and a final bonus comes in the shape of the impressively handsome and strong Château de Montmort rising, or so it seems, from the very surface of the D18.

If you seek out the Cheval Blanc between mid July and mid September you should make certain you arrive in the village after lunch because now the privately-owned château is open to the public from 2.30 to 4.30 (except Mondays). It's a remarkable place and there's still plenty of evidence on hand to show just why it was such a strong fortress. Among the more unusual aspects of the building are the deep, 'dry' moat, the vast kitchen with its interior well and the intriguing tower — designed to allow horses to climb or descend it by using a 'stepless' path and with a central, pedestrian-only staircase. Monsieur and Madame François Crombez de Montmort are the delightful, English-speaking owners; the château has been in their family's hands since 1704.

But the real reason why so many readers have headed for Montmort is not the château but rather the unpretentious, value-for-money home of the Cousinat family: Pierre, the father, does all the cooking with little help; Janine, his smiling, charming wife; and their grown-up children – Anne, now 21, Catherine, aged 17, and 15-year-old Frederic. (Anne is making a big effort to improve her English and the six months she spent in '86 at The Bell Inn, Aston Clinton, should help.)

It's clear why the whitewashed *logis* has been such a success: modest prices for the basic bedrooms and a 'cascade' of six menus which give you a price choice ranging from £5 to £20. The fare is *cuisine Bourgeoise* at its best: among dozens of alternative dishes are treats like *pâté de campagne, plateau de hors d'œuvre, tête de veau sauce Gribiche, jambon de Bayonne, canard de Barbarie rôti, sole grillée Béarnaise, coq au vin rouge* and *poire Belle Hélène*. No small helpings here and no large, unwelcome bills either.

The list of wines is excellent when you consider how humble the Cheval Blanc is: 70 different Champagne 'sparklers' are the main attraction, with 30 Coteaux Champenois whites and reds coming a close second. There are dozens of cheaper varieties, too, from the other wine regions of France. It all adds up to a typical French family-run establishment: nothing is too much trouble, hard work is a way of life, and service is given naturally – and always with a smile. And, remember, if it seems a long time between courses, Pierre is doing all of it with minimal help!

Don't miss the Moët & Chandon cellars at Epernay – one of the most unusual underground 'sites' in France.
category 2(S) *menus* A-C *rooms* 12A-B
closed Mid Feb-mid Mar. Fri.
post 51270 Montmort, Marne. (S of Epernay on RD51)
phone 26 59 10 03 *Mich* 237 *map* 22 Epernay 18 km.

58

REIMS   Boyer 'Les Crayères'

Luxury hotel
Quiet/Gardens/Tennis/Lift

In his memorable book *Champagne: The wine, the land and the people*, Patrick Forbes describes the family histories of all the great Champagne houses. One of the most famous is Pommery & Greno – founded in 1836 by two Reims traders.

Monsieur Pommery died in 1858 and, in the three decades that followed, it was his widow, Louise, who established the great name of Pommery & Greno. It was she who, in the last years of her life, arranged for the present-day château grounds to be landscaped by Redon, the artist – her objective being that at some point in the future her family could build a château home in a mature, natural-looking park. She died in 1890 and a decade or so later, just after the turn of the century, the stunning Château des Crayères was indeed built by her descendants. Today it's the home of one of France's greatest chefs, 45-year-old Gérard Boyer.

My pencil drawing gives you an idea of the perfectly balanced proportions of the mansion. If you stood on the steps and looked the other way you would see grounds falling slightly away from you: a circle of carefully planted trees, none too tall, allows you a glimpse of the 11th-century Basilique St-Rémi; Reims Cathedral can only be spotted from the second floor rooms. If you want to marvel at an exquisite 'picture' of the front of Les Crayères ask Elyane, Gérard's attractive, blond wife, to show you the work of art created by Davina Judis, an American living near Frankfurt. She and her husband, Harold, have

LES CRAYÈRES

become reader friends of mine: make absolutely certain you share Davina's creative secret with the lucky Boyers.

Les Crayères has been a big favourite with readers: the stylishly furnished house – with chandeliers, tapestries and wood panelling giving it a warmth and intimacy that larger châteaux can never match – is one major appeal of course; a second is the friendly welcome of the staff with none of the stuffy 'nose-in-the-air' superior attitudes so often encountered in luxury palaces; another attraction is the care and attention of both Gérard and Elyane, rarely absent from the kitchen and dining room respectively; and, finally, the greatest of all the benefits of this Reims crown – Gérard's glittering cuisine.

Incidentally, the two underground floors beneath the dining rooms are an eye-opener: a gleaming, modern, factory-like 'surprise' housing central-heating plant, the cool *pâtisserie* section of the kitchen, large laundry, a huge Aladdin's *cave* of magical bottled treasures and much else besides.

All clients should ask Werner, the long-serving *maître d'hôtel* (I met him first at the Boyers' previous Reims base), or Pascal, his deputy, to organise a *dégustation* meal for you; the printed menu doesn't make this option clear. The wine list leaves you gasping; not surprisingly as you'll not see its like, as far as Champagne sparklers are concerned, anywhere else. For once I'm not going to list Gérard's culinary repertoire; from beginning to end you'll see why he's a modern-day master. (If you cannot afford the luxury bedrooms and their 'luxury' prices, my *En Route: The French Autoroute Guide* gives you details of nearby, cheaper hotels where you can sleep.)

Finally, why 'Les Crayères'? Let me quote from a reader's letter in which Jennifer Harland makes it all crystal clear.

'In spite of having twice visited the Champagne region, it was not until reading Noel Barber's novel *A Farewell to France*, that we learnt of the Roman chalk pyramids and network of galleries which lay hidden from view underneath Reims.

Our visit to the *crayères* (chalk-pits) of Pommery & Greno was quite an experience. To reach them you descend a colossal flight of stairs inside the Pommery château (near the Boyer 'hotel'). The galleries, which are used to store champagne, were cut in the 18th century. These connect at base level ancient 'pyramids' hewn by Roman slaves for chalk. The base of a pyramid can be the size of a large room and, as you peer upwards, a tiny aperture, at ground level and some 30 metres above your head, permits daylight to filter down.

We found the *crayères* cold and awesome. To lighten the atmosphere Madame Pommery commissioned the artist Navlet to chisel his bas-relief masterpieces into the chalk walls — Bacchanalian feasts paying tribute to the glory of Champagne: the result is inspired and boy, do you feel like joining in!'

category 3 *menus* C-D *rooms* 16**D2-D3** *cards* A AE DC V *closed* Xmas-mid Jan. Rest only: Mon & Tues midday.
post 64 bd Vasnier, 51100 Reims, Marne.
phone 26 82 80 80 *Mich* 237 *map* 23

AURIBEAU
Nossi Bé

Comfortable restaurant with rooms
Quiet/Terrace

French Leave readers have finely-honed instincts for spotting chefs who are going places and for those tobogganing downhill fast: they can quickly identify the winners and losers! Jean Michel Retoré is yet another of the Côte d'Azur favourites who, without exception, readers have appreciated for their good-value cooking. No compliments have arrived at Chiltern House praising the famous Côte d'Azur chefs but hundreds of you have written to say how much you loved the simpler places in the *arrière-pays* — the hill country behind the coast.

Jean Michel is 34 and hails from a village near Arras, in the Pas-de-Calais; he couldn't be further from home. Dark-eyed Anne-Marie, his wife, is from Cannes and proud of it. After a spell in the Southwest at Montauban, the couple started their Auribeau enterprise in 1980. Readers are on the ball in recognising a good thing when they taste it — but neither Michelin nor Gault Millau, at the time of my last visit at the end of 1985, had found a place for the couple in their annual guides. Let's hope that changes soon. (GM did in '86!)

Auribeau is one of the picturesque 'perched' villages in the hills behind the coast. It's a tiny place with a narrow 'circular' road within the ancient village. Nossi Bé lies outside the village walls and has the splendid advantage of an extensive view north-east towards Grasse. As a bonus there are six comfortable bedrooms fitted out in modern style.

What a competent *cuisinier* Jean Michel is: witness delights like a *soupe d'écrevisses* or, a bit of a 'mouthful', a *gâteau de ris d'agneau à l'estragon au coulis de poivron rouge et ses raviolis frais* (the latter, green-coloured — made with spinach — are delicious; stuffed with basil they come from a shop at the crossroads in Pégomas — see the entry for Le Bosquet) and desserts like a home-made *nougat glacé au miel et coulis de framboise*. What's so special about the menu at the Nossi Bé is that you have such a wide choice — some eight or so alternatives for both the first and second courses followed by a choice of six desserts. Cheeses are extra. The home-made *apéritif — kir maison —* is unusually good and 'different'.

All in all it's a formula of benefits that has given a great deal of pleasure to readers: good, inexpensive food, a smashing couple — Anne-Marie is a delight — and a quiet, anything but run-of-the-mill setting.

The couple are motoring 'nuts': Jean Michel runs an old 3.8 Jaguar — a handsome classic; and Anne-Marie's pride and joy is a Mark III Austin-Healey Sprite. We shared many happy minutes comparing notes about cars and the world's best motoring terrain in the hills to the north. Finally, before I forget, don't miss the magnificent new Motor Museum — financed by Adrien Maeght (see the St-Paul entry) — near Mougins. You can get to it from the D35 Mougins-Antibes road (the museum is on the D135) or from the westbound carriageway of the A8 autoroute. It's well worth a detour. I was lucky enough to see an additional exhibition of Ferrari cars; what a sight they were. *category* 2 *menus* B *rooms* 6B-C *cards* A
closed Nov-Xmas.Tues evg & Wed (only Wed midday in season). *post* 06810 Auribeau-sur-Siagne, Alpes-Mar. (S of Grasse) *phone* 93 42 20 20 *Mich* 245 *map* 46 Grasse 8 km.

FAYENCE
France

Simple restaurant
Terrace/Good value

Shortly after *French Leave 3* was published I discovered that Marcel and Rosette Choisy had called it a day at their Fayence restaurant. My embarrassment was considerable. Why? Well, I had chosen Marcel as one of my favourite 15 French chefs, alongside people like Marc Meneau, for the reason that he was the epitome of so many hundreds of hardworking French men and women slaving away at the bottom end of the culinary pyramid but, nevertheless, giving marvellous pleasure to tens of thousands of clients — at knock-down prices.

I needn't have worried because, though I received a few unhappy letters to start with, the new owner soon settled into a reliable groove — doing things in very much the old Choisy style that our family has loved for two decades. Guy Boury, the new *patron*, is a great *copain* (mate) of Marcel; they have known each other since the days when they were members of the Free French Army. Guy saw action in Italy and France and for a time served under General Patton. He's a fine *patron*, easy to get on with, and determined to continue providing quite exceptional value for money for those who seek out the France.

La cuisine d'autrefois sums up the approach at the France to a tee: family, *Bourgeoise* cooking with honesty and simplicity shining through the numerous menu bargains. Amazingly the three menus cost approximately £5, £7 and £11. The first is charity; the second is the essential choice and the third only necessary for those with gigantic appetites who 'have' to have an extra main course and a selection of cheeses as well. On the coast utter rubbish is often dished up, and it costs more!

So Guy has kept to the Marcel 'style'. The good news, too, is that the familiar face of *petite* Fernande still graces the geranium-lined, awning-shaded terrace and the cosy interior dining room; she was married a year ago. What can you choose from that £7 menu? Well, to start with there's a plate of ham *(jambon cru)*, or a massive slice of *terrine du chef* (back home it would cost at least £1 or more to buy), or a big bowl of *rillettes maison*, or *les raviers de crudités du jour* (remember the cover picture on the hardback *FL3*?). For me the latter is the best choice: ten alternatives like saffron rice, green Le Puy lentils, beetroot, carrots, red cabbage, luminous bright-red tomatoes, cucumber, celery, peppers and potato; all served with tasty dressings.

For the main course you can try a trout, or *poulet aux pignons, canard en confit, entrecôte grillée, caille fraîche rôtie* or the famous *tranche de gigot aux herbes* – the latter served with *haricots verts, sautée* potatoes and a heady aroma of local herbs. Various sweets complete the bill of fare; a featherlight, creamy meringue is still one of the best alternatives. A rosé from the Vignobles Kennel Pierrefeu (see *FL3* or *Bon Voyage* for the location) is an ideal wine to accompany your meal; the Kennels are from Alsace and their vineyard is well worth a visit if only to see the *cyprès* (cypress) *millénaire*, reckoned to be the oldest in Europe. Book ahead at the France!

category **2(S)** *menus* **A-B** *cards* AE DC V
closed Jan. Mid Nov-Xmas. Wed evg & Thurs (out of season).
post 83440 Fayence, Var. (West of Grasse)
phone 94 76 00 14 *Mich* 245 *map* 47 Grasse 27 km.

FAYENCE

GRASSE

Maître Boscq

Very simple restaurant
Good value

Patrick Boscq is honest at least. His small business card, in announcing his restaurant to prospective clients, states 'Tries hard to speak English'. His English is perhaps better than my French, but be that as it may, I can guarantee you one thing the courageous 49-year-old chef does really well: he offers a wide range of Provençal specialities, particularly those from the immediate locality of Grasse and Nice. Apart from Hélène Barale at Nice I know of no-one else in the south who makes such an effort to protect and present regional recipes.

Inevitably, considering the past history of the Côte d'Azur, the specialities have a strong Italian influence. Their names make mysterious and fascinating reading. Patrick describes each one on his menus in English – but even if he didn't, you would still be intrigued by the names, and I guess you would order some of them for that reason alone. Among the many head-scratching descriptions, consider for example these few: *lou saussou* – a cucumber salad with a light *lait d'amandes*; *tourteau Grassois aux herbes* – a 'pie' made from green vegetables like *blettes*, *oignons verts*, *epinards* and *courgettes* and numerous herbs; *fricot de cacho-fuou* – a tartlet of *morue* (cod) and leeks; and, finally, the quite exceptional *lou fassum*.

What on earth is that? Well, before I describe it, let me tell you that all those specialities require long hours of effort to produce. Modern cooking, as much as I like its simplicity, is not exactly time-consuming; old regional specialities on the other hand often require hours and hours of slogging work. *Lou fassum* certainly does: a huge green cabbage leaf is stuffed with a mixture of white cabbage, rice, pork, *petits pois*, other chopped-up vegetables and herbs, and Patrick's own extra ingredient – a touch of sage! He prepares these huge *choux farcis* twice a week and it takes about eight hours to make them. It's impossible to cut the finished dish, for serving purposes, within the first 24 hours because, if you do, it literally falls apart. Many of his specialities are made to order so it really does pay to talk to him in advance. There's also a fixed-price menu at the ludicrously charitable level of £7 or so: what value.

The 'restaurant' is the smallest you'll ever see – you can hardly swing a kitten in it, let alone a cat. At the very most only 20 clients or so can be shoe-horned in – all of them looked after with great good humour and charm by Odile Boscq. Both Patrick and Odile have an engaging sense of humour. He started his hair-brained, self-employed existence six years ago – at a time when he had had enough of managing hotel establishments for big conglomerates in Paris. I know what he must have felt like at 40-plus to take that brave step.

The couple's eldest son, Cyril, is soon to join his father in the 'business'. I don't know whether that will mean a change in the basic approach as the young man has had a thoroughly good training – including spells at Vergé's restaurant and at Thuriès' hotel, the Grand Ecuyer, at Cordes.

The restaurant is just off the place aux Aires (the small open-air market) at the fountain end. On no account miss this lovely couple with a difference. *Vive la différence!*

Grasse has always been a great favourite for Anne and me. We like its site at an altitude of just over 1000 ft above sea-level;

it's always a cooler place than the sweltering hot coast. The narrow streets of the old town are well worth exploring but, for us, most pleasure comes from the morning market held in the place aux Aires (see map) – at its best on a Saturday morning. Apart from fresh produce, you can also buy flowers and though it cannot match the fabulous Nice flowermarket (don't miss that either – behind the Promenade des Anglais and east of the Hôtel Négresco), nevertheless, it's a wonderful spectacle. Seek out the *fromagerie* and *pâtisserie* shops on the main road side of the fountain: both called du Thouron, these featured on the cover of the hardback edition of *French Leave 3*; also the Charcuterie de la Montagne in the *place* – a fine example.

Maître Boscq can be hard to find – the map below should help. In the evening, park in the place aux Aires. At other times, park in the underground park at the place du Cours – if coming from the direction of Cannes; or the car park at the bus station if you are approaching from the direction of Nice. These suggestions take account of the new one-way traffic system.
category 2(S) *menus* A
closed 1st week July. Fête days. Sun. Mon (out of season).
post 13 rue Fontette, 06130 Grasse, Alpes-Mar.
phone 93 36 45 76 *Mich* 245 *map* 48

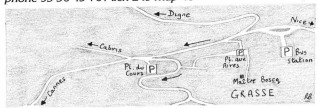

MOUGINS   Feu Follet

Simple restaurant
Terrace/Good value

The elm tree flourishes – and, what is even more important, the remarkably hardworking Micheline and Jean-Paul Battaglia have well and truly established themselves as a real hit with all those readers who have sought them out in famous Mougins.

It's a picture-book setting – the ideal location for a film set; you half expect to hear the shouted command "Take!" at any second. The good news is that the Feu Follet will not bankrupt readers – so you have no excuses for not visiting this honeypot village.

But first consider the financial facts of life behind an enterprise like the Feu Follet. If the price is right, clients will come. But high Mougins overheads and inexpensive menus (using 100 per cent fresh produce and with a welcome degree of fine skill applied to all the dishes) cannot make economic sense unless a good many clients are served every day. The formula works well here; it's always busy and tables are inevitably full. The key to success is in the number of clients served. But how welcome it is to see Micheline and her young team of waitresses keep their cool and show such patience – despite the crowded tables. I watched Micheline, without her realising it, deal most sympathetically with a young couple with their tiny baby in tow – despite other pressing tasks awaiting her. For a lot of readers the busy atmosphere adds to the pleasure; you have the choice of a terrace where you can see the 'actors' strutting by in the village 'pedestrian-only' street, or you can go indoors.

Jean-Paul Battaglia, the youngest of a family of six and one of three brothers earning their living as *cuisiniers* (see Valbonne), is an able 28-year-old chef. His training included stints in North America and he thinks nothing of spending part of his holidays in some of the great French restaurants, polishing up his skills. Micheline, his wife, was born in the States and thus speaks perfect English. The couple have recently taken the brave step of buying the restaurant for themselves with all the responsibility of a huge mortgage that that entails.

Menus range in cost from approximately £7 to £12. You have a limited choice but the alternatives could range from a *bisque d'écrevisses* or an authentic *soupe de poissons* to a *terrine de palangre* (a Mediterranean fish) or Sisteron lamb and *magret de canard* – just a few examples of the dishes available. Jean-Paul laughingly explains that he's often asked if his North Sea fish are frozen; not so, as overnight deliveries of fresh fish are as easy to get here on the south coast as anywhere else in France. And the joke now is that 'local' Mediterranean fish are very expensive – appearing mainly on the menus of more fancy restaurants. Only North Sea fish make financial sense!

Readers should realise, too, that a cheese board for any restaurant in France is a loss-making operation. You only have to price the variety of French cheeses in a *fromagerie* to see what I mean. Jean-Paul and Micheline get round the problem by offering just two varieties – at extra cost: an Auvergne blue, served with a salad, or a grilled goat's cheese. They, too, like all other restaurants, have been hit by years of Mitterrand's strict limits for annual price increases. What gives in the end? You employ less staff, you try to make a bit more on wines and you

cut back on anything too ambitious on the menus. Incidentally, Jean-Paul is capable of providing excellent dishes made to order – not in the high season but during the rest of the year. Give him two days' notice and you'll be pleased with his efforts.

(For the record those strictly-applied annual price rises are often given by hoteliers as the reason for the ever-lower standards of French breakfasts. Another moan is the 'commission' they have to give 'card' companies: five per cent is the norm – seven for AE.)

Finally, let me end on a happy note. Micheline's father, André Surmain, at his Relais à Mougins across the road from the Feu Follet, is back to his very best form. A traumatic divorce three years ago caused him a great deal of havoc: it was no wonder I received complaints and that the second Michelin star disappeared. But now he has got his grin back, has regained some lost weight and has assembled a first-class team.

There's Roger Heyd, a thoroughly-competent *maître d'hôtel*; Jean-Luc Gauffilier – a knowledgeable *sommelier*; and young Hubert Aviles, the chef, who in four years has added a sure, deft touch to his cooking skills. If the pennies count why not go at lunchtime when the quality/price ratio for this standard of high-class restaurant cannot be bettered in France. Two menus, service, tax and good-quality wine included, range in cost from £17 to £20: a typical menu could offer *rillettes de saumon fumé* with cherry tomatoes as an appetiser, a *salade de caille et blanc de lotte tièdes* (with a fried quail's egg accompanying it), then a *vapeur de sole et de saumon sauvage aux légumes 'en confettis'* (finely chopped peppers and courgettes), followed by a masterful creation of chicken breast and hot duck liver served in a sweet Ste-Croix-du-Mont cream

sauce. Finish with cheeses, three perfectly-balanced desserts and *petits fours*. At dinner there's a more expensive menu.

French Leave readers will know that André spent many decades of his life as a celebrated chef-restaurateur in New York. Quiz him about his culinary life and times and natter to him about his passion for cars and all things motoring.

category 2 *menus* **A-B**
closed 1st two wks Mar. Nov. Sun evg & Mon (out of season).
post pl. Mairie, 06250 Mougins, Alpes-Mar. (N of Cannes)
phone 93 90 15 78 *Mich* 245 *map* 49 Cannes 7 km.

PEGOMAS   Le Bosquet

Simple hotel
Secluded/Gardens/Swimming pool

Le Bosquet has always been one of a handful of the most appreciated *French Leave* favourites: but if one of that select band had to be voted the most 'loved' there's absolutely no question that this modest hotel would win the prize.

Jean-Pierre and Simone Bernardi opened their little gem of a 'base' 21 years ago, in 1965. Anne and I first 'discovered' it a year or two later – and, ever since, there has been no other hotel in France that we have returned to, time after time, more willingly and with such eager anticipation. Scores of you have written to me since 1980, when I first told readers about Le Bosquet; I suspect therefore that hundreds of you must have visited the hotel and fallen in love with it.

Why? Possibly it could be the setting, which is appealing: Pégomas is midway between Grasse and Cannes, at a point where the hills start their rise from the flat fields to the north of Mandelieu – so visitors are away from the worst of the concrete strip along the coast; and the hotel is in a fairly isolated site, quiet (though as I get older I find the distant church clock a bit of a 'pest' – maybe I sleep more fitfully now) and refreshing – ideal for those of you who want to sit back, relax, read and occasionally have a dip in the pool.

But material benefits, in the end, do not provide the answer to my question. Not surprisingly, as with most worthwhile enterprises in life, it's a super family who are the heart and soul of Le Bosquet. It will not take you long to meet them all: Simone is the 'locomotive' of the family – busy during every waking hour of the day, smiling, fastidious, energetically watching for any detail that needs correcting; Jean-Pierre, her husband, is a gentle, shy man with the most appealing of happy, smiling faces and, like all those who work on the land, he's a wise man – as you'll discover when you have a chat with him (unlike Simone, he speaks no English); then there's the remarkable Françoise, Simone's mother, who at the age of 87 reckons that retirement is for the lazy bones of this world – if you want to put her to the test watch the effort she puts into the daily washing of hotel linen; a third generation is represented by Chantal, the Bernardi daughter, who is a look-alike of her mother; and, finally, there's three-year-old Romain, Chantal's child, already a favourite with clients.

It's no wonder then that Britons, Danes, Dutchmen, Germans, Americans and 'some' French love Le Bosquet. It is the letter 'C' that counts most at Pégomas: cleanliness, character, courtesy, cheerfulness, comfort, care and calm are seven examples of what I mean. I have written elsewhere about that special down-at-heel 'charm' of many provincial French hotels; but that's not a description you can apply here.

You enter Le Bosquet down a long drive with fruit trees acting as a guard of honour (note how many perished in that cruel month of January 1985): on the left are plum trees, on the right apricot. The home-made jams you'll savour at breakfast are from the fruit from those very trees. (Interestingly, Simone reckons to use ½ a kilo of sugar to 1 kilo of fruit in making her plum jam.) High hedges, grass, flower beds, trees, driveways, exterior and interior walls, beds, bathrooms, terraces – all are smart but without being clinically oppressive. Originally the older building of the two was the property of a Grasse *parfumeur* – the gardens surrounding it a mass of jasmin and roses. Now the orchard, planted by Jean-Pierre, gives him an additional busy occupation.

Elsewhere I've given you plenty of detailed ideas of what you can see and do in the hills behind Pégomas – and more besides – in books like *Hidden France* and *France à la carte*. But there's a shop in Pégomas, by the bridge, which I would like to ensure you don't miss. Called La Bolognaise (Chez César & Pierrette) – what an evocative name – it's a treasure trove of Italian delights: *raviolis, pâtes fraîches, gnocchis, pâtes vertes, canellonis, lasagnes, tortellonis* and goodness knows what else. Everything is home-made: green *raviolis* (it's spinach that gives them their hue) stuffed with basil, mouthwatering *tarte à l'oignon, tarte aux courgettes* and *tarte aux poireaux*, pizzas – of course, *tortelloni* made with *fromage blanc* and *fines herbes*, *sauces maison* and, if you order in advance, paëlla.

Picnic lunches in Provence take on a different meaning from other parts of France – particularly between mid May and July. The shops in Pégomas or the bigger markets in Grasse and Cannes (and the rue Meynadier) are a joy: strawberries, asparagus, melons, cheeses, *pâtisseries, charcuterie*, breads – the list is endless. Le Bosquet has four studios with fully-fitted kitchens and small terraces where many a time my family have enjoyed the fruits of our morning market expeditions. Try to reserve one and count yourself lucky if you're successful!
category 1 *menus* No rest. *rooms* 25**B-C**
closed Nov.
post 06580 Pégomas, Alpes-Mar. (S of Grasse)
phone 93 42 22 87 *Mich* 245 *map* 50 Grasse 10 km.

PEGOMAS   L'Ecluse

Very simple restaurant
Secluded/Terrace/Good value

L'Ecluse has an unusual record. Over the years I have received no less than three postcards (from different readers at different times), all written on the spot, and on the spur of the moment, by happy, contented visitors to this isolated, riverside restaurant. It's an unpretentious place making no claims other than to provide value for money and the happy feel of a hardworking family at work. No wonder it appeals so much.

Raoul Tognarelli is the friendliest chef imaginable. He's proud of his newly-built kitchen block and the clever idea of an outside bar, sheltered by a handsome porch. His wife, Denise, together with their charming young daughter, Anne, and her husband, Antoine, look after the tables and their clients' needs.

The special 'extra' here is the position – alongside the River Siagne. In May and June it is at its best – the river is a shimmering green and usually full. A riverside lunch on the shaded terrace – or an evening meal during the hot months of July and August – is a pleasant experience. (At other times of the restaurant's all too short season, you'll eat dinner in a very modest dining room.) The setting in summer is perfection – an azure sky overhead and a wooded hillside on the other bank of the gently-flowing river. It's hard to leave this delectable spot.

The cuisine is simplicity itself; there's nothing chic about the dishes listed on the three menus. But how can anyone not enjoy the basic fare? Start with alternatives such as crudités, pâté de grive, pâté de campagne, terrine du chef, salade

Niçoise or, from the most expensive menu, a cascade de hors d'œuvre variés. Follow with one of these dishes: gigot aux herbes served with frites, haricots verts and a salad; lapin chasseur; a simple truite meunière or an entrecôte grillée; or a more complicated beignets de calamars or rognons de veau sauce Madère. Sweets will be equally simple.

Surprisingly, for this part of the world, the very short wine list includes two Vins du Bugey – from the hills east of Lyon in the area where the River Rhône leaves Savoie: a fresh Chardonnay white – with a slightly prickly feel to it; and a fruity young Gamay red. Both wines come from a good friend of Raoul's who lives at Culoz in Bugey. They're good – try them.

Despite its secluded setting L'Ecluse is easy to find: follow the signs as you head north out of Pégomas. Note, too, that it is open for tea, coffee, drinks and ice-cream during the afternoon. If you cannot manage a lunch – try those treats.

My family have known L'Ecluse and the contented Tognarelli family for 20 years. It has given us great pleasure to send so many readers down the narrow lane to their simple restaurant. We have seen Annie grow up from a youngster – and it has been nice, too, to see the family improve facilities over the years as profits allowed. The handsome new kitchen was built a couple of years ago and I gather other building plans are afoot. You can help them to materialise by paying the family a visit; nothing fancy, nothing sophisticated – but at the end of the day you'll leave as satisfied as you could possibly be.
category 2(S) menus A-B
closed Mid Sept-Apl. (S of Grasse: NW of village)
post 06580 Pégomas, Alpes-Mar.
phone 93 42 22 55 Mich 245 map 51 Grasse 10 km.

TOUR DE FORCE

To the north of Grasse is some of the best mountain terrain to be found anywhere in France. The recommended tour that follows is most certainly one of the best day drives you can make anywhere in this richly varied land. Ensure you do it: I guarantee you'll be spellbound. Use Michelin green map 195.

Mother Nature will hit you for six on the trip (a 'home run' to my North American friends). She's made savage cuts through the mountain rocks – and, for much of the trip, carpeted the hillsides with scores of different trees, both deciduous and evergreen varieties. From mid May to mid June you'll see dozens of differing wild flowers: some prosper on the sun-facing southern mountain sides – others cool themselves on the northern, more shady slopes; but one thing is certain – you'll spot them everywhere. During the spring and early summer the streams are full of rushing water – adding to the visual intoxication. And, for most of the route, you'll pass no coaches – that's for sure; and few cars, too, for that matter.

From Grasse, head north-east on the D2085 towards Nice and, after six kilometres, on the D3 towards Gourdon. Stop at the village for its aeroplane-like panorama of the mighty Gorges du Loup far below. Continue north as the River Loup gets closer to the road all the time. Eventually cross it and soon the D3 meets the D2; turn left towards Gréolières. Continue on the D2 until you reach Les Quatre-Chemins; then climb the Col de Bleine. At the summit, detour on the narrow, steep track to your right and continue climbing several hundred feet to the radio mast. A surprise awaits you to the north – extensive views of snow-capped peaks! The spot is a favourite haunt of hang-gliders; no wonder – you're well over 5000 ft above sea-level.

Descend to the north and then east on the D10. What an exciting road it is – and how interesting for geologists. You'll gasp at Le Mas on its dizzy perch – but even more so at the Clue d'Aiglun. It's an orange and grey gash – slashed through slabs of rock hundreds of metres high. Some seven kilometres later you spot the village of Sigale high above you – clinging on by its fingernails to the mountain edge; it seems set to start sliding down the slippery slope soon!

Use the D17 to traverse the village. Shortly you pass through a second *clue* – the Clue du Riolan. Then west on the D2211A to a third 'rift' – the Clue de St-Auban; here the road and stream share the narrow, deep slit in the rocks. Note the River Estéron is the same one that pierced the rocky barrier at Aiglun.

Retrace your steps to Briançonnet and climb north on the Col du Buis (a place where I once ran out of petrol with my youngsters aboard!) and then on to Entrevaux. As you descend you have a remarkable aspect of the medieval village and its citadel high above it – linked together by an umbilical zigzag wall. Total distance is about 135 km.

PEILLON   Auberge de la Madone

Comfortable hotel
Secluded/Terrace/Gardens

The evening before I was due to visit the Auberge de la Madone I had a strange premonition: something told me to telephone and ask for my written confirmation to be confirmed. It was the first time I had ever done it – but what an eerie premonition it proved to be: "No," the voice at the other end of the phone replied, "we are closed because of a death in the family."

So, for the only time in my long months of research for this new book I found the hotel's doors firmly shut. I wasn't able to stay overnight nor was I able to eat in the restaurant; but that was no problem as I was still able to talk to Christian Millo and his smashing sister, Marie-Josée – both of whom will continue to run this hugely-appreciated favourite of my readers. Despite their recent family bereavement they gave me two hours of their precious time to reacquaint myself with the joy of my last happy visit there three years earlier.

Your first sight of Peillon will make you gasp. Six kilometres after leaving the Nice-Est exit on the A8 autoroute you turn right off the D2204 Sospel road. Within three kilometres or so you see a tiny village 'perched' on top of a high, sharp needle of rock; you wonder how on earth you are going to reach the summit in a car. Soon a 3.2 km. (two miles) climb to the right proves the impossible is possible. At the summit of the 700-ft ascent you reach the Auberge and the village – the latter closed to all motor-cars; what a treat that is in this day and age.

The Auberge (once a nunnery) is to your left – sitting above its flower-bedecked terraces and with a spellbinding view southwards over the valley from which you have just climbed. Despite its remote and secluded site the hotel is fitted out with the most modern of bedrooms – those on the southern side having real sun-trap terraces. Apart from the delightful Millo family, who run the hotel with such charm and grace, you also have the extra special bonus of a highly capable chef, much in love with his *pays* and the rich larder of local produce it provides for his considerable number of regional specialities.

The menu names the first one that appeals so much to me as *le tourton des Pénitents* – hot fritters where eggs are used as the *liaison* to bind together *pignons* (pine nuts), almonds and a mixture of about a dozen Provençal herbs; a *coulis* of tomatoes and basil is the accompanying sauce. Don't miss this super dish. Another seasonal speciality you may be lucky enough to see on the menu in the autumn is *la charlotte tiède aux champignons et basilic* – where Christian uses the regional *sanguines* varieties; at lower altitudes in the Alpes-Maritimes these are reddish-hued *champignons* – at high altitudes, like the Col de Turini for example, they are orange-coloured.

Two further regional dishes that are personal creations of Christian's are a *bouillabaisse en gelée*, cut and served in cold terrine-like slices with *croûtons* and *rouille* – a rare treat; and *des raviolis de la Madone* – thumbnail-sized, transparent *raviolis* served with a *daube* made from beef, *cèpes* and red wine. Do both of them make your mouth water?
category 2 *menus* B *rooms* 18B-C
closed Mid Oct-mid Dec. Wed.
post Peillon, 06440 L'Escarène, Alpes-Mar. (NE of Nice)
phone 93 79 91 17 *Mich* 245 *map* 52 Nice 25 km.

ST-MARTIN-DU-VAR   Issautier

Very comfortable restaurant

I wonder why it is that I have received during the last five years so many critical letters for the three famous culinary shrines on the Côte d'Azur: Vergé's Moulin de Mougins, Outhier's L'Oasis at La Napoule and Jo Rostang's La Bonne Auberge at La Brague? And yet why is it that a score or more of my readers have written to suggest that I seek out Jean-François and Nicole Issautier at their restaurant in St-Martin-du-Var – a place I have yet to recommend in any of my books. Because of that unsolicited support I have decided to break the 'rules' and include the Issautier restaurant as a 'favourite'.

A dozen or so years ago my family and I had lunch at a remote restaurant in an isolated village called St-Etienne-de-Tinée. You'll have to search hard to find it: it's to the north-west of the Var Valley at the foot of the mighty Col de la Bonette – at 2802 metres the highest pass in France. We had a super lunch and marvelled at the skill of the then 28-year-old chef, Jean-François Issautier. We questioned, too, how he would ever make his name or fortune at such an out-of-the-way spot.

During those years, a decade and more ago, my family enjoyed our many visits to the simple Auberge de la Belle Route, in the Var Valley about 15 miles north of the Mediterranean coast. Nine years ago the Issautiers decided that enough was enough at St-Etienne and moved south, buying the Auberge from the Costes, the previous owners, in the process. What a transformation has taken place – it now befits the reputation Jean-François has gained of being one of the best French chefs. The proud holder of two Michelin stars, the 40-year-old chef is still his humble, happy self – and Nicole, too, has lost none of her unspoilt charm. The restaurant has none of the clinical soullessness of the more famous Riviera culinary temples. The chef is *in situ*, too!

With today's modern style of cooking – light sauces, sensible proportions and fresh produce – it's a delight to report that Jean-François has built up a formidable personal collection of specialities based on classical traditions. His style is just as modern as anybody else's – but the unmistakable print of the past is clearly stamped on his '80s repertoire. Consider two examples: a *soupe d'écrevisses en tasse, quenelles, huîtres et petits croutons frits* – crayfish tails with tiny quenelles of John Dory and salmon, a few oysters and croutons all served in a creamy lobster 'soup'; and a *suprême de poularde et légumes* in a tarragon butter sauce – the breast looking like a 'leg' and, as a stuffing within it, the same vegetables (*haricots verts*, carrots, *navets*, cauliflower and minuscule broccoli florets) that also appeared on the plate alongside the chicken.

You see similar touches of classical skill in other ways, too: for example, a *gratin* of hot raspberries and the smallest *millefeuilles* you'll ever enjoy. Add to these benefits a wine list which includes some of the best Provençal vintages (including the nearby Bellet) and you have every reason in the world to head for St-Martin. (For overnight rooms use the nearby Servotel: same postcode but phone is 93 08 22 00.)
category 3 *menus* C *rooms* See text *cards* AE DC V
closed Feb-mid Mar. Sun evg. Mon.
post 06670 St-Martin-du-Var, Alpes-Mar. (On N202 in Var Valley)
phone 93 08 10 65 *Mich* 245 *map* 53 Nice 27 km.

ST-PAUL

Le Hameau

Comfortable hotel
Quiet/Gardens

I hardly needed to be reminded just how awful the narrow coastal strip of the Côte d'Azur has become over the years: a ribbon of hideous concrete where so-called planners and architects have created a monstrosity of all that's worst in 20th-century urban development. Add to that the deafening sound of traffic in an environment where cars appear to outnumber people – and that's saying something; where pollution in both sea and atmosphere is rampant; where burglary has reached epidemic proportions; and the constant hassle in avoiding rip-offs in restaurants. I had a taste of it all while carrying out my autoroute project – that following on letters I've received from readers complaining about the coast.

No wonder then that all readers' Côte d'Azur favourites are to be found inland. Though the 'menace' is creeping nearer St-Paul, it has yet to overtake this little hotel – an oasis of calm and pleasure. In the shadow of the village, perched high above it to the east, Le Hameau is a delightful 'base' – several old buildings with 'honest' names like Le Pigeonnier, La Treille, L'Olivier and L'Oranger, all of them surrounded by fragrant gardens, full of orange, tangerine and apricot trees. You can have breakfast, which is of a high standard with good home-made jams, either on a shady patio or on a sun-trap terrace.

Le Hameau was once a farm – the oldest part of which is thought to be two to three hundred years old. Over the years I've stayed in all four sections of the hotel; on my last visit I had a bedroom in Le Pigeonnier. In fact I wrote these words on the bedroom's tiny terrace alongside a *pigeonnier* (dovecot) with a dozen or so white *paon* (peacock) pigeons as company; the word 'peacock' is an apt description for their fan tails.

Xavier Huvelin is a friendly *patron* and he speaks English well. He explained to me in some detail a hazard facing his continuing ownership of Le Hameau. Apparently he owns it in partnership with his mother and other members of his family; his mother is nearing 75 and, in the event of her death, the State would demand 40 per cent of her estate (her share in the hotel) as death duties. The legal experts say the only way out would be to sell the property now. Be that as it may, it will be a shame if Xavier is not on the scene in the years to come.

Once you have given your time to the local man-made villages and towns of St-Paul itself, Vence, Antibes and Haut-Cagnes, and, of course, to the Maeght Foundation (only a minute or two away), the Chapelle du Rosaire in Vence (created by Matisse), the Picasso Museum in the Château Grimaldi at Antibes and Renoir's old home, Les Collettes at Cagnes, why not head north for a day with Mother Nature?

Drive north up the Var Valley and, just beyond Plan-du-Var, turn right, heading north-east through the Gorges de Vésubie. (Michelin rate the latter *vaut le voyage*: no way!) The first essential detour is to climb the winding road from St-Jean-la-Rivière to the celebrated viewpoint at Madone d'Utelle – a 15-kilometre run that takes you from 285 metres above sea-level to 1174 metres. Towards the end of the ascent the road passes through a kilometre or two of mixed woodland – a surprising treat and unusual in that the trees are so green and cool. By the time you reach the summit the hillside covering is the more normal scrub-like variety. At the end of the road there's an observation platform under a strange umbrella-like roof; I hope you're lucky and have a view of Corsica, far to the south-east.

Descend and continue north up the Vésubie Valley, through St-Martin-Vésubie and then north-east to Le Boréon. You're at the door of the Parc National du Mercantour — one of six in France. Just before you reach the small lake and the few houses at Le Boréon stop and admire the cascade to the right of the road. At the junction beyond the lake turn right and continue for a couple of kilometres until the road peters out. It's super wooded country — at its best in late spring. This is a walker's paradise: set off up the valley and who knows — you may be lucky enough to spot some chamois, marmots or even, at much higher altitude, the *lièvre variable* (or *blanchon*), a hare that changes its coat from brown to white during the winter.

By this time you may postpone to another day the exciting climb of the Col de Turini — you'll have passed the turn to the pass halfway up the Vésubie Valley. But on no account miss this drive. It's a famous Monte-Carlo Rally stage: held on closed icy roads in January, the testing timed climb runs from the perched village of La Bollène-Vésubie to Moulinet on the D2566; the latter part of the climb runs through superb forest terrain. At the summit, turn north and complete the clockwise tour of L'Aution — glorious views will be your reward and, once again, at the observation platform where the circular trip starts, see if you can spot the elusive view of Corsica far to the south.
category 1 *menus* No rest. *rooms* 14**C** *cards* A AE V
closed Nov-Jan.
post 06570 St-Paul, Alpes-Mar. (NW of Nice)
phone 93 32 80 24 *Mich* 245 *map* 54 Nice 20 km.

ST-PAUL

COLLINE DE PEIRABELLE

The Auberge Fleurie (the next entry) is just over one km. from Valbonne – on the D3 as you head south towards Mougins. Less than 100 metres past the Auberge there's a sharp turn right: drive about 500 metres up the road and, to your right, you'll see a high arched gate – hiding behind it are neatly-trimmed low hedges and an extensive olive grove. The sign is simple enough: Colline de Peirabelle – Olives et Huile Oliviers. But what a remarkable individual lives behind the gate: a larger-than-life, bearded dynamo with a fascinating story to tell. His name is Marc Streitz and every one of you should seek him out for the various reasons I'm about to explain in some detail.

Marc is now close to 40 I would guess: he was born in Valbonne and, at the early age of four, attended a Cannes school where both English and French were used in equal proportions. Couple this with the fact that his mother was an Oxford undergraduate and you'll not be surprised to hear that his English is perfect – providing as he says "I get the chance to use it." His mother bought the property after the last war when her father died leaving her his estate; so for a long time, both mother and son had their toes literally 'in manure' as Madame Streitz was fond of saying. At 20 Marc went off to earn his fortune – to Paris where he qualified as an architect.

Six years ago, when his mother died, he gave up his career in the French capital to come back to the 2,000 olive trees she had so lovingly nursed for over three decades. "To put my fingers back in the earth – a much better way of life than being a bad architect," Marc colourfully and laughingly explains.

And what a life it has turned out to be. Let me first describe the trials and tribulations of the huge olive grove. Climatically, 1985 was a disastrous year in France – particularly in the south. Snow falls there regularly every decade or so but in January it snowed for ten days, several inches of it, and then the temperature plummeted. The blanket of snow froze on every tree in the Côte d'Azur: thousands of them died – orange, lemon, palm, olive and every fruit tree imaginable. Marc's orchard suffered a terrible fate – the olives literally froze.

In Marc's case, the crop is picked from December through to April. His usual harvest is 20 to 25 tonnes – of which 60 to 75 per cent is put aside for the sale of his quality olives (using the best fruit) and the balance is used to make his magnificent olive oil. Normally, in a good year, he is able to make nearly 2,000 litres of oil; six to seven kilos of fruit is needed for one litre of the golden liquid.

Fortunately, in January 1985, he had already picked quite a lot of fruit – but the olives remaining on the trees were destroyed completely (though many growers used 'ruined' fruit to produce some poor-quality oil). So, in the summer of '85, he was unable to sell any olives at all – using his precious harvest of just 5 tonnes to produce a very small pressing of oil, primarily to keep his long-term, loyal clients happy and satisfied. He also knew that the crop for 85/86 was going to be very poor indeed – again as a result of that savage January.

What followed was equally disastrous: the summer of '85 was one of the driest on record. Because of poor growth on the branches, where the new leaves all grew too close together, and because of the resulting small amount of flowering in the spring of '86, he faced not just poor years in 1985 and 1986 but also in 1987! It will be 1987/88 before a crop returns to a normal harvest – with no further climatic disasters that is.

It was his other 'interest' that saved him financially in 1985. Two or three years earlier a great friend of his mother, a relative of the world-renowned Eric Tabarly, suggested he used his 'green fingers' to grow and supply local chefs with high-quality herbs and vegetables. She introduced him to Guy Tricon and Jean André at nearby Mouans-Sartoux. They gave him a start – and, today, he has a number of customers, famous and not-so-famous, all of whom are within a ten-minute drive of Marc's estate: Vergé's Moulin de Mougins, the Amandier de Mougins, the Ferme de Mougins, André Surmain's Relais à Mougins and the two Battaglia brothers.

Why do his clients have to be so close? Marc's crops are grown 100 per cent naturally – they taste of what they really are: they drink no water laced with fertiliser and no greenhouse glass or plastic covers 'force' the growth – the vegetables grow in their own time and are picked when very young indeed. Marc gathers them in during the early hours and he delivers them to his clients by 10 a.m. at the very latest.

Under those natural growing conditions the season is short – starting in July and finishing in early November. And what a priceless list of Nature's finest produce emerges: artichokes, *fèves*, *petits pois*, carrots (so young, so tender and so small), *poireaux* (tiny ones where a dozen weigh no more than a normal bulb-sized leek), *haricots verts* (18 inches and longer), fennel and a score of other herbs. Marc's tomatoes are his pride and joy: the usual 'cherry' varieties – tiny, juicy red gems; but you should see his pear-shaped yellow mini-tomatoes and the more normal 'olive' and 'plum' shaped varieties. He worked hard to find the initial seeds and then, later, to multiply them.

But his interest doesn't stop there. He showed me many Vietnamese herbs that he's carefully nurturing: one, tasting like garlic but looking like chives, is called He; others, too, are unusually fragrant and useful – if only chefs would learn to use them. He makes his own peach liqueur where the ratio of pure fruit juices is one part to five parts white wine – it's a heady nectar. He also creates a home-made wine, similar to Beaumes de Venise, from his small vineyard of Muscat grapes.

His intelligence and knowledge shine forth: he told me, too, about 'Servan' grapes, famous in Valbonne, Opio and Plascassier (all with entries in *FL3*). Similar to the Chasselas variety, they are harvested in late October and November but are cut from the vine with stalks 20 to 30 centimetres long. Believe it or not, they are then stored indoors with the stalks resting in water; the grapes thrive and, during the period from Mardi Gras to Easter, they are sold as prime-condition table grapes. The production of the water 'containers' was how the now famous Biot glass 'industry' started decades ago.

I learned more about *sanguines* (see Peillon) – red and orange-coloured mushrooms: apparently both the red and orange varieties grow at an altitude of 1500 metres plus – the red ones under pine trees, the orange ones under larch trees which shed their needles every year.

Marc has brought his intellectual reasoning to bear on the horticultural needs of clients. He labours 'like a peasant' – to quote his own words; but complements that slogging work with a passion for the arts – books, the theatre and painting are all among his loves. All of you should 'invest' in his super olive oil and excellent olives. Pay him a call – and pray that no more bad weather decimates his annual harvests.

VALBONNE

Auberge Fleurie

Comfortable restaurant with rooms
Terrace/Gardens/Good value (meals)

What a transformation has taken place at this comfortable restaurant *avec chambres*. At last Jean-Pierre and Dominique Battaglia have won the success they deserved – and the limited financial rewards that go with it. For six years now I have been imploring readers to seek out the couple. Why? To put to the test my claim that the quality/skill ratio of Jean-Pierre's menus, in my opinion, could not be bettered on the Côte d'Azur. Considerable numbers of you did just that – and how much that has helped the Battaglias. But surprise, surprise: Gault Millau woke up to the same fact of life a year ago. Since they published an article in their monthly magazine suggesting that Jean-Pierre served one of the three best menus under 100 francs on the south coast, clients have flocked to the Auberge. (1986 saw the Auberge gain an entry in the GM Guide.)

The transformation is best seen in the improvements to fixtures and fittings. The dining room is now a handsome modern place: good lighting, huge picture windows, smart furniture, a new floor, and much else besides, has smartened it all up no end. Other facets have been polished up, too: the inexpensive, basic bedrooms are a bit smarter and the terrace should have been revamped during the summer of 1986. A new green and white awning has been added – next door to the old walnut tree.

Jean-Pierre is now 35. Anne and I first met the couple at Mouans-Sartoux where, after training stints at the Auberge de Noves, L'Oasis at La Napoule and Le Cagnard at Haut-de-Cagnes, the young chef decided he wanted to be his own boss. They moved to Valbonne 11 years ago.

In 1975 Dominique was carrying Stéphanie; since then she has had two more girls, Corrine and Laura, the latter now aged eight and six. In those early years Dominique slaved away; it was hard on her having to share her time between the children and the pressures of the business. Mercifully, oh how mercifully, she has now taken a back seat as a healthier Profit and Loss Account has meant help could be hired. All this came just in time because some years ago Stéphanie was found to have a heart problem and, after several operations, needed careful nursing back to full health. In addition Dominique's mother has suffered from very bad health for some years and she, too, needed a lot of her daughter's careful, loving nursing.

But Jean-Pierre is still the excellent chef he always was and what's more, you now see him in the dining room. Before he did everything in the kitchen – chatting with clients was an impossible dream. Two menus are offered – one about £8, the other approximately £13. The lower-priced version is a winner: four masterly first courses, four equally skilful second courses, a variety of cheeses and a choice of several light desserts.

The chef's classical skills shine through his repertoire: a *gâteau de poissons et son coulis* is pastry covered and is accompanied by an ideally-dressed mixed salad with a cherry tomato from Marc Streitz; a *filet de carrelet aux poivrons rouges* is perfectly balanced – the not-too-sharp sauce complements the bland, smooth fish well; and a *pigeonneau aux grains de genièvre* is worth a lot more than the modest sum you pay – red, tender meat with *haricots verts*, a stuffed tomato and a *gratin Dauphinois* as the accompanying vegetables. If you can afford the more expensive menu then relish Jean-Pierre's home-made *foie gras frais de canard* – as good, in my opinion, as you'll find anywhere in France.

You'll be impressed by the quality and variety of fresh cheeses; the selection is small, about seven or eight, but remind yourself they are included in the £8 menu! Why not go and see for yourself where Jean-Pierre gets them from?

Head for Antibes and park as close as you can to the Vieux Port – it's right at the north-eastern end of the town. Like all French markets the covered Marché Provençal is a delight; it, too, is at the north-eastern end of the town. Off a side street, the rue Sade, you'll find Roger Casoni's 'L'Etable' *fromagerie*. Tell him Jean-Pierre sent you: with pride he'll show you his selection of over 200 cheeses. The *chèvre* varieties, at their best in September, are amazing; you will never have seen so many shapes, sizes and tasted so many variable strengths of goat cheese. Most are from Provence: one from Peymeinade, west of Grasse, is allowed to ripen for over a year – the resulting 'kick-in-the-mouth' comes as quite a shock.

Finally, let me tell you about the third Battaglia brother, Mario. At 39 he's the oldest and, together with 'Nanette', his wife, runs a restaurant serving primarily good-quality fish: it's called Chante-mer and you'll find it at Les Issambres – between St-Raphaël and Ste-Maxime. It's easy to get to on the autoroute and the phone number is 94 96 93 23.

category **2** *menus* **A-B** *rooms* 10B
closed Mid Dec-Jan. Rest only: Wed.
post 06560 Valbonne, Alpes-Mar. (N of Cannes: S of village)
phone 93 42 02 80 *Mich* 245 *map* 55 Cannes 12 km.

SEILLANS

Seillans – see *Alluring Hinterland*

ALLURING HINTERLAND

I imagine 99 per cent of visitors to the Côte d'Azur see nothing more than the world-famous, 'honeypot' towns that line the Mediterranean coast: Monte-Carlo, Nice, Cannes and a score of other smaller resorts. All are attractive enough – and I'm glad that over the years I have not passed them by. But, if I had a limited amount of time, and I had to choose between those tourist traps or the sleepy hillside villages linking Grasse and Draguignan like a string of pearls, I wouldn't need a second to decide; without hesitation I would head for that alluring hinterland. Make certain that you do not pass it by.

All the villages are on southern-facing slopes – at altitudes between 1000 and 2000 feet above sea-level. Heading west from Grasse they include Cabris, Spéracèdes, Montauroux, Callian, Fayence, Seillans and Bargemon. (Beyond Draguignan others, too, appeal in a magnetic way – see the Provence entries for Cotignac, Tourtour and Fox-Amphoux.) The villages are ideal if you need a rest to restore lost energy, or if you just want to sit and read, or perhaps draw and paint.

At any time the wooded hillsides are an enchantment. But in May and June it's a magical show where every inch of ground seems to be a splash of differing colours. Climb the roads that zigzag up from the villages – and gasp at the variety, shades and profusion of wild flowers. The gardens, terraces and walls of the villas between the villages are blanketed, too, with roses, oleander, bougainvilia, veronica, hibiscus and countless other plants. Here Nature is an artist and in these hills she clearly must have dropped her box of brightly-coloured paints.

The villages have narrow streets – it seems as if houses almost touch in places. Their shaded 'squares' vary from the minute – like Bargemon – to biggish ones at Fayence and Montauroux; all have 'umbrellas' of chestnuts and plane trees and cool, twinkling fountains (Callian has an unusual 'waterfall' to add to its allure). Most are 'perched' villages, clustered around a church or, in Callian's case, below a château. The views from the villages and the roads connecting them give differing aspects from corner to corner; it's a scenic wonderland.

At the very least give the villages a day of your time. Follow the roads that link them together. There's many a shaded terrace café to enjoy a drink or a meal – and there's many a tree to sit sleepily under and take your time over a picnic lunch. Relish some *charcuterie*, bread, cheese, tomatoes, strawberries, a *pâtisserie* and perhaps a bottle of wine. All of them can be purchased easily enough *en route*.

AGEN — Résidence Jacobins

Comfortable hotel
Quiet/Gardens

This is another of my 'bases' in France which, when discovered, can prove to be such a godsend. This one is the perfect overnight hotel for a visit to Puymirol or Poudenas (see Southwest), or to break a journey on the autoroute from Bordeaux to Narbonne. The Résidence is in the heart of Agen.

The *logis* is loved by readers because it meets, spot on, all the requirements of the ideal 'base': friendly owners in the shape of Serge and Gisèle Bujan; comfortable facilities in a 19th-century house; a tranquil situation with a cool terrace and gardens – in the shadow of the 13th-century Eglise des Jacobins; off-the-road parking; and it's within a couple of minutes' walk from the magnificent Agen museum (like all museums in France it's closed on Tuesday).

Breakfasts are above average with little pleasures like a soft-boiled egg, tiny dessert grapes and two excellent local jams; one is a *confiture* made from Agen prunes – don't ignore it!

The Résidence can be tricky to find. If you are approaching the town from the autoroute exit, cross the Garonne and take the road that circles around underneath the bridge (not the first road to the right). Continue north and, just past the Chamber of Commerce, turn right up a one-way street.
category 1 *menus* No rest. *rooms* 15**B-C**
closed Open all the year.
post 1 ter pl. Jacobins, 47000 Agen, Lot-et-Gar.
phone 53 47 03 31 *Mich* 235 *map* 56

CHAMPAGNAC DE BELAIR — Moulin du Roc

Very comfortable hotel
Secluded/Terrace/Gardens

For many readers water has an irresistible fascination. Combine the most entrancing of small tree-lined streams with a 17th-century mill and you have the essential ingredients for the perfect hotel setting. There must be many sites in France that start with similar advantages – but the special ingredient at Champagnac that has made the Moulin du Roc such a favourite with *French Leave* readers is the human touch of an immensely talented *cuisinière*, one of the very best in France.

Solange Gardillou is a gentle, shy, attractive woman; you'll probably never see her in the dining rooms – she has always insisted that her 'place' is in her modern, gleaming kitchen. Solange's slight frame means, inevitably, that she has the lightest of touches – you sense this immediately whenever any dish is put before you. She also has huge reserves of culinary good taste: no dish is over complicated; helpings are modest; and sauces, even those using *foie gras* as a base, remain light and easily digestible – unusual in the Dordogne. For some her cooking is 'lack lustre'; the price she pays for a simple style.

Over the years I have enjoyed a host of specialities that meet those sensible culinary objectives spot on. Consider two: first, her famous *truite de rivière aux cèpes*. The fish is completely deboned and skinned, the two halves are then reassembled and between them is laid a thin layer of Limousin *cèpes*, renowned for their delicate and fine texture; the accompanying 'sauce' is no more than a few teaspoons worth surrounding the trout. The second has a complicated-sounding description — *l'eminçé de lapereau au serpolet et pâtes fraîches au basilic*. Yet the dish is simple enough: six or seven thinly-sliced rounds of young rabbit with just a hint of wild thyme and, beside them, a small mound of *pâtes fraîches* — an intelligent presentation.

Solange is well known, too, for her desserts — particularly the variety of fruit-based tarts. They come in all forms: pear, apple, strawberry, raspberry, assorted fruit tarts and more besides — depending very much on the season. Success has meant high standards are now easier to maintain; she has five assistants in the kitchen and about 30 diners at any one sitting.

Lucien Gardillou runs the 'front of the house' with a very firm hand and he, too, sets equally high standards. He has a staff of five in the two dining rooms and though these days it has all become rather sophisticated, intense and formalised, nevertheless, the intimacy of the mill, the setting and the small number of clients means that few visitors leave unhappy. It's expensive — but not unduly so for the luxury on hand.

The couple opened the Moulin in 1970 — a restored 17th-century walnut oil mill. (Previously they had owned a restaurant at nearby Villars which was destroyed by a fire.) How the mill has changed over the years; one of the most recent improvements is the block of six new bedrooms behind the kitchen — using an existing part of the old mill. By the time this book goes to press a further addition should be a small private car park on the west bank of the Dronne — linked to the mill by a new footbridge. One feature continues to improve year by year - Lucien's formidable cellar; his wine list now offers a choice of 600 wines from a *cave* of more than 20,000 bottles — 90 per cent are Bordeaux vintages. It's a remarkable roll call of

Bordeaux wines — from the greatest to the most humble. (If you want to buy walnut oil or *foie gras* then ask Lucien for nearby farm suppliers.)

Solange's sons are currently in the middle of the obligatory culinary training tour of some of France's great restaurants. François is 20 and Alain is 17; it will not be long before they'll be working alongside their mother.

The neighbouring terrain never fails to please. I first fell in love with Brantôme nearly 30 years ago: its abbey with its riverside setting, alongside the Dronne, is a spellbinder; and, just downstream from the town, is Bourdeilles — a château, part Renaissance, part medieval, sits above the river.

But seek out, too, some less well-known spots. First, to the

MOULIN DU ROC

north-east of Champagnac is St-Jean-de-Côle. Drive off the D707, along a street the width of a car, and marvel at the most evocative of Périgord villages. A small square, flanked by a most unusual 11th-century church, an ancient covered market and a modest château, is today just what it must have looked like in the Middle Ages – with the addition now of two humble cafés and their equally simple terraces. Walk down to the Gothic bridge that spans the Côle and continue for 100 metres for a view of the church's cloisters.

The Dronne changes its nature upriver from the Moulin. Park the car at Champs-Romain and walk to the Saut du Chalard where the stream cascades over rocks in a steep wooded valley. Beware: it's an easy downhill walk – but the opposite coming back! On your way visit two different attractions: the château at Puyguilhem – with its lone, sentry-like, pepper-pot tower; and the Grottes de Villars – open in the high season only.

Well downstream, west of Ribérac, is the hillside village of Aubeterre – what character it has. The site, narrow streets, a *place* and the Eglise St-Jacques will all please; but even more so perhaps will the *église monolithe* – carved out of rock. It's similar to the one at St-Emilion.

The countryside is at its best in May: unploughed, emerald green pastures; soft, wooded hills – the newly-opened tints a joy; flowers everywhere – lilac, bluebells, cowslips and endless others; and, if you're lucky, a blue sky for the perfect backdrop. No wonder the Dordogne is loved so much.

category **3** *menus* **C** *rooms* 12**D** *cards* A AE DC V
closed Mid Jan-mid Feb.Mid Nov-mid Dec.Rest.Tues.Wed midday
post 24530 Champagnac de Belair, Dordogne. (N of Périgueux)
phone 53 54 80 36 *Mich* 233 *map* 57 Périgueux 27 km.

LES EYZIES-DE-TAYAC   Centenaire

Very comfortable hotel
Terrace/Gardens/Swimming pool

Two talented young couples – both have that rare but invaluable instinct for hotelkeeping – are slowly but surely establishing the Centenaire as one of France's nicest hotels. There's nothing de luxe in either the hotel's setting or its style; but genuine interest and care comes in bucketfuls from the people who run it – always the most appreciated of client benefits. There's also a gilt-edged bonus; the brilliant *cuisinier* and his team – but more of that talented group later on.

Let me tell you a story that makes my point perfectly. A reader arrived one day from his 'base' miles away in the Dordogne; he had booked a family birthday lunch. But, to his distress on entering the hotel, he discovered that he had forgotten his wallet – he literally had no way of paying nor of proving his identity. Alain Scholly and his attractive wife Geneviève put him at ease immediately. He was told he could settle the bill when he returned to his 'base' – and, what was more, his birthday *apéritif* would be champagne all round. The reader was so grateful he rang me to relate the tale.

The hotel's fixtures and fittings improve year by year. Now there's a sun-trap swimming pool at the rear – with a steep terraced garden running down to the River Beune. Space is tight – it's a clever bit of building work. Alongside the pool is a small gym – marvellously equipped for guests to shake off those extra pounds they put on in the restaurant.

Many, many readers wrote to say how enchanted they had

MONPAZIER

been with the hotel's annexe — a couple of kilometres away to the south. I sought it out on my last visit. It's easy to understand why the five bedrooms, large garden, utter seclusion and its unique view of Les Eyzies have charmed you all so much. Nicole Mazère, elegant and pretty, is another good reason, too; the annexe is part of her home incidentally. Ask for a room at the annexe — Les Eyzies can be noisy.

Nicole's husband is Roland Mazère — Geneviève's brother. Now 37, he's one of France's most brilliant young chefs. His style is *cuisine moderne* with a vengeance; but here great

reliance is placed on the use of *foie gras* and *truffes* and some of the classic culinary sauces — *Périgourdine* and *Bordelaise* for example. The 30 or so dishes offered (not counting desserts) are a rich mixture of modern, regional and classical.

I tried many of the chef's creations: *foie gras d'oie chaud aux capres et à l'échalote* — tiny rounds of hot liver on mouthful-sized triangles of toast with minuscule capers and just a taste of shallots; Roland's famous *ravioles* — this time with a duck, truffle and *pistaches* stuffing; fresh bits of cod, caramelised in a soya sauce with a julienne of nine different vegetables; and from a choice of about 25 sweets I chose a 'brick' of hot apples, pears and bananas served with a vanilla ice cream. The cheese trolley was weighed down with 20 or so local *chèvre* varieties – and about a dozen of France's great classics.

Roland spends most winters on cooking trips to places like Hong Kong, Singapore and Australia; only the odd dish gives the clue to his eastern travels. His main influence is the greatest of current French chefs – Joël Robuchon in Paris.

Every visitor to Les Eyzies will undoubtedly give some time to the series of famous caves lining the Vézère Valley. The same applies to the picturesque towns and villages near or alongside the Dordogne. But let me try to entice you on a day's drive south of that legendary river – to three appealing sites.

First to Monpazier – 40 km. south-west of Les Eyzies; it's one of many *bastides* in the terrain between the Dordogne and the Lot. Built in 1284 by Edward I, King of England and Duke of Aquitaine, it is, for me, much the best of them. The arcaded square at the heart of the fortified village is a joy – with its perfectly proportioned stone buildings.

Nearby, further south, is the dark sullen château at Biron. With its elevated perch it must have been the ideal site for a fortress; commanding views stretch for scores of kilometres in all directions. Within its walls are an intimidating *donjon*, a chapel and a grass-covered *place*. Not too far away, to the south-east, is another amazing castle – marrying grace with formidable strength. Hollywood has yet to better Bonaguil.
category **3** *menus* **B-D** *rooms* 30**C-D2** *cards* AE DC V
closed Nov-Mar. Rest only: Tues midday.
post 24620 Les Eyzies-de-Tayac, Dordogne. (SE of Périgueux)
phone 53 06 97 18 *Mich* 235 *map* 58 Périgueux 45 km.

LES EYZIES-DE-TAYAC   Cro-Magnon

Very comfortable hotel
Terrace/Gardens/Swimming pool

What sensation do you feel when you address an envelope to a dearly-loved hotel? Or in the days before you arrive in its familiar surroundings? For me it's a silent glow of happy anticipated pleasure – like meeting an old trusted friend.

That's the ideal way to describe my appreciation for the Cro-Magnon. Anne and I have known the hotel all our married lives – nearly 27 years. We took our children there, too – when they were toddlers. Many is the time our family rested and played in the large, informal garden that surrounds the annexe; it's across the road – and the railway line – from the hotel. We remember, when our son was nearly three, the ringing of the level-crossing bell – warning of the approach of a single-carriage, local train. Andrew's eyes would light up; all else would have to stop – he had to see the train. Perhaps it was there that he first got the bug for his life-long passion for railways? (There's no problem with train 'noise' – although road traffic does bother some readers.)

We recall, too, on many hot days sitting under the chestnut and plane trees that shade the hotel's terrace – the sort of days when the rustling leaves and the azure sky above would hypnotise you into sleep. Sally, just turned one and learning to walk, must have fallen many times on the terrace's gravel floor – grazing knees and elbows continually in the process.

Throughout all those years we have got to know well Jacques and Christiane Leysalles, the owners of Cro-Magnon.

Indeed, their own children, Claire and François, are only a little older than our two. Jacques and Christiane add that special touch to this beguiling hotel; at the end of the day human beings mean more than bricks and mortar.

Jacques is the third-generation owner. His grandmother started the family business in 1906 – when it was the two-room Relais du Diligence. Before that she had run a tiny inn, very near the Grotte du Grand Roc on the western bank of the Vézère. There was no bridge or road by the cave in those days; visitors would shout from the eastern side – and grandmother would row both ways to get her guests back to the inn!

What changes have taken place over 80 years. Today, Cro-Magnon is a warm, welcoming hotel – and the garden has the benefit of a pool. But the family touch is its greatest asset.

After the publication of *French Leave 3* I was taken to task very severely by a reader for being somewhat unenthusiastic about the new chef's culinary abilities. Alain Guillois was finding his feet then and, in fairness, I could not compare his cooking with the form of Mazère down the road. But Alain, now 28, who hails from Brittany (his first job was in the modest kitchen of Chez Pierre at Raguènes-Plage) has grown very much in stature and ability. His style is modern and less inclined to the over-elaboration sometimes seen at Centenaire.

He's loyal to Périgord's famous products of course. Try a delicious soup, typical of those served in many a farm in the area; *tourin blanchi* – a 'white' soup with chicken, eggs and onions. He's skilful with fish; a *turbot à la saveur douce* is superb – steamed in a deep, pastry-sealed dish with a variety of herbs and vegetables. Be sure to relish the aroma before you tuck in. (Vegetables and herbs come from that same garden across the road.) He's innovative; a *pannequet de ris de veau aux champignons* is a good example.

Les Eyzies is the 'University of Prehistory'. It was in the cave-riddled limestone walls above the village that the skull of Cro-Magnon man was found. But, for me, the magnetic marvel of the Vézère Valley is the cave at Lascaux – one of the world's great wonders. I regret bitterly that Anne and I, in those early years of the '60s, didn't visit the cave before it was closed to the public on April 30, 1963. Today, there's a truly fantastic facsimile called Lascaux II – built underground just 300 metres away from the original (closed Mondays).

Those magical paintings fill me with a massive feeling of mystery. What made the Magdalenian hunters enter the subterranean cave? What were the gigantic problems facing early man in the cruel, harsh world outside the sanctuary of the dark cavern? It must have been a world of unimaginable fear and an unbearably lonely one at that. Yet early man, seventeen thousand years ago, had the ingenuity to create those paintings – full of vitality and technical wizardry. What a treasure the four boys from Montignac opened up for the world on September 12, 1940; all because a small dog, Robot, fell though a hole in the ground!

After Lascaux other sights tend to pale. But head north for 30 minutes or so from Montignac to Hautefort. Dominating the horizon is a huge château with pepperpot towers and, tumbling down the hill below it, is the village of Hautefort.

category **3** *menus* **B-C** *rooms* 27**C-D2** *cards* A AE DC V
closed Mid Oct-Apl.
post 24620 Les Eyzies-de-Tayac, Dordogne. (SE of Périgueux)
phone 53 06 97 06 *Mich* 235 *map* 59 Périgueux 45 km.

BEYNAC

Beynac, overlooking the Dordogne

LES EYZIES-DE-TAYAC   Moulin de la Beune

Comfortable hotel
Fairly quiet/Gardens

French Leave 3 readers will spot it straight away: this 'base' was not included in the last edition. But in 1983 it was too new for that. Because so many of you wrote praising it highly I investigated: and, without any shadow of doubt, it merits a place among my readers' favourites. It fits my 'base' objectives exactly – in every possible way.

The *moulin* sits beside the swift running River Beune – its name derives from the old wooden mill just behind the modern building. The hotel is modern with cool, airy bedrooms which are furnished in a light, refreshing way. Modern or not, it has character and really friendly owners; Madame Thérèse Dudicourt has won the hearts of many readers.

It makes a splendid alternative to the more expensive, more renowned and noisier hotels in Les Eyzies (there's too much lorry traffic these days). Being *sans restaurant*, it allows you to choose at will from the Michelin-starred restaurants at the Centenaire or the Cro-Magnon or more modest places like the Centre in the village or the much-liked Laborderie at Tamniès – in its hill-top setting above the Beune, upstream and to the east. Or how about a day's drive to Puymirol, near Agen – and a lunch at Michel Trama's restaurant?

category 1 *menus* No rest. *rooms* 20**B-C** *cards* AE DC V
closed Nov-Mar.
post 24620 Les Eyzies-de-Tayac, Dordogne. (SE of Périgueux)
phone 53 06 94 33 *Mich* 235 *map* 60 Périgueux 45 km.

LAGUIOLE

Lou Mazuc

Very comfortable restaurant with rooms
Lift

In *French Leave 3* I wrote these words: 'for Michel Bras to flourish at Laguiole is nothing short of a culinary miracle.' Well, the miracle continues to flourish and, judging by my most recent visit (in 1985), I have no hesitation at all in predicting that, within two or three years, the 38-year-old pencil-thin, bespectacled genius will be one of the French culinary greats. Wherever you live be sure to seek him out.

Not that that suggestion is easy to follow: for some it would be akin to seeking out The Scarlet Pimpernel! Laguiole is hardly a tourist trap and it's not exactly near any of the major routes used by foreign visitors in France. The terrain surrounding the very humble town is famous in France for its cattle – the area is nothing more than a plateau of lush pastures where the animals chomp away contentedly. Some Frenchmen would perhaps also know that Laguiole gives its name to two cheeses: a hard one, similar to Cantal; the other, a 'fresh' variety, is used in the regional speciality, *aligot*.

But, increasingly, the town is going to become renowned throughout the world for the fantastic talents of Michel Bras. What an amazingly innovative chef he is, bursting with original ideas and the technical skills to turn them into tempting reality. Some of his culinary ideas are so original that, frankly, he makes many three-star chefs look as if they have been left behind on the starting line in the creative stakes race. For all but one or two of his specialities he shuns the use of cream, flour and butter. He acknowledges openly on his menu that he searches for simplicity and he makes splendid use of regional products, herbs and natural flavouring ingredients – some long forgotten. No wonder Michel's hero is Girardet; well, Frédy, I reckon you have a talented competitor who one day may well be your equal.

And to think that all this explosive talent burst forth with no spells in 'famous' kitchens and no hotel school training! His parents opened the simple *pension* 32 years ago; Michel's apprenticeship consisted of one month at the Hôtel Fusiès in Lacaune (no great shakes – see *FL3*) and the rest of his training period was at his mother's side in her kitchen.

Three menus – ranging in price from about £7 to £23 – plus an à la carte list are available. The simplest is in fact prepared by Michel's mother who still works in the kitchen with him together with three young helpers. This menu is likely to include dishes like *saucisse du pays grillés avec aligot* and *tarte aux pommes confites au miel de pays*. But you must turn to the more expensive menus for Michel's skills to be put to the test.

You get a taste of what is to come with an *apéritif*: a tiny round of home-made black pudding on a bed of cooked apple purée accompanied by chopped onions, marinated in vinegar and red wine. A first course could be *la croûte aux cervelles, gaspacho d'épinards et d'oseille* – the small helping of brains on a lightly-toasted bread base, surrounded by a cool *gaspacho* of spinach and sorrel.

Dishes that follow could be specialities like a *terrine chaude d'escargots de Bourgogne aux noix sauce perlée et oignons fanes* – within the hot, soft terrine are *escargots*, nuts and chopped-up leek, and in the accompanying reduction, some onion 'fans'; or a *ballotine de pigeon poêlée au jambon, son jus et radis* pink, perfect, simple and delicious.

The highlight of my meal was the best salmon dish I have ever encountered. I was not keen to order it but Ginette, Michel's wife, was tactfully insistent. The menu description read – *filet de saumon d'écosse tiède, huile en maceration de ciboulette, asperges vertes*; what arrived was a slice of salmon, shining and tasting so moist and with the deepest of pink hues – the top lightly sprinkled with salt and chives. It would be worth visiting Laguiole for this one speciality – and Michel's desserts.

The latter are so numerous it's impossible to list them all. What took my fancy was not the conventional *assiette des sorbets* – which are very good – but an *assiette des sorbets d'un 'autre temps'*. I had encountered none of them in sorbet form before: myrrh, orange flower essence, nutmeg, cardamon,

ESPALION

Espalion, south of Laguiole and astride the Lot

clove . . . what unusual flavours. A *terrine de fraises à la pulpe de noix de coco* with a *coulis de framboises* and a *crème glacée à la vanille en gousse et à la nougatine de noix, arrosée d'un vin de noix vertes* were just two of fifteen or so original gems.

Provided it is ordered in advance Michel can prepare a special menu where he serves five courses – each one using different parts of a lamb combined with vegetables and herbs to match the separate dishes. What is interesting is that for each course the lamb is cooked in differing ways – *rognon poêlé, joues* (cheek) *en ragoût, filet mignon grillé* and so on. Sweets follow; the whole menu is a rare bit of culinary creativity.

What was once a modest *pension* is now a comfortable establishment; clearly the family have gambled a lot in the additional capital borrowed to pay for the modernisation – but Michel's talents will assuredly return a handsome dividend.

One pleasant surprise was to find, displayed in the new reception area, the ceramic pottery creations of Suzy and Nigel Atkins. Suzy is well known for her gifted skills. Her pots are functional – designed to be used; but they are so pleasing to look at, too, with brilliant, unusual colours and finishes on their surfaces. The Atkins' skills complement Michel's talents so perfectly. Their 'Poterie du Don' is south-west of Montsalvy – in an isolated site west of Montoursy, near the River Auze; follow the arrows from Montsalvy or from the Lot Valley. Try to visit Conques – to the west of Laguiole and south of the Lot; it's an enchanting village and its Romanesque church is superb.

category 3★ *menus* A-C *rooms* 13B-C *cards* AE
closed Mid Oct-Mar. Sun evg & Mon (except July & Aug).
post 12210 Laguiole, Aveyron. (SW of St-Flour)
phone 65 44 32 24 *Mich* 240 *map* 61 St-Flour 64 km.

PUYMIROL   L'Aubergade

Very comfortable restaurant
Gardens

Go! Every one of my readers should follow the advice of that simple one-word entreaty. I have always wanted to reduce an entry to the shortest message possible; in Michel Trama's case, it would be a shame not to give you the reasons why I am so enthusiastic about his skills. Even if you have the tightest of budgets you should make whatever sacrifice is needed so that you can head for the perched *bastide* of Puymirol — east of Agen and just to the north of the main road to Toulouse.

Apart from any other talents Michel and Maryse, his attractive, blond wife, may or may not have, you can be certain of two things: they both have courage and a tried and tested competitive spirit. What a decision it must have been back in 1978 to leave Paris, where Michel was a *maître d'hôtel*, and buy the old post office in Puymirol: today the restaurant is a 13th-century 'gem' but eight years ago it was in need of extensive renovation. A self-taught chef, Michel opened the doors of L'Aubergade in 1979 — encountering in the months before they started up all sorts of hostility from the locals.

If you judge success by Michelin stars (and, please, never make that mistake) then Michel's record is as good as anyone's; his first star came in 1981 and his second in 1983. And, for my money, I rate Trama the equal of any of the best half dozen or so three-star French chefs today.

So how has that spectacular success come about? It starts with the couple having a profound love and respect for their *pays*; they believe, passionately, that this is where the best of the real France is to be found. Despite those initial problems with the locals, long since resolved, they have found contentment in their 700-year-old home. What is equally important is that their children have too: Muriel, the eldest, who is married to Philippe, the young *maître d'hôtel* — the couple have a year old son, Michel; Dominique, Muriel's brother and now 18, who is at a hotel training school; and Christopher, the youngest, who was born in the village.

Another factor, of great importance to Michel, is that the best larder in France is on his doorstep. All the bountiful harvest of the Southwest is available in Paris, too, but at Puymirol it means the chef literally has one hand in his own culinary 'pot' and the other in the rich earth to be found encircling the village. Whether it is ducks, geese, pigeons, vegetables, cheeses, red fruit, or whatever, then you can be certain that Michel knows just exactly how, when, and where the produce is cultivated or reared. I visited Erminio and Santina Zanese who grow all his vegetables, herbs and flowers; what pleasure they take in the Trama success and, though in their 70s, what enthusiasm they display for their smallholding of delights.

Put simply Michel has been and still is inspired by his *pays* and his family: what more could any man or woman want?

Like Frédy Girardet, Michel is blessed with exceptional ability. He's a powerhouse of physical and mental energy. Just under 40, he's a bearded dynamo — crackling with passion, ideas and good humour. Unlike Frédy he speaks fluent English. He's a carbon copy of the great Swiss chef in other respects: he's a master organiser; and attention to detail and an utter refusal to take short cuts are two more Trama hallmarks.

His modern, 'contemporary' cooking style means vast amounts of time-consuming work — for himself and his six-man team; marry this to his creative skills and you have a chef who I reckon is as good as anybody.

Where does all this culinary magic leave you, the contented client? Well, you see signs of it before the first *plat* ever arrives. With your *apéritif* come five or six appetisers — all of them a world apart from the often dried, 'out-of-a-packet' variety so-called 'chefs' serve up. Then, to further tickle your palate and tease your senses, another small plate of mouthful-sized treats arrives: tiny tartlets, *beignets* with surprise fillings and all sorts of other simple, contrasting tastes and textures. The latter are served 'gratis' and Michel takes great pride in making sure he uses inexpensive produce for them.

Then follows whatever you have chosen from about 40 or so personalised specialities (that includes about a dozen desserts); each one reflects the man as all great cooking inevitably does. You could settle for the 'Menu Surprise' or the 'Menu Gourmand'. I tried the latter; let me describe parts of it.

The first course was an *assiette de canard*. Displayed beautifully on a large plate were six differently prepared morsels of duck meat — a duck *hors d'œuvre*: dried slices, *foie gras*, a roll of meat and *foie gras*, a ravioli of minced meat, slices of *'jambon'* and a little parcel of *canard* and spices. Another course was *mignons de saumon aux jaunets* — a fillet of Scottish salmon in a chives and saffron sauce; centuries ago all villages in the south had their own field of saffron — called *jaunets*. Accompanying the salmon was a stuffed courgette flower — from the Zanese smallholding.

A *pigeonneau aux épices* was perfection: a crisp skin with a red interior and resting in a red wine sauce with a hint of pepper, ginger and a pinhead of curry powder. The green 'parcel' with it was some chopped-up celery-like Swiss chard, wrapped within its own dark green leaf. Another speciality was Michel's interpretation of a regional classic — prepared in his personal style: duck *confit* with lentils, tomatoes stuffed with herbs and other vegetables served as an accompaniment on the same plate (I had this dish the next day). All this may sound stomach-filling — but, no, each dish was a sensible portion.

Of the superb desserts let me describe two: the *millefeuille de nougatine glacée au pralin* was ice cream piped between wafer-thin layers of biscuit; and the *soufflé froid de mangues, petites fraises des bois confites* was a stunning cold mango soufflé with a hot interior of wild wood strawberries.

I present Michel Trama to you — the equal of any three-star chef. Will Michelin award the accolade at Puymirol? In 1934 they would have done so — but now, whatever his talent, a chef must 'buy' the trappings of luxury to 'complement' his skills. And ditch the family waiters for professionals! How sad and idiotic. If I'm wrong, (how I pray I'm wrong,) Michelin would do a great service to all the up and coming chefs of the future. Or, if I'm right, will it mean in a few years that Michel will move to a site where three stars are guaranteed?

Use the Résidence Jacobins in Agen or the Parc at Bon-Encontre, near Puymirol, for bedrooms. Or enjoy a lunch in the cool, shady garden with its distinctive umbrellas.
category **3**★ *menus* **C-D** *cards* AE DC V
closed Mon (except July & Aug).
post 47270 Puymirol, Lot-et-Gar. (SE of Agen)
phone 53 95 31 46 *Mich* 235 *map* 62 Agen 17 km.

SARLAT-LA-CANEDA   La Hoirie

Comfortable hotel
Secluded/Gardens/Swimming pool

The ancient Périgord hunting lodge is a couple of kilometres south-east of Sarlat. New owners took over in 1984 – Arlette and Robert Sainneville-de-Vienne; they've done much to improve the facilities. There's a spanking new swimming pool and six modern bedrooms have been added. The spacious bedrooms in the old house still appeal – some of them have huge stone fireplaces. Another change is the availability of evening meals; these are not compulsory and I cannot recommend them. Use La Hoirie as a 'base' and eat at the many nearby restaurants.

Sarlat has changed so much since I first saw it 30 years ago. Most of the centuries-old houses have been restored and their golden stonework cleaned up – what a dramatic difference it has made. The town is more commercial these days – but not to an overwhelming extent. For me the special charm of this base is the terrain to the south: a landscape of glistening brown earth, of huge chestnuts, ancient oaks and twisted walnut trees, of drooping giant sunflowers and drying tobacco, of mellow old houses that seem to complement Nature's designs so perfectly, of perched castles and a tree-lined, magical river. Drive down as many of the lanes as possible.
category 1 *menus* B (see text) *rooms* 13C *cards* A AE DC V
closed Mid Dec-mid Mar.
post 24200 Sarlat-la-Canéda, Dordogne. (SE of town)
phone 53 59 05 62 *Mich* 235 *map* 63 Sarlat-la-Canéda 2 km.
90

SERRES   Fifi Moulin

Comfortable hotel
Quiet/Gardens/Swimming pool/Good value (meals)

As you head south from Grenoble to the Mediterranean, you cross the Col de la Croix Haute and descend to Serres. It's then that you begin to get that satisfying feeling that Provence, at last, lies ahead. It's a glow of anticipation that does wonders for the spirit – depression quickly evaporates away. Beyond Serres you spot the first all-important clues: olive trees, regimented rows of lavender (at their best in July) and the rich shades of terracotta roof tiles. Your sense of smell, too, will be awakened by the perfume of herb-scented pastures.

I first fell in love with the Fifi Moulin over 30 years ago; it's nice to say that that affection has not dimmed one iota – indeed it's stronger than ever. For that I must thank the 'new' owners – Philippe and Isabelle Frenoux; hardly 'new' as they have been here 10 years and are now in their mid-thirties. Before them the Martin family had owned the hotel for generations and, alas, towards the end of their tenure the Fifi Moulin had begun to get a bit jaded. But not any more: English-speaking Philippe – he worked in England years ago – has that special touch instantly recognised in all talented hoteliers.

Value for money, reasonable comforts and sound cooking standards are the highlights at Fifi Moulin. The latest addition to the hotel's 'features' is a swimming pool; but perhaps the best 'bricks and mortar' improvement over the years has been the new dining room. When you enter the hotel from the road, it's on the ground floor; when you sit down in the dining room

CRÊTE DES AIGUILLES – JARJATTE VALLEY

at the back, it's on the third floor! Huge glass panels give it an open-air feel – even on spring evenings; yet it's perfectly warm inside. On summer evenings the glass panels are opened and it becomes a delightful terrace – with extensive views south.

Philippe knows that prices must be held to sensible levels; in consequence he performs an excellent balancing act between quality and value. The two menus and à la carte list are short – hurrah for that. Every dish provides satisfaction and Philippe sticks, as far as he can, to regional produce. So *agneau* appears most often – in many forms: *tranche de gigot grillée aux herbes*, *carré d'agneau rôti* or a *souris d'agneau au thym* (small fleshy muscle on the leg) – a first-rate speciality; all come with an accompanying *gratin dauphinois*. Starters could include a selection of fresh *crudités* or local home-made *charcuterie* (try a wafer-thin slice of ham for breakfast).

Cheeses are fresh and one was new to me: a cow's milk variety called Carré du Trièves – from a tiny dairy nestling in the shadow of a massive, hypnotic slab of rock, Mont Aiguille. (Don't miss the astonishing view of it – just before you reach Clelles, 20 km. north of the Col de la Croix Haute; stop and look west.) A pleasing white wine is the Domaine du Plot from Saillans – wearing a Clairette de Die *appellation contrôlée* label. Sweets, too, are splendid: a not-to-be-missed *tarte aux prunes* (a local delight and made from Philippe's personally-picked plums – his father is responsible for the winter-long treatment given to the fruit) and several light-as-air *pâtisseries*. Everything is unpretentious and, for my money, is as enjoyable as fare served at most starred restaurants.

Can I persuade you to stay two nights or longer? There's plenty to see and do. First head for a new 'discovery' for me –

HAUTES-ALPES

the dead-end valley of La Jarjatte. Where is it? Six kilometres south of the Col de la Croix Haute turn off the N75 to Lus-la-Croix-Haute and then follow signs for La Jarjatte. Continue up the valley road as far as you can go. It's a miniature Chamonix Valley: on the right is a jagged jaw of sharply-pointed peaks and alongside the road is the crystal-clear water of the infant River Buëch. In June there's the bonus of many wild flowers and warm sun – yet plenty of snow is still on the mountain tops. See *Elephants, Mapoholics and Enthusiasms*.

Another fine drive – and one where you are unlikely to see any tourists – is the road west from Eyguians (11 km. south of Serres) through Orpierre and across the Col de Perty. At the summit climb the 150 metres to a *table d'orientation*: to the east are the snow-capped peaks on the Italian border; to the west the sulking hulk of Mont Ventoux.

Other totally deserted roads include a series of *cols* that surround Serres – many of which are used annually on the Monte-Carlo Rally. Exciting roads they may be – but my recommendations are made on the strength of their scenic value, not their rallying merits! The Col de Carabès is one – heading north-west out of Serres; a lovely fishing stream and, in June, the possible sight of gentians on the col itself, gives it extra appeal. Another is the Col de Faye to the south-east of Serres – with fine views east from the summit as you head towards Ventavon. Ask Philippe to prepare a picnic lunch for you: question him and follow his advice to the letter.

category 2 *menus* A-B *rooms* 25B *cards* A AE DC V
closed Mid Nov-Feb. Wed.
post 05700 Serres, Hautes-Alpes. (S of Grenoble)
phone 92 67 00 01 *Mich* 245 *map* 64 Grenoble 109 km.
92

ST-ANDRE-LES-ALPES **Grand Hôtel**

Simple hotel
Quiet/Terrace/Good value

Modest everything may well be – but so are the prices. There's no chance of you filing a bankruptcy claim after paying your bill at this Grand Hôtel – an inappropriate name if ever there was one! A couple sharing a room with a shower/WC can have dinner and bed and breakfast for as little as £12 per person per night. Add to that good value benefit the advantage of a quiet site, glorious country in all directions and the bonus of one of France's best private railways on hand. (The hotel is next door to the station: don't fret – it's not a busy terminal!)

Robert and Liliane Bruni are the first to admit that they run an unpretentious *auberge* – looking smart these days in its two-colour livery. One link with England is that Liliane's two sons from her first marriage, Alain and Jean-Louis Ivaldi, regularly present Provençal dinners at the Copper Inn, Pangbourne. Alain is a chef-instructor at the Toulouse Catering School and Jean-Louis teaches at the Nice Hotel School. Each year the brothers spend their vacations at the hotel – and then you're able to order an additional more ambitious menu.

Liliane and her sons grew up in Nice – where the family ran a restaurant many years ago. Menus therefore often have a strong Niçois element running through them: *salade Niçoise* and *tripes à la Niçoise* are examples. Other dishes could include *hors d'œuvre variés* (*charcuterie* and *crudités*), *truite meunière*, *lapereau aux morilles* and some simple desserts.

You should try to spend at least two nights here – putting

aside a day or two of your holiday for some exciting trips. The first is to take a ride on the metre-gauge railway line that runs from Nice to Digne – owned by the Chemins de Fer de la Provence. Four trains a day pass each way through St-André. Take one that heads south-east towards Nice and get off at Entrevaux – a medieval gem, capped by its lofty citadel.

Another must, from June to October, is the crossing of the mighty Col d'Allos (2240 metres high). When it's first cleared of snow – at the end of May or in early June – the newly-opened alpine flowers, in the pastures where the drifts have melted, are a stunning feast for the eyes.

You could, of course, spend a whole day climbing cols: the Allos first and then returning via the even higher Col de la Bonette – 2802 metres above sea-level. If you do this clockwise trip it will give you the chance, at the southern foot of the Bonette, to head west to Beuil where you should use the D28 for a truly exciting surprise – the Gorges du Cians. Steep cliffs, coming so close together that they almost touch, overhang the narrow road; dark rocks add extra splendour to the rushing torrent as it falls steeply down to join the River Var. It's quite different from the mighty Verdon, south-west of St-André (see the entry for Fox-Amphoux), but it's equally thrilling.

Another trip, ideal for a hot day and a picnic lunch, is the climb east from the village of Allos to the large natural lake at an altitude of 2229 metres; you can park half an hour's walk away. It's spectacular stuff and worth the effort.

category **2(S)** *menus* **A-B** *rooms* 22**A-B**
closed Oct-mid May. (SE of Digne towards Nice)
post 04170 St-André-les-Alpes, Alpes-de-H.-Provence.
phone 92 89 05 06 *Mich* 245 *map* 65 Digne 43 km.

VARENNES-JARCY   Moulin de Jarcy

Simple restaurant with rooms
Secluded/Terrace/Good value (meals)

I have often been asked to suggest a hotel or restaurant that meets these objectives: somewhere close to Paris; not too dear; and, ideally with a secluded, attractive site.

Impossible? No – not at all. The Moulin fits the bill to a tee. Considering the tiny mill is only 25 miles from the heart of Paris its setting is unusually picturesque. On a summer's morning the view from the terrace and dining room is one of utter calm: the River Yerres flows gently by on both sides of the mill – the building is literally squeezed on to a minute island; to the north the tree-lined stream meanders away into the distance; and

MOULIN DE JARCY

alongside the eastern bank are pastures where geese, ducks, cows and ponies sun themselves all day long.

You can have the best of all worlds here. Within ten minutes' walk is the railway station at Boussy-St-Antoine (on the main TGV line south) – you can be in Paris within half an hour (Gare de Lyon). So leave your car and enjoy the trip in a relaxed way – returning in the evening. Alternatively, you are within easy reach of some of the best treats in the Ile de France: the gorgeous Renaissance château at Fontainebleau – associated with so much of France's history – is down the road; surrounding the town is the Forest of Fontainebleau – superb in autumn; near the town are the Seine and Loing rivers that inspired Sisley, Monet and other Impressionist painters – visit Barbizon, Samois and Moret; and, finally, north-east of Melun, is the magnificent château at Vaux-le-Vicomte.

Don't expect miracles at the ancient *moulin*. Rooms are comfortable enough – but very basic (no showers or baths); three of them have particularly big terraces overlooking the scene I described earlier. Gilles and Claudine Le Moign are friendly enough hosts. Cooking is very modest with a wide choice of inexpensive alternatives like *terrine de saumon*, *jambon de Bayonne*, *gigot d'agneau* and *truite meunière*.

The appeal of the *moulin* is its site, so utterly different from anything in Paris. Directions: from N6 (Croix de Villeroy traffic lights) use D33, D94, under railway and *moulin* is 200 metres east of the Euromarché supermarket.

category **2(S)** *menus* **A** *rooms* 5**B** *cards* V
closed 1st 3 wks Aug. Xmas-mid Jan. Tues. Wed. Thurs.
post Varennes-Jarcy, 91480 Quincy-sous-Sénart, Essonne.
phone (1) 69 00 89 20 *Mich* 237 *map* 24 Paris 40 km.

94

CHATILLON   Chez Yvonne

Simple restaurant with rooms
Secluded/Terrace/Good value

Thank heavens this isolated, simple haven of good value is off the beaten track. You'll not see the village named on Michelin's small-scale maps – instead, like a true member of my readers' unofficial 'mapoholics' club, you'll need to be prepared to work just a little to reap the dividends (both pleasurable and financial) awaiting you. It's an especially good investment for those of you with only a few francs to spend.

The little *logis* took its name from its previous owner – the legendary Jura *cuisinière*, Yvonne Peltier. Born in 1901, she worked for over 50 years in the modest kitchen; her prodigious half-century of effort was honoured in 1977 by the richly deserved accolade of an *Ordre National du Mérite*. Sadly, she died just a few months after receiving it from the President of France himself – Valéry Giscard d'Estaing.

Now Madeleine Garnier continues the traditions started by Yvonne. In spirit the menu is the same – though, alas, today's high prices for some of the ingredients Yvonne used make it impossible to emulate her renowned specialities. Consider, for example, the *volaille de Bresse au vin jaune* that was one of Yvonne's masterpieces; Bresse chicken cooked in the stunning deep yellow, dry Château-Châlon wine – one of the world's great classics. Anthony Hogg, in his very useful *Guide to Visiting Vineyards*, describes it as 'France's longest lived wine'; it's like sherry (though not fortified) and reaches its peak after 20 years. The expensive wine comes from vineyards

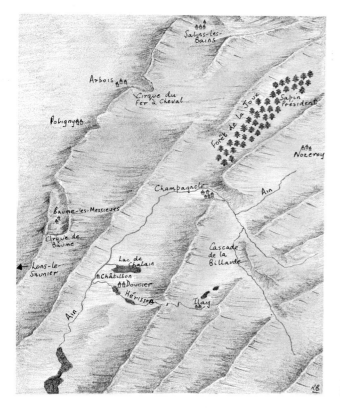

just a hop, step and jump away to the north-west.

So, today, Madeleine presents the dish in more modest form; her menu calls it *poulet de Bresse bagué*. The *bagué* refers to the small numbered metal ring around the chicken's leg. It guarantees authenticity – and to make sure you know it, Madeleine serves the roasted *poulet* with the much-singed ring still in place! Accompanying it is a simple salad – no more. Before this course you will be offered a home-made *terrine de foies de volaille truffée*, followed by a *truite belle meunière*; the latter, as so often now in France, is a farm variety.

After these two 'starters' will come a *timbale de morilles du Jura* – delicious honeycombed fungi served in a cream sauce. The *morilles* are from the woods that line the infant Ain – the whitewashed Chez Yvonne sits alongside the river, on the D39 to the east of the village. If you're lucky the *morilles* will be fresh – at their best after a wet spell, followed by hot sun which has a greenhouse effect on their growth. More likely they'll be *sec*, dried by Madeleine herself for year long use. Cheeses will follow – all local, all perfect: a Comté from the east, a Morbier from the village to the south-east, a Bleu de Bresse from the Saône Valley and a young *chèvre* variety.

Chez Yvonne is a modest, unassuming place – don't expect miracles. The countryside is gentle, peaceful and so green; its soft, tranquil charms will blow away any cobwebs of depression, I promise you. There's much to seek out; I'll highlight some of the best sights – see the adjoining map.

First the Cirque de Baume. View it from the belvedere at its southern end – high above the natural amphitheatre. Then descend to Baume-les-Messieurs – a tiny village where, from its 6th-century abbey, monks went west to establish the abbey at Cluny – and the unusual valley floor with a pretty waterfall, tumbling over green, mossy rocks; the latter caused by a resurgent stream that disappears underground miles away.

Another equally famous *cirque* and resurgent stream *(reculée)* is further north – the Cirque du Fer à Cheval.

Near Châtillon is the Lac de Chalain – summer sees it very busy with watersports of all kinds. But the walks in the woods flanking the southern banks are quiet enough. More spectacular is the Forêt de la Joux to the north-east – one of France's largest pine forests. Hidden within its 6,000 acres is an arboretum and the Sapin Président – a huge pine tree with a circumference of four metres (it's a long walk from the road).

Another pleasant port of call could be ancient Nozeroy – a 'lost', fortified, medieval village; after exploring it why not follow the Ain from its nearby source for a few kilometres and then head south to the Cascade de la Billaude – a thundering sight after very heavy rain, as are all waterfalls.

An even more rewarding trip – seen at its best on foot – is the Hérisson Valley. Use the D326 from Doucier as far as you can go – then walk the four kilometres upstream towards Ilay. You'll be thrilled by two dozen or more cascades – the river falls over 250 metres in those few kilometres. Of course they're at their best after heavy rain; so, if your visit coincides with a spell of wet weather, don't despair – this is the time to get out your mac and walking shoes. You'll not regret the effort – it will bring a smile back to your wet but happy face.

category 2(S) *menus* A-B *rooms* 8A
closed Dec-Feb. Mon evg. Tues. (SE of Lons-le-Saunier)
post Châtillon, 39130 Clairvaux-les-Lacs, Jura.
phone 84 25 70 82 *Mich* 243 *map* 25 Lons-le-Saunier 20 km.

CRISSIER   Girardet

Very comfortable restaurant

Anne and I made our first visit to Girardet nine years ago – primarily because of a passionate recommendation by Seppi Hunkeler at Nebikon. Our newly-acquired Gault Millau Guide – the third we had bought and one of the unwieldy early editions – confirmed Seppi's enthusiastic testimonial. At that time Girardet was unknown in the UK and was just about to be 'discovered' by Craig Claiborne in the US – something I didn't know until years later when I had the pleasure of meeting the knowledgeable writer from East Hampton.

A decade ago a pound note bought considerably less than three Swiss francs. Not surprisingly therefore, we clenched our teeth and made the necessary financial sacrifice for our first visit. We arrived at Crissier begrudging the small fortune we had set aside to pay for the yet unseen bill.

Four hours later we left quite speechless. We both knew we would have gone without almost anything to pay for that revelation of a meal; I know of no better way of complimenting any chef. In the years since, we have returned eight times and, astonishingly, our last visit was perhaps the best of them all. It will not surprise you either to be told that Girardet has been the most popular of readers' favourites.

It was in 1980 that I first wrote about Girardet in the earliest edition of *French Leave*. About a year earlier, with others in Europe, I had bullied Allan Hall into making his initial pilgrimage to Crissier; he did so, and I believe Allan was the very first British journalist to write about the 'King of Chefs' in NOW!

I'm pretty certain I was the first to sing Girardet's praises in any UK guide. My generous words left me nervous but I needn't have worried – I only know of one reader who has travelled to Crissier and has returned home disappointed.

You must still make a 'sacrifice' to eat at Girardet's *tour de force* restaurant. But it's not so excruciatingly painful any more. These days a strong pound helps and with both inflation and VAT doubling UK restaurant prices during the last few years (compare that with the annual 2 per cent inflation rate in Switzerland) the francs you must set aside are not as excessive as they seemed nine years ago. Every reader should head for Crissier. I promise you that you will not regret the effort.

What is it that makes Girardet so repected, so loved and so admired by tens of thousands of loyal, passionate supporters? I have tried to analyse it before and I'll try yet again. Since 1981 many journalists, writing for British magazines and papers, have taken my advice and discovered for themselves just what makes this Swiss genius tick. One journalist, more than any other, has captured best the magic of the man and his restaurant – Richard Kann. I would like to quote from Richard's richly sympathetic article in *Chef* magazine: 'Fredy is an anomaly. He never studied with a master chef and his training was entirely in Switzerland. He was 35 before he gave up playing football and devoted himself to cooking. He seldom goes to France. He gives no cooking classes and he doesn't run a consultancy.'

I'll add my thoughts to Richard's statements. For me Frédy is the Leonardo da Vinci of *cuisiniers* – an inventor second to none, a 'scientist' able to turn his innovative culinary concepts into reality, and an artist *par excellence*. It's not just the specialities arriving at your table that make the man such a creative chef. It's the original thinking that goes into how food is prepared in the kitchen that makes Frédy so unique; no other chef knows so intimately the tastes and textures of every single one of the ingredients he uses. He is the chef who, almost without exception, is most respected by his peers; I've asked enough of them in Britain, France and Switzerland – and I have yet to hear one that puts any other chef above Girardet. It is he, and others like Robuchon, for example, who have brought *cuisine moderne* to such a polished peak; a spontaneous, light style based on classical traditions.

You instinctively sense honesty, humility, sympathy and love when you talk to the man: his eyes, his hands and his deep, calm voice are instantly reassuring; his character and strength of personality are like the sun. It's these facets that in the end set him apart from the rest. He's an inspiring individual – you recognise that by watching his youthful staff and by talking to them about their extremely respected 'boss'.

At senior level there are few staff changes. After many years at Frédy's side, Michel Colin, a Frenchman, has set off to run his own restaurant. Frédy's new head chef is Gérard Cavuscens, a Swiss from nearby Bulle; before his promotion he had already worked in the kitchens for many years. Louis Villeneuve, the chief *maître d'hôtel* and one of the very best I know, is a Frenchman – he's been at Chez Girardet for 11 years. He has two assistants: Jean-Louis Foucqueteau, from Mâcon, has worked for Girardet for 15 years, and John Davey, an Englishman from Shirehampton, near Bristol, has had a nine year stint at Crissier. The three work together like a multi-jewelled Swiss watch: quietly, efficiently and in harmony.

The end result is that there's a family atmosphere in the anything but pretentious dining rooms. The ambience is never intense – there's a carefree, but very professional, feel to it. You'll not be made to look like an idiot if you don't understand something; just ask – there's no nose-in-the-air superiority here, common to so many great restaurants. Clients do not whisper, and though the percentage of visitors from other countries is higher these days, the majority are Swiss clients, booking months ahead for their tables. Only 60 or so *couverts* can be reserved; when you consider that 30 people work in the restaurant and Frédy has a passion for using only the freshest and finest produce available, then you'll quickly see why each table must be full twice a day, five times a week, for the Profit and Loss Account to work in Girardet's favour. Don't book a table and then not turn up – the latest pitfall for restaurateurs; it's mainly Americans who are guilty of this wretched way of demonstrating bad manners. Please – don't do it!

Attention to detail is another foundation on which the Girardet reputation has been built. You spot it immediately you sit down and study the menu. In his youth Frédy had wanted to be a typographer; you'll not come across a more beautifully designed menu anywhere. (Readers will be amused to know that he took my advice to install a word processor; the menu that changes each day is now printed in a far more satisfactory way. Long before my constructive criticism appeared in *FL3* I had sent him ideas on how to operate a simple machine – the least I could do after 20 years in computers!) The bread rolls offered at the start of the meal are another sign; six or so varieties are freshly baked twice a day in the village bakery – and a different assortment of bread accompanies the cheese.

That last meal I talked about earlier was a succession of brilliant creations. An appetiser appeared in a tiny earthenware *cocotte* – a brawn-like mouthful or two of young rabbit in a jelly and studded with *persil* and carrots. Then followed a *galantine de ris de veau* – combined with *foie gras* and contained within a cabbage leaf covering. Next a Crissier-grown *courgette* flower with a *fricassée d'encornets* alongside it; the flower itself was stuffed with the same cuttlefish and a mixture of vegetables – all of it chopped to pinhead-sized proportions.

Next came a dish named simply as *les rouelles de St-Pierre en verdure* with a *sabayon léger pimenté*; a wafer-thin stuffing of peppers encircled the 'rounds' of John Dory – all of them encased by tender cabbage leaves. A superb *canard confit au citron et légumes rissolés* followed the fish course; how proud Alforns Lehni from Egolzwil (see Nebikon) must be to supply Girardet with his lovingly-tended young vegetables. The famous Girardet cheese trolley appeared next. Don't miss the chance to taste slivers of the finest Swiss varieties; my favourites are the different Gruyère and Tête de Moine cheeses. Finally, the equally renowned selection of desserts: smooth creamy ice creams and six sorbets which are not bettered at any other restaurant I know; a trolley with an assortment of *pâtisseries* and fruits; or a selection of half a dozen sweets from the menu. Perfect *petits fours* added the final detailed touches to a meal without fault – where, at the end of it all, we still had an appetite. That's the hardest trick for any cuisinier to pull off!
category 3★ *menus* 130-160 SF *rooms* Use Novotel (see *FL3*)
closed Last wk July-mid Aug. Xmas-mid Jan. Sun. Mon.
post CH-1023 Crissier, Switzerland. (4 km. NW of Lausanne)
phone (21) 34.15.14 (Switzerland) *Mich* 243 *map* 26

GOUMOIS

Taillard

Comfortable hotel
Secluded/Terrace/Gardens

The Taillard family, from father to son, have been pleasing clients for 112 years at their off the beaten track hotel – lost in the Jura hills on the border of France and Switzerland. I'm writing these words on the hotel terrace and, just a few minutes ago, I overheard a telling comment from a contented guest – high above me on his bedroom balcony: "If there's a more marvellous place to be this day, I don't know where it is."

Below me the late afternoon sun is illuminating the woods and meadows on the Swiss side of the Doubs Valley. The Doubs itself is hidden by trees and the village church – but that's not a problem as a short drive or walk provides scores of different views of the pleasing river. As I write I can hear the distant sound of Swiss cow bells – as their owners munch away contentedly at the thick green blankets of rich grass.

Anne and I have known the Taillards for more than 25 years. We took our children, too, when they were toddlers and when Andrew was getting over a bad attack of measles. The week we spent at the 2000 ft above sea-level hotel, where the air is so invigorating, had a spectacular effect on the youngster; we saw, before our very eyes, how each day he made a speedy return to good health. You'll not be surprised to hear that the Taillard hotel has been one of the most loved and appreciated of all *French Leave* favourites. I could have predicted that six years ago when I first sang its praises.

Why is it such a great favourite? Well the pleasures are many.

But the first and foremost reason must be the Taillard family. There's Henri, now 72, and his sister, Henriette; a younger generation is represented by Jean-François and his wife, Brigitte – and, in years to come, no doubt their son, Pierre, will carry on the unbroken Taillard line. In 1875 it must well have required considerable effort to seek out the hotel; but not today as the A36 autoroute is less than an hour's drive away. From it's entrance, at Montbéliard, there's not a traffic light to stop you until you reach Ardres, near Calais!

I've described the setting already but all the nearby terrain is equally seductive. There are walks galore: the Taillards will highlight the best of them but I suggest you head south along the GR5 footpath, which follows the Doubs upstream or, alternatively, drive to a spot just north of Le Boulois (on Michelin map 243 about 8 km. south-west of Goumois), and then take any of several marked paths. Ask the Taillards for their booklet called *Guide des Promenades*; it's an enterprising document – full of ideas for trips and visits of all kinds.

Further afield are other scenic alternatives: the Dessoubre is described elsewhere; the Saut du Doubs, a spectacular cascade where the river 'shoots' over a 30-metre-high rock face, is upstream; and, across the border, are many Swiss attractions. There's La Chaux de Fonds, famous for watches, and, south-east of the town, the viewpoint called Vue des Alpes where all the mighty peaks of the Alps lie to the east and south. With the Swiss autoroute system now covering most of the country you can be in places like Berne, Interlaken and Lucerne within 90 minutes or so.

Let me suggest just one example of what I mean. Cross the frontier below the hotel and head for Bienne – 25 miles away.

GOUMOIS

Then use the 55-mile stretch of motorway to Berne and Interlaken; within two hours of leaving Goumois you can be in the heart of the Bernese Oberland. Grindelwald, Wengen and Murren are on the doorstep. But continue east – using, by 1987, a newly-completed autoroute to the south of Lake Brienz. At its terminus, east of Brienz, visit the remarkable Swiss Open-air museum at Ballenberg where there's an ever-growing collection of ancient Swiss rural buildings – taken from their original sites and restored cleverly in a wooded setting. Finish with an exhilarating drive: head south from Meiringen up the Rosenlauital – sparing time for the walk from the road to the top of the Reichenbach Falls, the spot that Conan Doyle chose as an appropriate end for Moriarty.

Back at Goumois be sure to visit one of the many scores of *fromageries* that lie on the rich pastoral plateaux of Franche-Comté. I recommend the *fromagerie* at Fessevillers, to the north of Goumois where, thankfully, traditional methods are still used to make Comté and Morbier cheese.

At the hotel treat yourself to a mixture of culinary pleasures where both regional and modern creations appear side by side. I'm glad that Henri and Jean-François insist on 'guarding' local specialities and it's good to see them making extensive use of *morilles* (I understand some English visitors push them aside on their plates – heaven forbid), *jambon de Tuyé au genièvre*, *saucisse de Morteau* (*Jésus de Morteau*) and so on. (*Tuyé*, or *tué*, is the name given to the huge chimneys found in Franc-Comtoise farms – it's there that hams and sausages are smoked. You can visit one, the Ferme des Guinots, owned by Monsieur Guillaume, which is south-east of the crossroads at Les Cerneux-Monnots, a hamlet on the D414 from Charquemont to Le Russey, both of which are to the south-west of Goumois.)

The more modern creations served these days are in large measure due to the co-operation between the Taillards and Jean-Michel Turin and his 'Vauchouxfrais' enterprise (see Alsace – Port-sur-Saône). Fresh fish and high quality meat are just as much a reality here on the eastern border of France as they are anywhere else in the country. The family smoke their own salmon in an old garage at the back of the hotel. And Jean-François is the artist who painted the menu cover in a modern style; many of his paintings hang in the bar and dining rooms.
category **2** *menus* **B-C** *rooms* 17**B-C** *cards* A AE DC V
closed Nov-Feb. Wed (in Mar & Oct).
post Goumois, 25470 Trévillers, Doubs. (NE of Besançon)
phone 81 44 20 75 *Mich* 243 *map* 27 Besançon 95 km.

THE UNSPOILT DESSOUBRE

There's a 20-mile stretch of French countryside which I think can hardly be bettered anywhere else in France. That's a bold statement about a country where there's such a wide spectrum of alluring natural treasures. I've returned many times during the last three decades to this delectable, unspoilt corner of eastern France – a tiny river hidden in the Jura hills, just a few miles to the west of Goumois.

My last visit to the Dessoubre Valley was a stunning few hours of scenic wonder. My luck was in – even though it was late October; the sun beat down strongly from a clear blue sky and, what is more, I had the valley completely to myself. For many people cities are a magnet and motor vehicles are to be avoided at all costs: but this was a day when one blessed the motor car as mine had taken me to the perfect landscape.

I have seen the Dessoubre at various times of the year. In late October it's a dazzling, breathtaking show. Trees are everywhere and, for much of its short length, the majority are deciduous varieties. An eye-catching array of colour sweeps the hillsides – shining reds, burnished golds, rich browns and bright yellows. Occasionally one passes newly-cut pine trees, their barks scraped away, and the air full of pine smoke from the fires that foresters have lit to burn the surplus trimmings. At two or three places alongside the river there are small workshops where furniture is made or where timber is cut into endless varieties of planks; then the strong scent of pine wood takes its turn to awaken your sense of smell. What a joy it all is.

Dotted along the length of the stream, from its source to St-Hippolyte where it joins the Doubs, are just a few houses and only one hamlet of any size – Rosureux. There are one or two modest *auberges*, happy to serve you a *truite* or perhaps some *brési* or a *saucisse* from Morteau. But it's the unspoilt character of the valley that pleases most. The hillsides, not too high and, most importantly, not too close together, are covered in trees for the entire 20-mile length of the valley. There are dozens of spots where you can enjoy a picnic or even a paddle in the stream. Here and there meadows line the banks or, alternatively, there are several pocket-sized squares of maize. The stream itself is at its best in late spring.

Seek out the Dessoubre and absorb its beauty. I suggest you travel from the source downstream – south to north; that way the sun is always behind you and this helps to provide sharp scenic views. Start by parking at the viewpoint called Roche du Prêtre. On your right is a classic example of a *cirque* (amphitheatre); far below is the 17th-century abbey of Notre Dame de Consolation. Descend to the abbey park, taking care not to miss Pierre Favre's splendid little hotel which sits above a cascade. It's the perfect spot for a light lunch if you have the time. The abbey grounds, further down, are a wonderland of springs, streams, waterfalls, grottoes and marked woodland walks. The Dessoubre literally 'springs' from a score of different spots – where water has seeped down from the vast Jura plateau, high above you, re-emerging at the foot of the limestone *cirque*.

I pray that you have a fine day. I hope, too, that you have the great good fortune to see a *milan royal* (kite) gliding in the thermals below you at the Roche du Prêtre – as I did on that unforgettable October day. Don't miss the Dessoubre Valley – where you can put **all** your senses to the test.

NEBIKON   **Gasthaus Adler**

Very comfortable restaurant

"Gasthaus Adler, Nebikon?" I can sense your exclamation as you read the heading. "Where on earth are we?" you ask.

I have deserted France and made for Switzerland – to the home of one of the most talented chefs I know, Seppi Hunkeler. Nebikon, like so many hundreds of other Swiss villages, is an unpretentious place; in the past its only claim to modest regional fame has been the village's brass band. Not any more because Seppi – an irrepressible bundle of enthusiastic fun and energy – is one of the very best chefs in Switzerland. He has a hugely enjoyable and highly distinctive personal style.

The village is easy to locate – bang in the very heart of the country. It's not far from the point where the N1 and N2, the two most important Swiss motorways, cross. Use the Dagmersellen exit from the N2 as it heads towards Lucerne (34 km. to the south-east). Nebikon is to the west of the exit.

The Gasthaus, built over 150 years ago, is full of character. It has always been the village 'pub'; the 'bar' is likely to be used by villagers at any time of the day – making brief calls to enjoy perhaps a beer, a plate of local ham and a chat. Seppi's family have been the 'publicans' in Nebikon for many centuries – service runs in the blood. Within the building are two small dining rooms; their panelled walls and ceilings give them a warm feel. Seppi seems to be just as at home whether he's sharing a joke with his mates in the public bar or, alternatively, when he spends a few friendly moments in the restaurant with his clients from Basle, Zurich or Lucerne.

Apparently the Gasthaus was considered for membership of the *Relais et Châteaux* chain a year or two ago. The 'bar' part of the inn was thought to be not quite the *R&C* image! Three cheers; it's that that gives the Adler a down-to-earth character. On a Saturday evening it's possible you may even be able to share in the fun of a local wedding reception – held in a big room at the rear, then the place is alive with music.

You could say that none of this makes Seppi any different from many other inn owners in Switzerland. True enough; but it's what the culinary magician gets up to in his small kitchen – aided by seven assistants – that makes the Adler so very different. From Seppi's *'répertoire de ma cuisine'* you can choose from a short à la carte menu or order one of the two expensive *menus surprises.*

Take the latter route. Seppi and his wife, Sylvia, both of whom speak fluent English, will explain that either *menu surprise* is not just a random serving of dishes using what's left in the kitchen. Far from it. "It's like composing music," Seppi enthuses, "with changes of mood, colour and balance." What follows confirms his definition. From start to finish he demonstrates his skill with specialities you'll not find in France.

Like his great hero, Girardet, Seppi has an eye for detail – nothing is missed. Every day his local baker bakes half a dozen different sorts of bread rolls – offered at the start of the meal. Accompanying the cheese course is another quite different selection of six special breads. Sylvia, not to be outdone, looks after the table decorations; every day she artistically 'creates' a distinctive display for each table – using, in the main, greenery from the local forests. Wedgwood crockery, a wine list of over 350 alternatives, including dozens of Swiss varieties (even a

Dagmersellen vintage!) and friendly waitress service complement the professional culinary touches.

What is a *menu surprise* likely to include? Here are a few examples of the six to ten small servings that could be put before you. A starter could be a lobster terrine – looking as pretty as a picture and served with a side bowl of sour cream, shrimp, chives and chopped tomatoes. Then a cup of piping-hot cucumber soup – a tantalisingly tiny serving. A *ragoût de saumon au trèfle* follows; dice-sized cubes of salmon, crisp on the outside but with meltingly-soft interiors – *trèfle* is clover.

Next a finger-sized fillet of *féra aux cipolottis* – the latter are spring onions. A *foie de canard* could follow – a masterpiece; a *bouchée* of hot duck liver on a bed of *chanterelles* and, sprinkled on the top, some fried slivers of what the French call *brési* – wafer-thin slices of dried beef. Then Seppi's version of *râble de lièvre*; six minute slices with accompanying small vegetables – carrots, *navets*, *mangetout*, thumbnail-sized tomatoes and a help-yourself dish of *gratin Dauphinois*.

Earlier in the day I had quizzed Seppi about supplies. "Where do you get them from?" I asked. "Jump in the car – I'll show you," came the reply. A couple of minutes later I was in nearby Egolzwil meeting Alforns Lehni who grows Seppi's vegetables especially for him; the young farmer is pleased as punch to be associated with the chef's increasing fame. What is more he now supplies Girardet and Stucki in Basle. *Féra*, perch and pike come from the Sempacher See and crayfish from the small lake of Mauensee (both south-east of Nebikon). Trout are fished from local streams and game comes from the nearby forests (admire the bronze of 'hunter' Seppi and his dogs in one of the dining rooms – created by a friend and exchanged

for a free meal or two!). Meat is local – only ducks being imported. Seppi's training included two years at the Savoy.

Your 'surprise' meal will finish with a selection of cheeses (mouthful bites of several – French and Swiss), some 'marbles' of various sorbets, wild strawberries, and a paper-thin biscuit of pastry topped with fruit like rhubarb, apple and pear. It all sounds like too much food; in reality it's not so – as each course is no more than a sensible tasting. 'Music' it all is; you leave contented – the expense is not begrudged.

Overnight accommodation? The modern, inexpensive Löwen is in nearby Dagmersellen. Sursee has several good hotels – the best of them is called the Sursee. Ask the Hunkelers to make reservations. Lucerne is a 30 minute drive away – down the N2. What I would like to do is to highlight two of my favourite corners overlooking Lake Lucerne.

The first is the view from Seelisberg – on the southern side of the lake. Use the new N2 and leave at the Emmetten exit. Continue on the minor road eastwards and then gasp at the simply breathtaking view below you. The jelly mould Fronalpstock and the Mythen molars are across the lake. Walk down through the woods to Rütli – the Runnymede of Switzerland; but allow plenty of time for the steep climb back. The second is Morschach – above Brunnen. Again lovely views – both west and south – and restful walks abound. For four decades my family have shared with me the joys of the meadows and paths surrounding the village.

category **3** *menus* 65-140 SF *rooms* See text *cards* A AE DC V *closed* 1st 3 wks Aug. Tues. Wed.
post CH-6244 Nebikon, Switzerland. (36 km. NW of Lucerne) *phone* (62) 86.21.22 (Switzerland) *Mich* 216 *map* 28

COLLIOURE   La Frégate

Comfortable hotel
Terrace/Lift/Good value (meals)

I visited Collioure in early November, at the end of what was one of the driest six-month periods ever known in the southern *départements* of France. Even the day I spent in the high Pyrénées – normally such lush, 'green' country – was an eye-opening surprise: the countryside everywhere had the look of a heavily-wrinkled peroxide blonde – well past her best. Normally verdant pastures were scorched sheets of lifeless hay-coloured stubble. Apart from six weeks in July and August I had spent most of those six months in France, and astonishingly, I can only recall rain falling on three occasions – and that was during May in the far north. Modern painters have always had a great affection for this corner of France – Collioure and Céret inspired Matisse, Bracque, Picasso and Chagall to do some of their finest work in the nearby terrain – but it was unlikely any painter would have gained inspiration there in 1985.

The sun was still burning brightly out of a clear blue sky the day I visited Yves Costa at La Frégate. It was a day or two before he closed down for his winter break. I had never seen him look so tired and clearly so exhausted – he admitted to feeling quite ill. It was a vivid but sad reminder how much a long ten-month season, without any break, can take out of a chef – something all readers should bear in mind during the months of October and November when holidaying on the Mediterranean coast.

During the last six years I've received seven letters and verbal reports from Fleet Street editors and journalists about their visits to *French Leave* recommendations: an amazing quirk is that three of these reports, favourable ones I may add, all concerned the anything-but-conventional Yves Costa. Perhaps those individuals, working in the Fleet Street 'jungle', take more kindly and more readily to maverick Yves than many readers appear to do. He really is his own man; some would say stupidly so – others, like me, would counter by admiring his refusal to toe the conventional line. He's an honest, likeable character.

At the start of 1985 Yves made some tough decisions. His profits for the previous year had been poor and he realised that if he was ever going to make improvements to his already cramped hotel he would have to do something about the 'bottom line'. He concluded that he would have to fill his restaurant with more clients – so the days of aiming for the heights of *haute cuisine* were put behind him; expensive wines, cutlery, crockery, glasses and linen and a menu laced with products like *foie gras*, lobster and *loup* were all put aside. Expensive *haute cuisine*, he reckoned, like *haute couture*, was for those establishments where Americans and Japanese appear so eager to fritter their dollars and yen away.

He scrapped all his existing menus and decided that quality at bargain prices was going to be his simple objective (the French have the perfect word for the relationship of price to quality – *rapport*). I think he has succeeded very well. The new fixed-price menus and his à la carte list provide visitors with a chance to try a wide selection of specialities from an individualistic repertoire: not just the odd classical dish, but many original specialities inspired by Catalane *cuisine* and a host of his own highly unusual 'modern' recipes.

Among the dishes offered under the menu heading of

cuisine Catalane are delights like *terrine de ratatouille aux anchois* (the anchovies come from Italy these days incidentally) — served cold with the anchovies ringing the vegetable *pâté* and all of it lying on a base of olive oil; *moules à la 'sang et or'* (those last words describe the colours of the Catalan emblem) — mussels in a tasty saffron sauce with tiny bits of red pepper giving a bright contrasting colour to the golden liquid; and *la crème Catalane* — a cold dessert, served in an earthenware dish, and described by Yves as 'Catalan cream, aniseed egg custard powdered with sugar and caramelised.'

Yves' modern creations include *les dominos de rouget frits à l'huile d'amande et au chou vert* — a clever marriage of tastes where the almond oil is a foil for the mullet; and *le mille-feuille de poissons 'mer rivière'* (Yves' passion is fishing) *sauce langoustine* — no pastry in this dish as the *mille-feuille* refers to the ten small rounds of various fish and the way they are presented in the *Américaine* sauce.

Will Yves succeed? I'm sure he will. More and more French chefs, depending on French custom, will have to walk that path sooner rather than later. By the time this book is published many changes will have been made to the hotel's fabric.

Finally, let me comment about the nearby Casa Païral. If ever there should have been a favourite 'base' this should have been it. But Madame Pons wins thè prize for the most unpopular hotelier in *FL3*. Use it if you want calm rather than La Frégate's clatter; but please don't get into a tiz about Madame.
category **3** *menus* **A-B** *rooms* 24**B-C** *cards* V
closed Mid Nov-Dec. Rest: Thurs evg & Fri (out of season)
post 66190 Collioure, Pyr.-Or. (S of Perpignan)
phone 68 82 06 05 *Mich* 240 *map* 66 Perpignan 27 km.

ST-MARTIN-DU-CANIGOU

St-Martin-du-Canigou, west of Collioure

NARBONNE   Réverbère

Comfortable restaurant

If you stay overnight at the hotel La Résidence it takes four minutes 50 seconds brisk walking to reach the value-for-money La Réverbère. So often readers say "We must eat where we sleep." Well, if you belong to that band of play-safe individuals, then you're missing some of France's best treats.

Claud Giraud is a marvel. He marries the highest standards of culinary excellence with the most modest of prices. While Yves Costa at Collioure has decided to take a different path, Claude, with the huge advantage of a restaurant at the door of two major French autoroutes, has chosen to keep to the same road he knows so well. And what a yellow-brick road it is! The restaurant is always packed so don't go without booking.

What's so nice, too, is that the majority of his clients are French; and that, more than anything else, is perhaps the best recommendation of all, because, make no mistake about it, the French don't willingly part with their francs these days in up-market restaurants. Why should Anglo-Saxons miss out on such largesse? Make your reservation now – after I've given you several reasons why you should not miss La Réverbère.

Let's deal with the staff first: Bernard is the *maître d'hôtel* – always willing to explain the subtleties of any dish; Bruno is the young *sommelier* – only too keen to try out his halting English on you; there's attractive, slim Sabine, Claude's wife – it's likely, too, you'll spot her eight-year-old son, Lionel; and, finally, there's the chef, 33-year-old Claude himself – and what a young genius he is, that's for sure.

In 1986, £16 bought the following meal, served in a panelled dining room with a happy, warm feel about it. To start with, an enterprising appetiser of an egg cup filled with a *mousse de chou-fleur*, topped with tiny bits of cauliflower *à la grecque* and accompanied by a tiny 'finger' of toast spread with *foie de canard*, *grattons* and *champignons*. The first course was a small cup of piping hot *crème aux cèpes des bois parfumée de cerfeuil* – it was so nice it was a shame there wasn't some more; then *huîtres et St-Jacques aux poireaux, sabayon de la mer* – it tasted of the sea; followed by a small slice of *saumon frais au pistou* – the latter a tomato and olive-oil sauce.

Then a breather before a *granité de menthe poivrée à la girofle* – it was more like a sorbet with the mint and clove combining well; a *rable de lièvre sauce civet* followed with *tagliatelles* and an unusual *tian de céleri* – a mound-shaped celery flan; the cheese course was exceptional – *chèvre frais à l'endive* turned out to be five endive 'petals' with a 'pistil' of goat's cheese mixed with *fines herbes*; and, finally, *a pavé de chocolat* served in a light cream sauce, followed by a selection of 12 *pâtisseries*, poached fruits, sorbets and ice creams.

Claude cuts no corners: witness the selection of ten alternative coffees (served with a glass of Banyuls *sec* and *petits fours*), eight different teas and a dozen *infusions spéciales* – based on all sorts of different herbs. A wine list ranges in cost from 50 francs to a 1924 Barsac at 1,500-plus francs! Of the various *apéritifs* I enjoyed a Muscat de Rivesaltes, laced with a touch of lemon and some *marc*.

When you've finished, and assuming, of course, that Claude is clear of his kitchen duties, ask him to show you his IBM Personal Computer. A wide range of package programs –

FONTFROIDE

bought with the hardware from a Toulouse computer dealer – makes it easy for Claude to do his accounting work: not just clients' bills but different sorts of valuable analysis and, more interestingly, it gives a cost breakdown of every speciality he offers – as the computer holds the details of all the ingredients and their costs.

Most of Languedoc-Roussillon is an ocean of vines: I call it the 'Vinsee' – a vast wine lake. It really is quite ludicrous where vines are planted – in every conceivable nook and cranny. And to think that a great percentage of the plonk made there is never drunk – it just fills up the EEC's own 'Vinsee'!

The countryside around Narbonne does not fit the description 'pretty as a picture' – but, as compensation, man has provided a host of interesting sites for you to visit. (Nature's best contribution is in November when the vineyards are a splash of colour – a patchwork quilt of reds, yellows and orange hues.) There's Narbonne itself, dominated by the Cathédrale St-Just. To the south-west are half a dozen spots I would hate readers to miss: the 800-year-old Abbaye de Fontfroide in an isolated wooded setting – once a Cistercian treasure but now privately owned; the ancient ruined fortresses of Peyrepertuse and Quéribus with such dominating positions – the former built on a high narrow ridge of granite, the latter looking for all the world like a fingernail added to the top of a rocky finger; the last Cathar fortress to fall at lonely Montségur, west of Quillan; the unnerving Rennes-le-Château – a hill-top village that played an important part in the controversial book *The Holy Blood and the Holy Grail*; the modern-day Montaillou, south-west of Quillan – be sure to read the classic *Montaillou* (published by Penguin), the story of the Cathars in this remote

107

hamlet during the period 1294–1324; and, finally, the detour to the little village of Tautavel.

I can sense your question: "Where on earth is that?" It's about 25 kilometres north-west of Perpignan and the site of a fascinating museum. Just to the north of Tautavel is a remote cave, sitting high above the River Verdouble. In July 1971 it was the scene, after some crafty detective work by the archaeologist, Henry de Lumley, of the remarkable discovery of the skull of a 20-year-old man who lived in the cave some 450,000 years ago! A newly-built and skilfully-designed small museum, high above the village amidst scented pines and herbs, tells the story of Europe's first *Homo erectus*.

The museum is open every day from 10.00 to 12.00 and from 2.00 to 4.00. Don't miss it. The cave can be seen from the museum through a specially-sited telescope; if you want to get closer to it then drive north 2.3 km. (1½ miles) and turn off the D9. The museum visit will set your imagination alight: it's intriguing to think of man living such a shatteringly lonely life surrounded by multitudes of animals including elephants and rhinoceros. What a fight it must have been to survive. And to think that in 1986 all some of the local inhabitants have to do is plant vines, make some wine, (which more than likely will never be drunk as it simply adds to the 'Vinsee') and the EEC will guarantee them an income. How our taxes get wasted!

Use La Résidence as a 'base': quiet, beautifully furnished, it's a town house *par excellence* and good value, too.

category **3** *menus* **B-D** *rooms* See text *cards* AE DC V
closed Feb-mid Mar. Sun evg. Mon.
post 4 pl. Jacobins, 11100 Narbonne, Aude.
phone 68 32 29 18 *Mich* 240 *map* 67

ST-GUIRAUD   Le Mimosa

Comfortable restaurant
Quiet/Terrace

Early in March 1985 I received a small pocket-sized French book from Georges Renault – a do-it-yourself publisher who, each year, researches and markets a splendid guide to the restaurants on the Mediterranean coast of France. He knew of my own publishing venture and the reason for his delightful gift, the newly-published 1985 edition, was to bring to my notice a most unusual culinary tale.

The entry for Le Mimosa, like the one for the Bansards at Javron in faraway Normandy, is one of only two in this guide that has not come about as a result of readers' letters. That matters not one iota. In both cases the recommendations are fully justified for many reasons; I'm just pleased as punch to be able to tell readers the good news of talented cooks working hard to make their mark in culinary France.

Can you envisage the scene where, in a tiny Languedoc village, well off the beaten track, a French businessman entertains a dozen Chinese clients to a meal cooked by a New Zealand-born lady chef – who, just two years earlier, had been dancing as a professional ballerina – and served by her violinist husband, Englishman David Pugh? That amusing tale tickled my fancy and it sets the stage for what is an intriguing story.

The couple are now in their late thirties. Until 1982 both Bridget (née Taylor) and David Pugh had worked for 11 years in Oslo – as members of the Norwegian National Opera and Ballet Company; Bridget had been the principal dancer and

David a violinist in the orchestra. They had met and married in the late sixties when she was a member of the Royal Ballet in London and David was working for the orchestra accompanying the dancers on a British tour. They recount, with happy chuckles, how their present-day Languedocienne life started – on a train from Aberdeen to Glasgow. They became friends on that journey – and all because Bridget offered to help David with his bag, violin and Burmese cat!

In 1982 the couple decided to have a year's sabbatical at their holiday home in minute St-Privat, 14 km. east of Lodève, a town on the road from Millau to Montpellier. Both had had a longtime interest in cooking and wine – and, early on in that year off, they both agreed that their own restaurant was what they wanted. It had to be a quiet start because they had no idea what success, or otherwise, they would achieve. Lara, their 12-year-old daughter, remembers clearly how every meal seemed to be an animated time – when all the complicated plans of starting a restaurant were discussed endlessly. During that year Linnet, their second child, was born.

In their search for a suitable property they eventually discovered a marvellous house in St-Guiraud, a tiny village of 128 souls. Once the property of a prosperous vineyard owner it had all the right ingredients for their project: bags of character, cool, airy rooms, a terrace, ancient beams and stones and, as an interest-arousing bonus, a *cave*, where wine had been made for decades beforehand, which still had *in situ* huge oak casks and an ancient wine press. Later the couple built a stunning small swimming pool; half of it in the *cave*, the other half in the courtyard at the foot of the terrace.

Despite many setbacks they opened on February 29, 1984.

And what a success they've made of it – though to be fair it's still tough going financially. At such a remote spot they need to be known and I can only hope that many Anglo-Saxons will seek them out, adding important numbers to their local clients.

The couple have created a happy 'home' – and it's the dining room décor which immediately gives the clue for the choice of Le Mimosa as the restaurant name. You walk past the open-plan kitchen as you enter the dining room; you'll see Bridget working away as she does all the cooking on her own. And she does that with great flair; using only fresh produce and building up a self-taught repertoire she has done well enough to gain an entry in the 1986 Gault Millau Guide and has won a most rewarding recommendation from Georges Renault.

Most produce comes from Béziers market – but they have also built up good contacts with local suppliers, particularly for the excellent beef they buy from a nearby butcher. Bridget's specialities are an enjoyable mixture of styles: a *salade grande ferme* with local Roquefort and bacon, *terrine maison* with a Cumberland sauce, *baudroie au safran et à l'estragon*, *symphonie de la mer* and *filet de bœuf Daumas Gassac* are just a representative few dishes from her ever-growing culinary repertoire. She works hard – that's for sure: as a ballet dancer she always had a problem to keep her weight down; as a *cuisinière* her biggest difficulty now is to put on extra ounces!

The beef dish reminds me to tell you about the best *vin de pays* (and most expensive) you'll drink in France: a modest label, Vin de pays de l'Hérault, gives no clue to the quality of the Mas de Daumas Gassac from nearby Aniane. It's a 'rogue' wine for these parts – as it's made primarily from Cabernet Sauvignon grapes. David, an enthusiastic, friendly man, is rapidly developing a great interest in the local wines.

The couple deserve some support. Bridget is not the first self-taught lady chef who will make her mark in France – it's just that she has a much harder task in a country where *cuisinières* are not taken too seriously these days, particularly one from the other side of the planet. David is 100 per cent behind her and brings a lot of personal warmth and style to what is already a splendid house full of character. I assure you your navigational efforts will be rewarded. (Talking of planets it seems appropriate that I visited St-Guiraud on a night when I was lucky enough to see a full eclipse of the moon.)

Where is St-Guiraud? Follow the N9 14 km. south-west from Lodève to its junction with the N109 – the Montpellier road; a couple of kilometres to the north is St-Guiraud. The A9 autoroute is just 25 miles away to the east at Montpellier. Where do you stay? Use the *French Leave 3* 'base', the Hauts de Mourèze at Mourèze (p. 153) – ten miles away – or the Hôtel de Sarac at even-closer Clermont-l'Hérault. Or, better still, when you write or phone to reserve a table ask the couple if they can put you up in a newly-created bedroom above the *cave* or in private rooms in the village.

If you don't stay overnight then try a lunch at least. Combine it with a tour of some of France's greatest countryside to the north – the forests and mountains of the Cévennes and the incomparable Cirque de Navacelles; read the chapter called *Captivating Cévennes* in the Massif Central section.

category 2 *menus* B *rooms* See text
closed Feb. Mon. Tues (Oct-May).
post St-Guiraud, 34150 Gignac, Hérault. (W of Montpellier)
phone 67 96 67 96 *Mich* 240 *map* 68 Montpellier 40 km.

ST-SERNIN-SUR-RANCE   Carayon (France)

Fairly comfortable hotel
Terrace/Good value

You could visit this hotel for lunch and leave – as I did years ago – without realising that the chef speaks fluent English. Pierre, 36 years old, is the fourth generation *cuisinier* at the family hotel – owned by the Carayons for over a century. After finishing his studies at the Toulouse Hotel School he spent two years in England at the Savoy and Dorchester; no wonder his English is perfect. He is passionately intense about his *pays* and regional produce; quiz him on both subjects – his enthusiasm is infectious. Claudette, his wife, is an attractive hostess and she brightens up the dining room no end. But first let me highlight other reasons for visiting the area.

I would suggest that all visitors to France, who rate getting off the beaten track as one of their prime touring objectives, should head for the Haut Languedoc Regional Nature Park. A mass of green, wooded hills, between Albi and Montpellier, it's full of visual scenic surprises.

If your itinerary through the park includes a visit to St-Sernin then be certain to approach the town from the south. From St-Pons you climb steeply up through wooded hillsides. Apart from the view south the first thing that strikes you so forcibly is how suddenly the terrain changes from the dry, dusty scrubland south of St-Pons. Lacaune is famous for its *charcuterie*; with its dark grey slate roofs, it looks more like a town in mid Wales. Much of the landscape from this point on reminds me of Wales – though the hills here are higher!

Climb north from Lacaune, using the D607 to the Col de Sie. The views to the east – and later to the west – are remarkable as you continue north. At Roquecezière make the one-minute detour to the viewpoint on top of a rocky outcrop. Share the fantastic panorama with the statue – but, be warned, you need to have a head for heights to climb those steps.

My last drive on this marvellous ridge-top road was on a Sunday evening in June. The sides of the road were ribbons of wild flowers – of every colour and variety imaginable. I have never seen so many French families out picking wild flowers – I must have counted at least twenty groups busily collecting blooms. (Early next morning I watched Ernest Carayon, Pierre's father, spend an hour filling the hotel's vases with wild flowers; he had already been up into the hills to pick his share.)

The road descends steeply into medieval St-Sernin – itself

above the River Rance. Be sure to take an appetite with you to the hotel because no-one can possibly complain about small portions being served here. It's a perfect example of what a great number of ordinary French folk want: solid, copious fare – *cuisine Bourgeoise* using local produce as far as possible. So loosen your belts a notch and tuck into some big helpings of value-for-money nosh. (Though, ironically, if you do ask Pierre to provide a specially-prepared 'light' dish he'll do so with pleasure – steamed fish for example.)

You can choose from seven menus – varying from £5 to £20 in cost. One is described as a 'Menu Rouergat' – priced at a modest £7 or so! First *une grand assiette de hors d'œuvre avec le jambon du pays* – three sorts of Lacaune *charcuterie* and a large slice of mountain ham; then *les petits ris d'agneau du Causse parfumés à l'ail et au persil* – a vast helping by any standards; then a massive *côte de mouton du Causse* – which I defy you to finish; next a superb example of *le Roquefort 'sélection spéciale'* – even a request for a small *tranche* brought a big slice which, back home, would have cost a fortune; and, finally, choose from any one of about 20 desserts! (The *causses* are the rock strewn, barren stretches of plateaux encircling Millau; sheep play a big part in the local economy.)

It's possible you may prefer to stay a few days, enjoying the good-value *pension* terms – joining the many French families tucking into the varied set meals offered each evening. Then you'll have a chance to see the local countryside.

To the north-east is Millau and the many marvels of Mother Nature (see the Massif Central). To the south-west is a small circle of country called the Sidobre. Within its wooded hills are some of the strangest quirks of Nature you'll ever see; weird granite rocks lie hidden among the trees – the strangest is the amusingly-named Peyro-Clabado, the rocky equivalent of a Centurion tank sitting on top of a Mini.

To the south of St-Sernin are two large lakes – both with roads encircling their banks. The towns of Brassac, Lacaune and La Salvetat-s-Agout are ideal examples of what life is like in rural communities throughout France. It's in places like this where you sense the real strength of France, where you recognise the immense importance of agriculture and where the 'family' and local traditions are put above all other aspects of life; long may those values continue to flourish.

Another pleasant day out would be to head north with a picnic lunch. Follow the Rance downstream to Plaisance (a young chef, Francis Roussel, is making a name for himself there at his medieval restaurant, Les Magnolias) and continue on the D33 until you reach the Tarn. Follow the river upstream to Brousse-le-Château: a ruined castle, a centuries-old bridge over the Alrance (a tributary of the Tarn) and rose-covered walls give the riverside village an entrancing atmosphere. For some extensive views climb the D54 and D25 until you reach the D31 – a panorama stretches away far to the south.

Finally, ask Pierre to show you the old stables (now a disco/bar) where the first generation Carayons kept horses – to provide passing travellers with extra 'horse-power' to enable their coaches to climb the steep D999 to Albi. Chuckle as you climb the 'col' in the comfort of your modern car.

category 2(S) menus A-C rooms 23A-C cards A AE DC V
closed Sun evg & Mon (Nov-Mar).
post 12380 St-Sernin-sur-Rance, Aveyron. (SW of Millau)
phone 65 99 60 26 Mich 235 map 69 Millau 63 km.

LES BEZARDS   Auberge des Templiers

Luxury hotel
Quiet/Terrace/Gardens/Swimming pool/Tennis

It doesn't take long at this extremely luxurious auberge to discover just why it's such a great favourite with readers. Expensive it all is – as it should be ; but that doesn't prevent one from feeling, the moment you step through the front door, the strong family atmosphere that I think is the big bonus at the Templiers. Luxury hotels are common in France but none of them can better the all-important detailed touches that come so easily from the talented staff – which, in the end, always seem to be more appreciated than material trappings.

The family touches start with the owners, Philippe and Françoise Depée. Philippe is a handsome host; his parents ran the Auberge des Templiers back in 1954 when it was one of the original eight members of the now hugely successful Relais et Chateaux chain. Indeed, Philippe is proud that 32 years later his hotel is the only one of the founding eight that is still owned by the same family and occupies the same site.

Françoise is for my money the most attractive hostess at any hotel I know. She and Philippe were married 15 years ago. After leaving school she spent some years studying commercial subjects like law and accountancy; but, not surprisingly, she soon became a talented fashion model – working for world-famous houses like Dior and Chanel. She has used those varied skills very effectively in the dozen years she has masterminded the behind-the-scenes running of the hotel.

Most of the staff are long-established regulars: Jean, the

porter, who welcomes you at the hotel entrance, has worked for the Depées for over two decades; Alain, the *maître d'hôtel*, matches that time span with 20 years service as well; Henri, the likeable *sommelier*, has been offering clients his massive store of wine knowledge for 15 years; and Guy, Alain's assistant, has been at the Auberge for 12 years. Most of the senior staff speak English; all of them are unpretentious, friendly individuals – skilled, patient service seems to be an effortless, unobtrusive talent for all of them.

There have been changes in the kitchens however. Jean-Claude Rigollet now works for himself in Chinon and Christian Willer, his successor, has headed south for Cannes. Roger Tillier, who seconded both of them for a long period at Les Bézards, is now the *cuisinier* in charge. Standards remain consistently high and they follow a classical path but with a light, modern style running throughout the menu.

Specialities change from season to season. Typical of the wide choice available are *rougets de roche au basilic – très simple* and as light a delight as you can imagine – and a *rognonnade d'agneau 'au vert'* – three small rounds of lamb served with a *gâteau* of vegetables which include aubergine, courgette and red peppers within the flat cake shape.

A *feuillantine de framboises et fraises des bois d'Orléans* (more about those woods later) arrives filling a sizeable plate. Between two huge pastry biscuits is an agreeable mixture of raspberries, wild strawberries (collected from the nearby woods) and cream; an enjoyable dessert and it's not difficult to finish it off though at first sight it seems a daunting task.

The wine list is formidable – one of the finest in France. Philippe and Henri work hard at maintaining its high standard, constantly acquiring the best wines available – from all parts of France. There are nearly 100 half-bottles on the list, prices starting at the low level of about 50 francs. At the other end of the scale there's a very rare *marie-jeanne* (2½ litres) 1947 Château Lafite-Rothschild at 8,500 francs! Complementing the fantastic number of Bordeaux and Burgundy vintages – the oldest dating back to 1897 – is a quality selection of Loire wines. Take Henri's advice – his English is excellent.

During the last few years Philippe has helped many young chefs from overseas by allowing them to work for brief periods in the kitchens at the Auberge. Two of those stars of the future are English – Craig Dent and Jeremy O'Connor. Both are friends of Jean-Claude Rigollet – see the entry for Chinon.

Most of the 30 bedrooms and suites are located in buildings scattered around the 14 acres of grounds: they include a thatched cottage, modern, stylish structures, an old bakehouse and some converted stables. The rooms are large, impeccably furnished and luxurious; this is a hotel for some special occasion when you want to give yourself a treat. I said earlier it's expensive but you will not begrudge the francs spent.

There's much to see locally; some of it, in my opinion, matching the more famous attractions to the west. Start a rewarding day tour by heading seven kilometres south to the château at La Bussière – set in a Le Nôtre designed park. Then continue south again for another five km., turn left off the N7, and enjoy the smaller château at Pont Chevron. Now due west to Gien; visit the factory that makes the splendid crockery that you'll admire in the Auberge's restaurant. Continue on the south bank to Sully – its handsome castle had close links with Joan of Arc. She visited the château twice. On the first occasion her visit followed the battles of Orléans, Beaugency and Patay — it was there that she persuaded the Dauphin to go to Reims to be crowned. From Sully continue downstream on the northern bank of the Loire to St-Benoît; revel in the glory of one of my favourite French abbeys — I particularly like the belfry porch.

I mentioned the Forêt d'Orléans earlier — one of the largest natural forests in France. When I was at Les Bézards I studied Michelin map 238 — my curiosity aroused by the 'Carrefour de la Résistance' in the very heart of the forest. I set out to find it; you should do so, too.

From Sully head north for 3 km., then use the D961, cross the D952 and, one km. north of Les Bordes, follow the signposted forest track to the *carrefour*. What a moving spot it is; large sequoias shade a memorial to the *maquis* of Lorris (a village to the north). During August 1944 over 50 patriots died fighting the Germans in the nearby woods — the vast majority were killed on the 14th. (Orléans was liberated by Patton only days later.) Crosses mark the spots where they fell and a map shows where each one died in the forest. Their leader, sent by de Gaulle, is buried there — even though he died many years later in Algeria; intriguingly his name was Colonel Marc O'Neill. There are many pleasant marked walks in the woods — watch out for the ancient oaks.

Finish by heading south-east to the D119; drive through Montereau and on to Langesse where you should stop to admire the old houses, church and *étang*.

category 3 *menus* **C-D** *rooms* 30**D-D3** *cards* A AE DC V
closed Mid Jan-mid Feb. (On N7 S of Montargis)
post Les Bézards, 45290 Nogent-sur-Vernisson, Loiret.
phone 38 31 80 01 *Mich* 238 *map* 29 Montargis 23 km.

114

CHINON   Au Plaisir Gourmand

Comfortable restaurant
Gardens

French Leave readers who, in the past, have used the guide in the Loire Valley will query why this entry should be a favourite as it was never recommended in any of the three editions. The reason why this restaurant finds a place in this new book is because the talented chef, Jean-Claude Rigollet, was a great favourite with readers during his four-year stint at the Auberge des Templiers at Les Bézards. Those of you who have *FL3* will know that Jean-Claude left Les Bézards to teach at the Orléans Catering School; his great *copain* (buddy), Stewart Cunningham, also left the Auberge at the same time, headed for Tahiti in the South Pacific. (Stewart, a Scotsman and great motor enthusiast, had been the *maître d'hôtel* at Les Bézards.)

The teaching stint didn't last long. At the beginning of 1984 Jean-Claude and Danielle, his wife, bought their own place — here in Chinon. They've made a great success of it; certainly I can think of few better places to set up 'shop'.

Underneath the castle walls, just 30 metres from the Vienne, the restaurant has a small, colourful garden and a dining room which seats no more than 25 to 30 clients. For the standard of cooking available prices are amazingly modest. Jean-Claude's style is based on thoroughly honed classical skills; sauces are his forte and he has a real master's touch.

Consider, for example, a *jambonette de canard à l'ancienne*; using the local red Chinon wine as a base, the dish is worth ordering for the sauce alone. *Vieux Chinon* is also used in an alternative *filet de bœuf* speciality. The menu describes another dish as a *feuilleté de bar au beurre de homard*; you don't get the normal puff-pastry top and bottom – rather it's a *pâtisserie*-like slice with a mousse of bar stuffed within the soft feathery covering. It's a brilliant example of *cuisine moderne* – based on a sound classical training.

I was thrilled to see the Rigollets using Wedgwood crockery – manufactured back home in North Staffordshire. At Les Bézards Jean-Claude's old bosses, the Depées, use the local Gien crockery. An unusual quirk is that in his time Jean-Claude gave both Craig Dent and Jeremy O'Connor the chance to have spells working alongside him at Les Bézards – both are among our best British chefs. Craig, would you believe, uses Gien crockery at his Midlands base, just an hour's drive from where Wedgwood plates are made. What a strange twist!

By the time this book is published you'll be able to order red Chinon wine from Jean-Claude's very own two-acre vineyard – which he bought in 1985. For your *apéritif* why not try a 1947 *verre de Vouvray*? At 38 francs per glass you may think that's steep – but it's not, as 1947 was a superb year for the magical Vouvray sweet wine. If you cannot afford that then order a glass of Coteaux du Layon at less than half the price.

Apart from Danielle, who'll take your order, you're also likely to see her eldest daughter, Laurent, serving in the dining room. Visit the family and enjoy the best thing to happen on the culinary front in the Chinon area for years.

However, whatever you do, Chinon is a must. It's a place where you should let your imagination work hard for you. Walk the narrow Rue Haute St-Maurice – past medieval houses and the historic Grand Carroi. Joan of Arc came this way on a day which was to prove in time one of the most eventful in the histories of both France and England. Her meeting with the Dauphin at Chinon in 1429 proved to be the beginning of the end of the English influence in France.

As you walk the walls of the great fortress high above Chinon, think of the castle in its great days, eight centuries ago, when the Plantagenets were such a formidable force in France – when Henry II, Eleanor of Aquitaine, Richard the Lionheart and John, his brother, made this small town the centre of their considerable empire. It's a stirring, inspiring site.

For overnight stays use La Giraudière – the next entry.
category **3** *menus* **B** *rooms* See text *cards* V
closed Feb. Last 2 wks Nov. Sun evg. Mon.
post 2 rue Parmentier, 37500 Chinon, Indre-et-Loire.
phone 47 93 20 48 *Mich* 232 *map* 30 Tours 48 km.

CHINON   La Giraudière

Simple hotel
Secluded/Gardens

La Giraudière is a 17th-century manor house in an isolated location about six km. north-west of Chinon. Surrounded by fields and woods the hotel is 500 metres from the River Vienne. It's a *sans restaurant* hotel of the kind that I've been trying for the last six years to persuade readers to use throughout France. The site of this 'base' has proved to be a success with most visitors – complimentary letters have arrived at Chiltern House from all parts of the world. What gives La Giraudière a special plus is that a score or more of man-made architectural treasures – of all kinds – are within a short drive. But before you seek them out let me tell you about the hotel.

It's a simple place with access to bedrooms on three sides of the old manor; two other outbuildings have bedrooms as well. There's a large garden; parking is easy; some rooms have *cuisinettes*; there are walks to the river; Jacques Ragli, who runs the hotel, speaks excellent English; and some of you will be pleased to know that the nylon sheets have been thrown away!

There's one feature of the hotel which is hidden away from clients' eyes; ask Jacques to show it to you. Called a *pigeonnier*, it forms part of one of the old outbuildings. It's a huge room where, within the four walls, are 920 pigeon *boulins* – literally, pigeon holes; made from the local tufa stone they were once used for just that purpose. The high timbered roof, with chestnut wood beams, is also well worth seeing.

Undoubtedly you will want to make your way to some of the great sights that are so close at hand: the châteaux at Langeais, Ussé, Azay-le-Rideau and Saumur; the great abbey at Fontevraud where Henry II, Eleanor of Aquitaine and Richard the Lionheart are buried; the tiny hamlet of La Devinière where Rabelais was born; and the site of Chinon castle. But let me also recommend others which are less well known.

The first is at La Herpinière, one km. south-west of Montsoreau, where an ancient windmill has been restored with loving care by Guy Petitfils. Nearby, at Candes-St-Martin, is a magnificent 12th-century church – full of character. (On your way there from Chinon pay a call on the *poterie* of Charles and Joanna Hair at Thizay, seven km. before you reach Candes.) To the east of Chinon is an equally old church at Tavant – in this case enriched by some splendid Romanesque frescoes.

Further afield, outside Tours, is another fantastic structure which, alas, is missed by the vast majority of visitors to the Loire. Built 700 years ago, the Grange de Meslay is a fortified farm where the 190-ft-long stone barn hides within its interior the most stunning maze of wooden rafters, beams and pillars; made of chestnut, some of the pillars are as thick as very sizeable tree trunks. Each year at the beginning of July a musical festival is held in the atmospheric tithe barn – it must be a thoroughly enjoyable way of listening to talented artists. To find the barn, head up the N10 from Tours – it's on your right just beyond the Tours-Nord entrance for the A10 autoroute. It's one of my great favourites; don't miss it.

category 1 *menus* No rest. *rooms* 25**C** *cards* A AE DC V
closed Open all the year.
post 37420 Avoine, Indre-et-Loire. (NW of Chinon – off D749)
phone 47 58 40 36 *Mich* 232 *map* 31 Chinon 5 km.

NOUAN-LE-FUZELIER

Charmilles

Comfortable hotel
Quiet/Gardens

If there's an ideal time to visit the Sologne then it must be in the four months following the first Sunday in October. The area between Orléans to the north and Vierzon to the south – a misty, flat landscape peppered with thousands of *étangs* (pools) and vast sandy acres of mixed woodland – comes to life with the start of the hunting season. Sportsmen take up their guns and, accompanied by their dogs, go in search of wild boar, roe-deer, hares, rabbits, pheasant and partridges.

La chasse dominates the fare appearing on the region's menus. This is the time for tourists to go in search of 'base'

hotels: establishments which are *sans restaurant* and which allow you the freedom to eat whenever and wherever you wish in the locality; Charmilles is a classic example. Within a thirty minute drive are many fine restaurants: La Solognote at nearby Brinon-sur-Sauldre is reputed for its game dishes – the Girards recently won their first Michelin star; young Monsieur Beurienne is highly thought of locally at his restaurant La Perdrix Rouge at Souvigny-en-Sologne; Didier Clément at the Grand Hôtel Lion d'Or in Romorantin is one of the best young chefs in France; Bernard Robin, like Didier, also has two Michelin stars – his home is Le Relais at Bracieux; and within walking distance is Jean-Luc Germain's Le Dahu restaurant.

Dominique Sené has made many friends, too, at his 'base' hotel in Nouan-le-Fuzelier. On a quiet side road (the sound of distant trains can be a problem if the wind's from the west) it

CHENONCEAUX

backs on to six acres of woods – ideal for a quiet walk or for the fisherman looking for a restful spot alongside the two small pools in the hotel's grounds. There's a shady garden for those of you who just want to sit and read. Bedrooms are comfortable and most have showers or baths.

Be certain to take some large-scale maps of the area with you (Michelin 238 is ideal). Then head up as many of the 'yellow' and 'white' roads as possible. For example just west of Nouan – on the far side of the new autoroute – are the lanes encircling the Etang de Marcilly and the Etang de la Grande Corbois. A handsome château at Favelle makes an excellent point to stop, desert your car and walk the banks of the pools. Woodlands are everywhere; you'll never be short of ideas for exercise. Inevitably there are countless streams, too.

On the edge of the circle of terrain called the Sologne are numerous man-made treasures: the château at Sully and the glorious abbey at St-Benoît are to the north-east, alongside the Loire; to the west are the châteaux at Chambord – from afar the myriad chimneys look like a distant town – the smaller Cour-Cheverny and glorious Chenonceaux, astride the Cher.

Apart from the harvests from the woods the region is renowned for its fish: *sandre*, pike, tench, carp, trout and perch are caught in the rivers, streams and lakes. Fruit, too, is very good – particularly pears from Olivet, a suburb of Orléans. Don't miss the chance to try the local *eau de vie de poire William*!

category 1 *menus* No rest. *rooms* 14**B-C** *cards* V
closed Mid Jan-mid Mar. Mon (in Oct, Nov & Dec). (On D122)
post Nouan-le-Fuzelier, 41600 Lamotte-Beuvron, Loir-et-Cher.
phone 54 88 73 55 *Mich* 238 *map* 32 Orléans 44 km.

118

NOUAN-LE-FUZELIER   Moulin de Villiers

Simple hotel
Secluded/Terrace/Gardens/Good value (meals)

Some years ago I recommended the Moulin de Villiers to a friend of mine. He was making an October trip to the south and Nouan was the perfect spot for an overnight stop. By the time he had crossed the Loire at Orléans it was dark and, what was worse, very foggy. He turned his car off the N20 at Nouans and, correctly, followed the D44 road, signposted to Chaon. He began to think he might be on the wrong track as he drove north-east through the swirling mist; luck was on his side as he caught sight of the Moulin sign on his left – usually, visitors wizz past, but the thick mist helped on this occasion. He headed left up the long entrance to the hotel – a tarmac ribbon through dense woods (watch the bumps) and unusually eerie in the blanket of fog that covered the Sologne. At last he reached his goal – still not sure of what I had led him to.

He and his wife awoke next morning to a glorious autumn day – one of those October marvels when Nature is at her most seductive. Even before breakfast they were out and about – relishing the clockwise walk round the large *étang* alongside the small hotel. What a surprise the site must have been; now my friend knew well enough why I had persuaded him to seek out the heavenly spot – a mini version of the Sologne.

The ancient *moulin* – once a water mill used to grind wheat – is at the centre of 25 acres of private woodland; surrounded by woods, it has its own very sizeable lake, streams and marshes. For the last 60 years the Moulin de Villiers has been in the ownership of Gladys Andrieux and her family – her grandfather bought it between the wars; for over two decades it has been run as a hotel by Gladys and her husband.

The original mill has been extended during that period – a small modern wing has been cleverly added to the old red-brick, timbered structure, so typical of the area. It's particularly popular with the French who stay and enjoy its many tranquil charms for several days at a time – rather than just pushing on after a single night's stop.

You should stay awhile, too. Enjoy the friendly welcome and humour of the two resident angels – Gladys and Gérard. Fish in the large pool and test the wits of the giant pike lurking in the still waters. Walk in the endless woods. And appreciate the really very modest cooking at the Moulin: home-made soups, terrines, *brochet* and other fish, beef of all types, French fries with everything, salads and basic desserts are the sort of fare you'll be offered. During *la chasse* in the autumn there'll be local game, too – from the nearby forests.

Wines and cheeses are all local. Wines will include cheaper varieties from Cour-Cheverny and Menetou-Salon – neither are well known – and also the more famous vintages from Sancerre and Pouilly-sur-Loire to the south-east. The *plateau de fromages* may have an Olivet Bleu or an Olivet Cendré on display (both are made from cow's milk) or, alternatively, a goat's milk cheese from perhaps Chavignol or a variety from Selles-sur-Cher, beyond Romorantin.

category 2**(S)** *menus* **A-B** *rooms* 20**BC**
closed Jan-mid Mar. 1st half Sept. Tues & Wed (Nov & Dec).
post Nouan-le-Fuzelier, 41600 Lamotte-Beuvron, Loir-et-Cher.
phone 54 88 72 27 *Mich* 238 *map* 33 Orléans 44 km. (On D44)

REDOUBTABLE SOLOGNE

Throughout the last war the Sologne was one of the strongest Resistance areas in France. There were many *maquis* groups operating in the woods and marshes and their sabotage work was not confined to just the Sologne – they instigated attacks in towns like Tours and Orléans. It's said that the Sologne *maquis* was the most formidable in France.

During the first eight months of 1944 some spectacular action caused havoc for the Germans. Many of the attacks were led by SOE agents: Philippe de Vomécourt who had been imprisoned for 14 months in France before escaping back to Britain in January 1944; Captain George Donovan Jones who, after enduring sadistic torture at the hands of the Gestapo, made an amazing escape back to London in 1943; Captain Stanislas Makowksi, a Pole; and George Wilkinson. By April 1944 the four were working in France – based at Salbris (south of Nouan) and St-Viâtre (west of Nouan). Later they were joined by uniformed units from The Special Air Services (SAS).

Perhaps the most amazing sabotage action organised by Vomécourt was when the Resistance and Allied Bomber Command combined to destroy the vast arsenal at Salbris – Michelin map 238 shows the many railway tracks within the area blown up in early May 1944. Makowksi led a *maquis* attack on German troops in the woods east of Souesmes (south-east of Nouan) on June 17th; nearly 200 Germans were killed or wounded. After further action near Neung-sur-Beuvron (west of Nouan) the Pole was finally captured in August 1944; he was tortured by the Gestapo at Romorantin and then murdered – only days before Orléans was liberated by Patton.

ROMORANTIN-LANTHENAY   Grand Hôtel Lion d'Or

Very comfortable hotel
Terrace/Lift

For over a decade I have watched with great interest how various changes have transformed one of my favourite French hotels; I have been delighted, too, that so many of you have enjoyed the differing pleasures that make the Lion d'Or really special. Today it's a very comfortable, modern hotel with all the creature comforts that any visitor could ever want; the standard of cooking is already amongst the best in France and will improve even further in the next decade – more of that later; there's a lot of agreeable terrain nearby; and there are many entrancing man-made architectural sites within a short drive.

All those 'benefits' apply to many fine hotels – but, here at this small market town, there's another which I rate even more highly: it's the personal touch and the feel of a family home. At Romorantin the family is represented by two generations – two charming, unpretentious couples. Colette and Alain Barrat, 'Mum' and 'Dad', are the owners of the Lion d'Or – it's they who have masterminded the changes over the last decade. The hotel has just 14 bedrooms – but how comfortable they are; their modernisation has worked well. 1986 saw extensive redecoration of the entire ground floor; many of you have commented on the new elegant atmosphere of the lounge and dining rooms. The 'terrace' at the heart of the hotel remains as appealing as ever.

The second generation is represented by the Barrats' daughter, Marie-Christine, and her gifted husband, Didier Clément; Hélène, their first child, was born on February 20, 1986. Didier is already a very talented cook, full of imagination and a seeker of perfection. Marie is an intelligent girl, speaks fluent English and has developed a great interest in a culinary field which helps her husband so encouragingly. It's worth explaining, briefly, what this is.

Three or four years ago Marie-Christine was preparing for her doctorate. One of the projects assigned to her was the study of medieval French cookery. It proved to be a daunting task following up different research paths all over France. During her studies of centuries-old books and texts Marie-Christine discovered, to her surprise, what great use was made of herbs and spices. It was the latter that intrigued her most. Many manuscripts referred mysteriously to a *poudre fine* (fine powder) – the latter being added to all sorts of ancient recipes. What were the ingredients of the *poudre fine*? Further enquiries and research indicated that the expression referred to a very flexible use of assorted spices – the latter cultivated not just in France but imported also from North Africa and the Far East. Marie has been able to track down some of the rare *épices* that were once so common in French cooking.

Her searches continue but already Didier has incorporated the use of spices to several of the specialities in his repertoire. The most stunning is a *langoustines rôties aux épices douces*; the accompanying sauce is just right – spicy but not excessively so. The mix of spices is a closely guarded secret; Didier is keeping it to himself. A nice extra touch is an onion and chives mixture, combined with a humble potato.

The use of ginger is more normal; Didier uses it skilfully with *noisettes d'agneau*. Most welcome is the accompanying selection of five vegetables. An unusual alternative — demonstrating the young couple's great passion for herbs — is a *cuisses de grenouilles au pourpier et la ciboulette*; read the chapter on the *Romorantin Market* for details on *pourpier* (purslane). *Mélisse* (lemon-balm) appears with *aile de pigeon* and several dishes make use of other *épices* and *aromates*.

Didier has spent a considerable time experimenting with salmon. One result of his efforts is a *saumon sauvage d'Ecosse aux radis roses*; wafer-thin squares of salmon assembled like a *millefeuille* with layers of alternating pin-sized morsels of radish — it works beautifully. Another dish is a *saumon sauvage d'Ecosse au jus de truffe* — the truffle reduction is both light in colour and taste and does not overpower the fish.

The *crépinette de pigeon au vinaigre de cidre*, which I described in early editions of *French Leave*, is still on the menu — what a masterpiece. The huge assortment of cheeses — served on four large straw 'plates' — similarly continues to beguile all those who visit the Lion d'Or. The restaurant's reputation for creative desserts has been enhanced even more recently: *soufflé aux pruneaux et à la creme de thé*; *millefeuille d'abricot au coulis d'abricot*; and a *tulipe de fraises des bois au lait d'amandes* are just a few examples of Didier's talents.

Lovely small touches abound: the appetisers are mouthwatering treats — quail eggs on minute rounds of toast, hot tiny slices of *feuilleté* with different fillings and a combination of melon and paper-thin ham are examples; *petits fours* are the real thing — and there's always a good choice; and breakfasts are super — with home-made breads and jams. And, please, don't ignore the saucer of dark liquid served at breakfast; it's rich, strong, 'wild' honey — collected by a friend of the Barrats deep in the forests of the Sologne.

Don't leave Romorantin without heading for the *étangs* and woods of the Sologne — the countryside to the north. If time is precious why not follow this short drive to the north-west of the town? Leave by the D765 and more or less immediately join the D59. Soon the Etang de Batarde appears on your right. Stop and find the sluice gate alongside the road — this enables the large pool to be emptied and cleaned periodically.

Continue on and if you're lucky you'll see a huge herd of about 100 brown goats in the fields on your left. The couple that own them milk each one every day by hand. Despite the size of the herd they all have a 'rhythm' of life that doesn't change from hour to hour; apparently you can set your watch by it. Following their leader, they feed, drink and visit particular parts of a pasture according to a strict daily pattern. In 1985 the pastures were covered by a fantastic show of wild flowers. The hard winter had killed off many insects in the ground; this severe spell of weather, combined with a wet spring, was the reason for the blankets of blooms.

The Etang de Paris comes next — in summer it's covered by water lilies, unless of course the sluice gate has been used to empty it; in the year following the 'cleaning-up' the blooms do not appear. Just beyond Lassay visit the 15th-century Château du Moulin — hidden in the forests. Continue across the lanes to the château at Fougères-s-Bièvre; it's a small fortress — ignored by tourists — and a great personal favourite.

category **3**★ *menus* **C** *rooms* 14**D** *cards* A AE DC V
closed Jan-mid Feb. (E of Tours)
post 69 r. Clemenceau, 41200 Romorantin-Lant., L-et-Ch.
phone 54 76 00 28 *Mich* 238 *map* 34 Tours 90 km.

ROMORANTIN MARKET

Market day in Romorantin is Wednesday. It's probably no different from the weekly markets held in hundreds of French towns – but, by choosing the Romorantin version as a typical example, it allows me to write, briefly, on what is one of the great pleasures of France. I'm always tempted by the sight of a bustling provincial market; lack of time usually prevents me from stopping but, if I can, I'm happy to spend an hour – looking, chatting, enquiring and perhaps buying, too.

The centre of Romorantin is alive and busy from an early hour on market morning. Scores of traders bring goods of every description into the town – they take over the streets and squares. But these are travelling marketeers – moving from one place to another every day. They are of little interest to me. What I get excited about is when I wander among the stalls of the local growers and producers. In Romorantin you'll find most of them under the protection of the covered market hall. You'll profit, as I did recently, by heading indoors.

The first stallholder I met proved to be the formidable Madame Barboux – a local legend. I saw her unloading trays of cheeses from an ancient Peugeot estate car, which, anywhere else but in France, would have been despatched to the scrap yard long ago. I'm not joking when I tell you the headlamp bulbs were hanging from their reflector holders – the headlamp glass covers had long since disappeared. It must be a frightening experience to encounter Madame's motor in thick fog! (She's from Billy, a northern neighbour of Selles-sur-Cher; the clue in that address is that she makes her own goat's milk cheeses!) On display is a range of different types – six in

all; from tingling fresh to very, very dry. The latter have an almost black exterior; they mature for up to three months.

Near her in a corner was an older, quieter woman – renowned for the quail eggs she had in baskets in front of her. These are the same eggs you will relish when you try the Lion d'Or's appetisers. Alongside her was the amazing Elisa Bouleau, mother of twelve; her eldest daughter, Annick, is the receptionist who welcomes you at the hotel. It seems unnecessary to say how hard Elisa works to keep her brood alive; she does it so successfully that she wins many of the local horticultural prizes for the quality of her produce – cheeses (goat's and cow's milk), chickens and vegetables.

Next came Lucien Carré – from Pruniers, eight km. to the south-west of the town; he's considered by the Cléments as the best *charcutier* in the Loire Valley. What a display: *boudins blancs*, *boudins noirs*, hams tasting quite different from the supermarket 'plastic' we all get used to, *saucisses* – both garlic and *sec* versions, *andouillettes* and, inevitably, *rillettes* and *rillons*. Both the latter derive from the world *rille* – lard. (During the hunting season you'll also be beguiled by several stalls offering their 'catch' of wild boar, roe-deer, hares, pheasants and all sorts of wild fowl from the 'peppered' landscape of *étangs* and woods that cover the Sologne.)

A few metres away from the butchers and *charcutiers* was a small dark woman – in front of her a table covered with both white and grey examples of *champignons de Paris*. Later that day I visited her 'caves' where the townspeople of Bourré, at the eastern entrance to Montrichard, alongside the Cher, earn their terribly hard living. The 'caves' were cut centuries ago – in tiers, one above the other; the stone was used to build châteaux, like the nearby one at Chenonceaux. Pass through Bourré during the day and the place is deserted; everyone is underground using miners' lamps to illuminate their task of picking, at just the right time, the continual harvest of mushrooms.

Madame Terreau, aptly named, earns her living differently – above ground near Cour-Cheverny. She is famed for her bedding plants and home-grown fruit. I counted at least 30 varieties of colourful plants ready to brighten up local gardens.

Across the aisle was a ten metre long 'display' of mouthwatering *pâtisseries* – of a much higher standard than is normal at markets. The family running the stall have made it such a hit that they now own their own *pâtisserie* in the town – the one immediately across the road from the Lion d'Or. Not bad after six years developing an appreciative local clientele in a modest market. Apart from the four dozen different cakes on

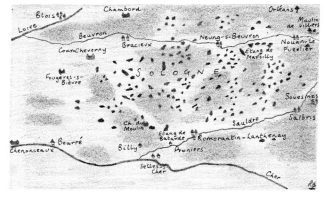

display the thing that took my eye was a *galette aux pommes de terre* – a shiny pastry-like surface with an amazing rubbery flexibility; you can bend it and roll it as you like. It has a rough, earthy taste – much to my liking.

Near the *pâtisserie* was Monsieur Gaullier's 'stand' – perhaps the biggest in the market. On the floor in a square around him was a huge assortment of vegetables – I counted over 40 different sorts. There was also a selection of six different types of potato – looking so good you could have eaten them on the spot. Everything was of first-class quality – but the *haricots verts, haricots beurres*, cabbages, different sorts of lettuce, radishes, chicory and courgettes looked particularly appetising. In May and June you will also see on stallholders' stands stack upon stack of the famed Sologne asparagus; during the season, in your travels through the lakes, woods and marshlands, you'll spot the regimented rows of rounded earth where the *asperges* is grown – be sure to taste it.

My last call was to meet Madame Leloup, surrounded by her small, but so interesting, selection of produce. She's a real character; tall with sparkling eyes and her skin shining with good health – so typical of anyone who spends their life outdoors. She must be about 60; later I was to meet her remarkable family at their simple two-acre farm (you'll understand soon why I'm not locating it precisely).

Around her in a circle was the evidence of the family's hard work: courgettes, *cornichons, ciboules laitues, échalotes, groseilles* and other vegetables and fruit; freshly-picked herbs like *menthe, marjolaine, absinthe, ciboulettes, estragon, sariette, persil* and others; dried herbs such as *thym, camomille, mélisse, laurier, basilic* and *thym citronelle*; and colourful 'everlasting' flowers (more about them later).

I was taken by her striking personality and amazing energy. Fortunately Marie-Christine Clément was with me and, on the spot, she agreed to accompany me to the Leloup smallholding. Fifteen minutes later we met Madame Leloup's daughter, working in the fields, her granddaughter and her 86-year-old mother, still active and full of vitality.

Our walk through the rows of plants, flowers, fruit bushes and herbs was a revelation. Growing there was all the produce listed earlier and lots more besides. The profusion of herbs was amazing – some unknown and one or two considered 'weeds' by the Leloup family but not by the Cléments. *Pourpier* is one; it's used by Didier in a *grenouilles* speciality, the 'weed' being perhaps the only one he knows which stands cooking in butter. There was tarragon – so strong smelling it was more like *anis*. Wild garlic – *rocambole* – was evident, too; in late evening its heavy perfume fills the air. What gave me the greatest surprise was to be shown *ache* – the original celery. When I sucked the thin stalk it was amazing how strong the celery taste was. Later I challenged the Cléments to find a way of using *ache* with goat's milk cheese – chopped up like *ciboulettes*. One day you may taste the result of their experiments. Last but not least were the rows of bright 'everlasting' flowers – of all types – hanging in the family kitchen for final drying.

Finally, can I ask you to keep a secret? Madame Leloup has a sense of humour. During the 'season' she collects edible wild fungi from the woods bordering her smallholding. She then sells them to the owner of the neighbouring château who, for the record, owns the self same woods. Now that's enterprise and it demonstrates an admirable survival instinct. Agreed?

124

SACHE   Auberge du XIIe siècle

Comfortable restaurant
Gardens

My favourite stretch of the Loire Valley is not to be found alongside the banks of the wide, characterless river that flows sulkily towards the Atlantic. Its waters are dark and murky – polluted by several cities and many nuclear power stations; you don't swim in the Loire these days – and I'm always amazed that any fish are caught at all. Instead, I have always preferred to seek out a tributary of the Loire, the Indre.

It's a river worth exploring all the way from its source near Châteaumeillant. In its early stages the stream flows through the Vallée Noire – much beloved by George Sand. Her home was at Nohant, not far from the river. But the Indre is at its best in the 30 km. before it joins the Loire. Near the point it meets the latter is the château at Ussé. Cross the river by the bridge in front of it and admire the imposing structure: it's said to have inspired Perrault who used it as the setting for *Sleeping Beauty*; enjoy the flowered terraces, towers, turrets and woods. Fourteen km. upstream is the château at Azay-le-Rideau – for me one of the loveliest in France. It's a gorgeous place – at the heart of a park and woods; the château seems to float on the Indre. From Azay I suggest you continue on the north bank of the river and six km. later turn right. A series of bridges takes you over the lush water meadows of the Indre to the village of Saché – another favourite of mine.

Spare time for the château. That word can have various meanings: it is used to describe a fortress, a castle, a vast structure like Chambord and often just a small house. The Saché version is one of the latter, surrounded by woods. Balzac spent great periods of time at the home of the Margonne family – from his childhood to his death in 1850. Today the house is dedicated to the life and work of the writer with letters, manuscripts, proofs, original editions and portraits.

Until a year or two ago Saché was also associated with the famous American artist, Alexander Calder. On the hill above La Sablonnière the garden of the family home used to contain many of his steel mobiles; now they are no longer there but one remains in the village square.

Since the beginning of this decade there has been yet another good reason for seeking out Saché – the restaurant home of Jean-Louis and Maryline Niqueux. The restaurant name gives a clue to the nature of the ancient house; stone

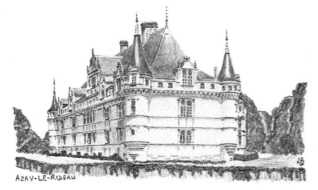

AZAY-LE-RIDEAU

floors and walls and wooden beams give it a real medieval feel.

Jean-Louis first made his name at the Château d'Artigny – an imposing member of the *Relais et Châteaux* chain; it sits high above the Indre just before you reach Montbazon. Today Jean-Louis delights clients in his own restaurant; his cooking is very much in the modern style, based primarily on a classical base with a welcome light, easy-to-digest touch.

An intriguing starter is called *œuf fermier à la coque, purée de morilles*. In fact three soft-boiled eggs arrive; two still in their shells and the third shell full of a *purée de morilles*. In addition a dozen strips of buttered brown toast 'soldiers' encircle the three eggs; what delectable dips!

A *matelote d'étang au bon vin de Chinon* shows off the chef's mastery of sauces; the red Chinon wine sauce is superb. The *matelote* includes eel, *sandre*, *brochet*, *pleurotes*, potatoes, celery and carrots. Another alternative on the menu is a famous regional speciality – *beuchelle à la Tourangelle*; a dish of kidneys, sweetbreads and *champignons*.

Don't fail to order the wines from the neighbouring vineyards. I'm able to enjoy Saché wines back home because Robin Yapp of Yapp Brothers at Mere, Wiltshire has for many years imported the dry whites and rosés of Gaston Pavy to the UK. (Gaston's home is near the northern end of the Saché bridges.) Jean-Louis doesn't stock Pavy wines but the Maurice Jahan alternatives are equally appealing; Saché wines take the Touraine Azay-le-Rideau *appellation*. Try a Saumur-Champigny red, too; the restaurant will serve it slightly chilled and I find it lighter than the Chinon or Bourgueil varieties.

Arrive early at the restaurant and ask if you can have an *apéritif* in the small garden at the rear. It's then that the Saché

125

whites can be enjoyed at their best; a magical treat in an ancient, atmospheric setting.

Before you leave the Indre Valley put aside a little time for two rarely-visited villages. Villaines-les-Rochers is five km. south-west of Saché; it's renowned for wickerwork products (*vannerie*) – chairs, baskets and scores of other products are made by some 60 families in the village. (Gaston Pavy is one of many who cultivate the osiers alongside the banks of the Indre.) Cheillé is just west of Azay-le-Rideau; see the oak tree that literally grows out of a wall in the village church.

For overnight stays use the 'base' at Chinon.
category **3** *menus* **B-C** *rooms* See text *cards* AE DC V
closed Last wk Jan. Feb. Tues. (SW of Tours)
post Saché, 37190 Azay-le-Rideau, Indre-et-Loire.
phone 47 26 86 58 *Mich* 232 *map* 35 Tours 35 km.

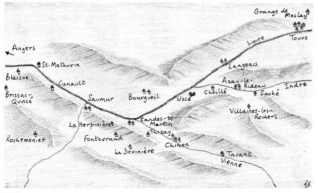

THE POTTERY AT MESLAND   Owen Watson

The Prior of Mesland laid out vineyards here in the eleventh century, for wine for his altar, his guests, his monks and for himself. Mesland is now at the northern limit of the vine in France, producing fine wines (*appellation contrôlée* Touraine-Mesland) if the long maturing season is kind. It also produces a certain kind of man: hard-working, convivial, not well off, full of human kindness. Puritanism and social snobbishness cast no shadows here in this corner of the Loire Valley.

I had the good fortune to come to this place 26 years ago (I was then 37), and also had the luck of finding a small farmhouse to live in just right for my work, my temperament, and my standard of life. It is in a small clearing on a wooded hillside, with room for Alpine goats, peacocks, fantails, bantams, and for old roses in profusion. The house lies in a little valley, where poplars grow beside the tiny Cisse. Oaks, hornbeams and acacias cover the low northern slope of the valley, alongside chestnut and wild cherry.

Now all this is not so far removed from potting as it may seem. A craftsman lives a solitary life, much shut in on himself in his workshop. William Morris taught me that liking to work where you work is of the first importance: that as the body is to the soul (as he put it), so is his place of work to the craftsman.

At Mesland I make ash-glazed stoneware for the table, in the Hamada-Leach tradition. For me it involves a certain refinement of form and appearance, rather tight throwing, and care over finish: these are sources of beauty, but can make for feeble ware. Now the old tradition in the centre of France is of vigorous peasant salt-glazed stoneware, wood-fired, the clay dominant, the finish minimal. (You can see it at its best in Bourges museum. St-Amand-en-Puisaye is at the heart of the tradition.) Of course stoneware in France is as much a middle-class affair now as it is in the rest of Europe, and no longer a peasant concern. But I have found that attention to this reference has improved my pots greatly. St-Amand pots are collected, prized, merchandized, catalogued, displayed, in a way their creators would probably not have thought well of, if ever the idea that it could happen had occurred to them.

In common with most French stoneware potters, I get my clay from the same seam that these old potters used. It not only throws supremely well, it fires to a lovely colour, has a dense, beautiful texture, and is immensely strong. (For 50 cm.-high slab pots I add no sand or grog.) Even going to get it is a pleasure, with an early-morning drive through Sologne (the country of lakes and silver birches south-east of Blois), and back home for tea: twice a year, two tons each time.

The ashes I use for glaze are apple ash (from the Normandy cider orchards near Caen), lavender ash (from the distilleries in the Drôme), oak ash (from my fireplace: in this part of France oak is still what you burn to keep warm) and vine ash (from the prunings in the Mesland vineyards). I think of the vine ash glaze as my main glaze. It is beige on a single dipping, bluey white on double dipping, yellow on iron, and flows well without running off the pot. The vines are pruned in the dead of the year, January and February, and I burn the stacks reserved for me in the spring. They make wonderful fires, all crackle and spit, with sheets of flame leaping and veering. Generally boys from the village share this work with me, liking bonfires as much as I do. The ashes are cold enough by nightfall to be collected, and in due course they are sieved, sacked and stored away.

In England I had a small experience of gas kilns and electric kilns, but promised myself a wood kiln when I could reasonably have one. My first care after settling in Mesland was to visit the studio potters using wood kilns at La Borne (near St-Amand-en-Puisaye), get a design from the porcelain factory at Sèvres, have refractory bricks of the first quality sent up from Bordeaux, and build a fine kiln of 1.3 cubic metres capacity that I had no idea how to fire. I did eight firings of my kiln without success (each firing involves 50 hours of sawing and splitting wood, but there are other designs that do not call for such a load of work). Then with advice from Leach and Hamada after a film show at UNESCO, and 24 hours of help from Michel Lavice, a French ex-potter who happened to pay a call at the critical moment and whom I had never met, I got to know how to make the kiln climb to 1300°, and the pots were wonderful.

The point about a wood kiln is the extreme variety of the atmosphere in which the pots bathe. Flame, smoke and fly ash play freely over the pots. They modify the clay and glazes in a thousand accidental ways. The presence of so much carbon and silica changes the colours and quality of the glazes fundamentally. A potter who uses wood can well cultivate a certain humility: much of his achievement is the gift of the kiln.

My 60th birthday was celebrated by an exhibition in the Grand Renaissance Salle des Conférences in Blois Château of 220 of these wood-fired pieces, whilst the walls were hung with splendid embroidered patchworks made by my friend Jacqueline Hauser at Castlebridge in Co. Wexford, Ireland.

But sixty is sixty, and a wood kiln is exhausting. Besides, mine is currently bedevilled by the roots of an ash tree that

127

refuses to be killed. I rely largely on a second kiln now, fired by propane and wood together. In both kilns I burn oak and hornbeam from local sources up to 1000°, and silver birch from Amboise Forest, 20 km. away, from 1000° to 1300°. The birch gives less heat but makes very little ash, so the fireboxes do not get clogged. I find longer firings are better (for the pots) than shorter ones, so I don't try to see how fast I can get to temperature. Young friends come in and help. Indeed, it is one of the happiest aspects of my life here that the work brings me friendship of some of the young people in the village. Their generation has a harder start in adult life than mine did, and I like their sturdy, life-loving attitudes.

I will end with a word on sales. I suppose it has always been hard to make a living out of a small workshop. It is hard now, and as hard here in France as anywhere else. Sales are precarious, costs and dues are hefty. There are probably fewer outlets for selling pots in France than in England. On the other hand, French people tend to be great present givers, and to buy generously for their own needs. My own practice is to sell direct to customers, and to work a great deal to order. I like best of all working to order for people I've watched grow up. But what puts the butter in spinach is selling to summer visitors, and singularly to the happy devotees of *French Leave*: who in one go discover Richard Binns, Owen Watson and the Prior of Mesland's true descendants.

(See the notes on *Contributors* for details of how to find Owen Watson's pottery. Within the Loire section of this book are several references to the fine Sologne countryside. If you do travel east to Burgundy, be sure to enjoy it; detour through St-Amand-en-Puisaye – between the Loire and Vézelay. RAB.)

ST-MATHURIN-SUR-LOIRE La Promenade

Comfortable restaurant
Good value

Jacques and Gillian Morisan have made many British and American friends during the 20-odd years they've been at their restaurant alongside the Loire. That's not surprising: they are friendly, easy-to-get-on-with hosts; Jacques' classical style makes fine use of local, fresh produce; and, as a useful plus, both speak fluent English. That's to be expected as Gill is English – she met Jacques when they were both working at the Plaza-Athénée in Paris over two decades ago. The Morisans have two sons; one is making his mark in the French Army and the younger boy is currently getting a first-class culinary training in the kitchens of Le Prieuré at nearby Chênehutte.

It makes an interesting conversation when you quiz Jacques and Gill about the severe headaches French restaurateurs have faced in Socialist France during the last few years. The first cruel blow was the 30% tax Mitterrand imposed on all business entertaining. That was followed by a price freeze and then, after a year or so, restaurateurs were allowed to increase prices – but only by a nominal percentage.

But it's another aspect of culinary life that makes Jacques angry. He always uses fresh produce – whether it be fish, vegetables or whatever. When he describes a dish as *brochet frais de Loire beurre blanc* – it means what it says. Nearby competitors call the equivalent a *brochet beurre blanc*. And guess where that comes from? From a bag in a freezer – 'created' by a factory hundreds of miles away. Don't kid yourself in thinking that French clients know better. They don't; and many appear not to care less – lower prices matter more.

For those of you who do care about regional produce, and fresh at that, then here's a place you should take a promenade to. Jacques' menu is likely to include local treats like salmon, pike and *sandre* from the Loire – usually accompanied by a *beurre blanc* sauce. Equally a *matelote d'anguille* may be offered – cooked in a Chinon red wine sauce. In addition you'll have the chance to try *rillettes* or possibly *rillauds chauds d'Anjou en salade* – strips of hot bacon served with a salad; and an extremely rich *crémet d'Anjou* – served with a few raspberries and a *coulis* of the same fruit. (The pig is taken seriously hereabouts. The morning after my visit I spent an hour in Brissac-Quincé where the locals were celebrating their annual 'La Rillaudée'; market stands were laden down with *rillaux* and every other pork product imaginable.)

If you want to buy some wine locally then head for a private enterprise – operating from an old château hidden in a fold of hills on the left bank of the Loire. It's called the Château de Cheman. Cross the river at St-Mathurin, head west to Blaison, continue for a kilometre or so beyond the village and then turn left, following a sign saying 'Cheman'. (On Michelin map 232 it's the building above the word 'Cotillon'.) Madame Antoine and her husband have their own vineyards which encircle the property. The reds, whites and rosés are inexpensive and good value; you'll enjoy, too, the remarkable tower and the spiral staircase within it. The Antoines let two fine apartments in the château – by the night if needs be; it's the weekly rate that makes them such excellent propositions. The post code for Blaison is 49320 Brissac-Quincé; phone 41 80 54 15.

An alternative overnight 'base' is the simple, quiet and modern hotel run by Suzanne Violleau at Brissac-Quincé. Called Le Castel it sits in the shadow of the town château; the postal code is 49320 and the phone number is 41 91 24 74.

Don't leave the area without visiting the unusual underground troglodyte village at Rochemenier – just north of Doué-la-Fontaine; the marvellous 12th-century church at Cunault; and the Musée du Champignon, on the D751 at St-Hilaire, just before Saumur. The left bank of the Loire is studded with caves; tunnelled out of tufa stone, they're ideal for the cultivation of *champignons de Paris*.

category 2 *menus* **A-B** *rooms* See text *cards* AE V
closed Feb. Sun evg. Mon. (SE of Angers)
post St-Mathurin-sur-Loire, 49250 Beaufort-en-Vallée, M.-et-L.
phone 41 80 50 49 *Mich* 232 *map* 36 Angers 20 km.

CHÂTEAU DE CHEMAN

FAREINS   Restaurant J. Fouillet

Very comfortable restaurant
Gardens

I'm glad so many readers took my advice, first given in 1980, to quit the A6 autoroute at Belleville and head west into the Beaujolais hills – to the 'bistro' home of a talented couple, Jean and Dalia Fouillet. I'm prepared to bet a larger wager that those of you who made the detour must have doubted my sanity when you drew up outside the Auberge du Pont des Samsons at Quincié-en-Beaujolais – a decrepit, run-down place in an isolated site under the dome of Mont Brouilly.

"Binns is out of his mind," must have been the typical exclamation of readers parking their cars; though I suspect some of you will have put it even more strongly! 'Simple' was the word I used to describe the building; as far as I know it was about the only Michelin one-star restaurant that carried a single crossed knife and fork symbol (called a *couvert*) for amenities. But in the Lyonnais appearances can be deceptive. Did you ever visit Georges and Jannie Berger at Priay? Working behind that ugly exterior was one of the world's best chefs and one of the most captivating hostesses I've ever met. The same is true of the Fouillets: Jean is a competent chef and Dalia is the most delectable *sommelière* you'll encounter.

1986 saw the couple installed in a smart new home – on the left bank of the Saône, in the *département* of Ain and at the door of Les Dombes. You'll find the restaurant on the D933, 6 km. south of Montmerle-sur-Saône and just 4 km. north of Villefranche, which is on the opposite or western bank of the

river. What a handsome building the new place is with light, airy rooms (air conditioning is a welcome bonus).

Common sense is the key to Jean's cooking: *la carte* is short and is built around fresh produce with Bresse treats predominating. *Poulet de Bresse*, of course, is highly recommended but so is the *andouillette Beaujolaise* and, in the words of Roy and Shirley Dixon, 'the cheeses and puddings are a joy'. In fact you can relish a menu called 'Poulet de Bresse'; the first three courses all make use of the renowned local poultry. You start with *rillettes de béatilles de volailles*, followed by a *petit ragoût de suprême aux huîtres* and then a *jambonette de poulet rôti au porto*; the last dish is a treat.

Dalia's wine list is formidable with a choice of hundreds of vintages; her Beaujolais section is perfection.

For overnight accommodation use the base at St-André or the modern Ibis which is just a few kilometres away on the eastern side of the Villefranche autoroute exit (*phone:* 74 68 22 23).

Before I pass on to other matters let me say how sad I was to have to omit the great favourite at Montmerle-sur-Saône – the much loved Castel de Valrose. There was no question about it: the Morillons were among readers' top favourites. I visited Bernard and Martine in 1985 and, as always, was enchanted by the ebullient, happy couple. But shortly before I went to press I heard that they had sold up and were looking for a new restaurant home in Nice. Martine mentioned they were negotiating to buy La Poularde: please check the '87 Red Guide to see whether the name Morillon is listed.

There's much to enjoy in Bresse country. Châtillon-sur-Chalaronne is for me still the best of the many villages that lie to the east of Montmerle. In the summer it's a vast splash of

CHÂTILLON-SUR-CHALARONNE

colour – with flowers everywhere; the ancient buildings – many of them incorporating attractive and practical use of timber – are a magnet for photographers and artists; and the stream that runs through the town is an additional eye-catcher. Be sure to see the Châtillon triptych (1527); it's in the town hall on the first floor – just enter and ask. If you make your visit on a Saturday morning all the better; the whole town is bustling and alive – its streets a colourful, open-air market.

But don't concentrate on Châtillon alone. Go armed with Michelin yellow map 244: drive the lanes that take you past the numerous *étangs* (meres or pools) that dominate Les Dombes. (Can you find the spot where I drew my trees' drawing? See *Odds and Ends.*) Stop for a while beside one or two and watch the wildlife. Quite different from the peace and quiet of Nature's handiwork is the dramatic line that the fantastic TGV railway has sliced across the landscape. Position yourself on one of the bridges and gasp at the speed of the futuristic bullet trains. You can get from the Gare Mâcon Loché (signposted from the Mâcon-Sud autoroute exit) to Paris in about 90 minutes – a distance of 400 kilometres!

Don't miss Beaujolais country to the west. Explore the famous villages like Fleurie for example – but make the climb in your car to the summit of Mont Brouilly. Relish the view and then descend to the east to St-Lager; don't worry – the road is quite safe. On the way down you can buy Côte de Brouilly direct from Jean Noël Gaze: what a nice *tip*ple to end on!

category **3** *menus* **B-C** *rooms* See text *cards* AE DC V
closed Mon evg. Tues.
post Fareins, 01480 Jassans-Riottier, Ain. (Site: see text)
phone 74 67 91 94 *Mich* 244 *map* 70 Lyon 42 km.

MONTLUEL   Le Petit Casset

Simple hotel
Quiet/Gardens/Swimming pool

Just the place for those of you who want a quiet 'base' near Lyon but without any of the headaches that go with sleeping overnight in a huge, noisy city. Montluel is ten miles east of Lyon – easily reached by the N84 or, better still, by the toll-free A42 (leave just before you enter the *péage* section – follow signs for Montluel). The hotel is one km. west of Montluel on the north side of the N84.

Le Petit Casset is a super little 'base': guests appreciate the modern rooms, the quiet site, the small garden, the protective trees and the swimming pool. The latter, incidentally, is well hidden behind a high hedge and is in the grounds of the handsome chalet-styled villa above the hotel.

Madame Jeannine Perronier, the owner, is liked as much by readers as any of the hotel's material benefits. She's a friendly, welcoming soul and it's very evident that she takes great interest in her 'investment'. You'll be tickled pink by her *perroquet* (parrot) who will entertain you royally during breakfast. Full of french chat – and what a whistle, too – it has yet to learn any English. Perhaps a reader with some time to spare can put that right some day in the future!

Apart from the many restaurants in Lyon there are others close at hand. The latter are easily reached and include starred establishments at Pérouges, Meximieux, Loyettes, Les Echets and Mionnay; Priay's La Mère Bourgeois has re-opened, too. Lyon-Satolas airport is also very conveniently situated.

Be certain not to miss Pérouges – ten minutes' drive away. Head for Meximieux and, on the western approach to the town, turn left off the N84 for Pérouges. Within 200 metres, slow down and stop beside the small plaque hanging on the railings to the right. It's in memory of Marin Antonin and Falcand Gabriel, shot by the Germans on 1st September 1944 – like so many others in the months after the Normandy landings.

Pérouges is a remarkable hill-top citadel. Four hundred years ago it was a thriving place with a population of 2,000; three centuries later it had all but fallen into ruin – with no more than 50 inhabitants. It came close to being demolished. Thankfully, that outrageous suggestion was scotched. Walk the cobbled streets, soak up the dream-like atmosphere of its ancient houses and seek out the huge lime tree at the heart of the medieval fortified fortress. Try to enjoy Pérouges in the twilight when the village is at its most captivating.

category **1** *menus* No rest. *rooms* 11 **C**
closed Open all the year.
post à la Boisse, 01120 Montluel, Ain. (NE of Lyon)
phone 78 06 21 33 *Mich* 244 *map* 71 Lyon 23 km.

MONTROND-LES-BAINS   Host. La Poularde

Very comfortable hotel

There's an extra ingredient in the 'La Poularde' recipe that makes it quite irresistible to all those who seek it out – the happy family at the heart of this special hotel.

I've explained the unusual twist to the family relationship before – but let me repeat it again. Joannès Randoing – over 50 years a chef – and his wife, Yvonne, are the 'parents'; Gilles Etéocle (the 36-year-old son of Yvonne from her first marriage) and his attractive, sparkling wife, Monique (Joannès' daughter from an earlier marriage) are the 'children'. These days Joannès takes a back seat and Gilles' fantastic culinary talents are now being given a free rein – with impressive results.

Gilles is an inovative chef. In 1982 he won the *Meilleur Ouvrier de France* (best cook) competition – a tribute to his skills. He's a supporter of *faites simple* – letting flavours count: thinly-sliced *coquilles St-Jacques* in a subtle orange and lemon sauce; a delicate morsel of hot *foie gras* – served on a bed of chicory; smooth sorbets – their flavours immediately recognizable; those are a few examples. Five exceptional menus are on offer – from about 150 francs to over 300; it's value for money in any terms – some of the best in France.

Joannès has retired on a high note. 1984 saw him win the award of the *Ordre National du Mérite* – a marvellous honour for a great *cuisinier* and equally great football fan. He's still like a schoolboy when it comes to soccer: eager to spend hours fervently nattering about the game. His connection with the *verts* of St-Etienne is still strong; just glance at the *livre d'or* to

Charlieu, north-east of Roanne   133

see what I mean. Many European soccer teams have been entertained at La Poularde after their matches at St-Etienne: Liverpool, Manchester United and Ipswich among them.

The good news is that the family traditions will continue. Gilles and Monique have three children – two boys, the eldest is 14, and a girl. Nothing is too much trouble for the so helpful family – as many of you have confirmed. One example is typical. A reader had trouble with his car, well to the north in Burgundy; he rang late in the evening to say he would arrive after midnight. No problem *monsieur*! When at last he arrived, to be shown his bedroom in a still, darkened hotel – by a young waiter assigned the temporary job of night porter – he found a tray with coffee in a flask, a *mélange* of tasty treats and a half-bottle of champagne to help it all down! Now that's service – and at a price which represents real value for money.

The newly-opened A72 autoroute from St-Etienne to Clermont-Ferrand is proving to be of great help to the family business – an exit is only two miles away. Access to Montrond is easy for those clients who don't want to work hard at getting off the beaten track. Another benefit that will appeal to readers is a brand new golf course at nearby Craintilleux; Gilles is a member and he can make the necessary arrangements. Monique, too, can arrange for hostess-accompanied day trips for parties of three or more – to a series of local sights.

But my readers are not usually shy about exploring out-of-the-way places. So, get out your map 239 and let's enjoy some rarely-visited treasures. First the château at La Bastie-d'Urfé – an unusual Renaissance building partly constructed by Italian artisans; next the strange-looking, formidable, fortified Romanesque church at Champdieu; then over the hills to

Ambert – making sure, east of the town, that you detour to the old Moulin Richard-de-Bas still making hand-made, heavy paper and with a fascinating museum on paper-making.

Now up the D67 to Valcivières – a lovely road through wooded, rounded hills – and then east to the Col des Supeyres. The map identifies several *jasseries* – lonely, stone-built buildings, all located at an altitude of over 3500 ft. They provide the ideal year round temperature and humidity for the making of Fourme-d'Ambert and Fourme de Montbrison – both blue-veined cheeses need three to four months to reach maturity. Few *jasseries* are used these days – the price of progress. Finally, order Montrond's own slightly gaseous spring water: ask for the 'Dom Pérignon' of mineral waters!

category **3** *menus* **B-D** *rooms* 15**C** *cards* AE DC V
closed 1st half Jan. Mon evg. Tues midday. (N of St-Etienne)
post 42210 Montrond-les-Bains, Loire.
phone 77 54 40 06 *Mich* 239 *map* 72 St-Etienne 27 km.

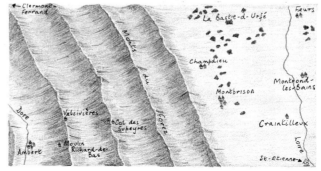

ST-ANDRE-DE-CORCY   Manoir des Dombes

Comfortable hotel
Quiet/Gardens

The Manoir is another much appreciated Lyonnais 'base' — three km. north of St-André-de-Corcy. From the main road, the N83, it doesn't look too inviting; don't be put off — it's much quieter than you think. Even Michelin, at long last, have acknowledged the fact; the guide now awards the hotel a black 'rocking-chair' symbol. The reason why it is quiet is that all the bedrooms are at the rear of the hotel; those odd, small windows you see as you drive in are in fact on the landings that stretch the length of the building. Another visual benefit is that the bedrooms overlook an *étang* — one of thousands in Les Dombes country, the terrain lying to the north of the hotel.

Les Dombes is a peppered landscape of *étangs* – the French word for ponds or pools. Use the minor roads and seek out the numerous *étangs*; arm yourself with a pair of binoculars and you'll spend many happy, inquisitive hours. Six km. up the N83, on the southern entrance to Villars-les-Dombes, is an excellent bird sanctuary. Laid out as a park, it contains hundreds of different species; some come and go as they please on the many pools, others are to be found in large 'open' cages.

The 'base' is well placed for a host of restaurants: from the humble, down-to-earth simplicity of the Aubert at Dompierre-sur-Veyle, to the world-famous temple of gastronomy, Alain Chapel's home at Mionnay — five minutes away towards Lyon.

That's where I headed for on my last visit to Bresse country. Not to research it afresh because it had proved to be one of my readers' great favourites — it certainly has not been that — but to reassess what turned out to be the most difficult page I had to write for *French Leave 3*. Had I been wrong?

The latest visit, yet again, was a disappointment. And that word sums up perfectly what so many readers experience at Chapel. No longer can a visit to Mionnay be considered 'special'; Chapel's three-star rating doesn't influence me one iota. My visit was a day or two before I ate at Laguiole; Chapel's efforts couldn't be compared with Michel Bras' golden touch.

One thing has changed for the better: Chapel now spends as much time walking through the dining rooms as he devotes to the kitchens — that's something he never used to do. But why can't he manage to include just one half-bottle of wine on his list? Jean-Pierre Silva, at Bouilland, manages 80!

Chapel's expensive 'Image de Mionnay' menu was no more than a succession of mediocre dishes — rich in menu description verbage but poor in plate and palate reality! Consider two courses: a *tranche de grosse langouste rouge bretonne rôtie et des pommes de terre, genre maxim's* (what a verbal mouthful) was a small, rubbery bit of *langouste* with warmish potato crisps – no more, no less; and a *crapaudine de pigeon au thym et un paillasson de vermicelles* proved to be a tough, stringy *pigeonneau* full of bones — refer to Jean-Pierre Silva's restaurant again. I gave the Mionnay dish the 'bird', returning most of it — something of a habit for me these days Chez Chapel.

category 1 *menus* No rest. *rooms* 16**B-C** *cards* AE DC
closed 2nd half Feb. (NE of Lyon and N of St-André-de-Corcy)
post St-Marcel, 01390 St-André-de-Corcy, Ain.
phone 78 81 13 37 *Mich* 244 *map* 73 Lyon 24 km.

THEIZE   Espérance

Simple hotel
Quiet/Good value

There's a small enclave of colourful terrain at the southernmost end of the Beaujolais hills – known by the equally colourful phrase of *au pays des pierres dorées*. Within the circle of villages that make up the area, buildings are constructed of the local stone – a golden-textured, warm material, much darker than Cotswold stone; hence the name.

Theizé is at the heart of *pierres dorées* – perched high up at about 1600 ft above sea-level and facing south. During the afternoon the village shines with glowing, gilt-edged health; from the ancient church you get vast views towards Mont d'Or (Lyon's northern, natural barrier) and, to the south, the Monts du Lyonnais (worth exploring one day – particulary Yzeron and the circle of countryside surrounding it).

More about the pleasures of man and Nature later on; first let us consider one of the best reasons for visiting Theizé – the much loved Espérance. Those of you who know it already will shed a tear when I tell you that Louis Clavel died on the 26th October 1984, at the early age of 51. However, his widow, Marie-Louise, and her 23-year-old son, Max, continue the traditions established by Louis and, before him, by his mother, Marie. Max has much to learn – but, in time, he will.

It's basic hotelkeeping: nothing pretentious – just value for money that will suit visitors hoping to keep as many francs as they can in their pockets. Bedrooms are modest (the toilet on the upper floor will make you laugh as it did Anne and me over

20 years ago on our first visit – I'm not saying why, just use it) and the cooking is conventional Lyonnais.

A typical menu could include as a starter an authentic, mouthwatering Lyonnais sausage, wrapped in its mantle of a light brioche. Served with it will be some vinegar-cured *griottes* (bitter red cherries) and small, green tomatoes – both have a sharp tang. Then perhaps an *assiette de poisson* – some *lotte* in a spicy *américaine* sauce. *Haricots verts* follow – served as a separate course; close on their heels comes an *entrecôte Charollaise* (beef from the northern Beaujolais), a few cheeses and a sweet – something like an apple tart or a sorbet.

An essential accompaniment to all this fare should be a light, fruity, local Beaujolais wine; not one of the famous nine *appellations* from the north – but, nevertheless, still of a very high standard. The reason is simple: be sure to order a bottle made by Antoine Pein – the home and office of this multi-award winning magician is just up the hill from the hotel. Some say Beaujolais became famous in the early 70s; well, let me tell you that New Yorkers got to know of Antoine's handiwork as long ago as 1964 when André Surmain (see Feu Follet in the Côte d'Azur) introduced his wines to the Lutèce customers.

The reds are best known of course. But I was fortunate enough to be offered a *dégustation* of two rare and unusual delights: a Beaujolais *blanc moelleux* (sweet) and a home-produced (it carries no *appellation*) sparkling white – made by the *méthode champenoise*. Call on Antoine and buy some of his young red wines: I cannot promise that he will have any of the others in stock as very few bottles are made. Try your luck!

Across the road from the hotel is a simple, newly-opened shop run by Max's brother, René, and his young wife, Evelyne.

Pay them a call before you leave the village.

Give the neighbouring countryside as many hours as you can. First seek out Oingt – once a strong fortress; climb the old tower for spectacular views. Due west – a few kilometres away – you'll spot the minute, perched hamlet of Ternand; centuries old, it's well worth a visit later. To the north of Theizé is *Clochmerle* country – made world famous by Gabriel Chevallier: soak up its charm and be certain to include Vaux-en-Beaujolais on your travels.

What else can I think of that will please you? Ah – just one thing: the 'music' that comes with your meal (and breakfast) is the sparkling song of a tiny, brown *canari* – caught, apparently, in the hotel's garden. There's no better start to a day than its tuneful notes. Come to Theizé with no great expectations and no great hopes; you'll leave Espérance knowing just what good value means. Long may that continue.

category **2(S)** *menus* **A-B** *rooms* **9A-B** *cards* A AE DC V
closed Mid Sept-3rd wk Oct. Tues evg. Wed.
post Theizé, 69620 Le Bois-d'Oingt, Rhône. (NW of Lyon)
phone 74 71 22 26 *Mich* 244 *map* 74 Lyon 34 km.

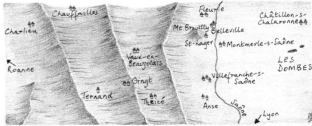

CAPTIVATING CEVENNES

The Cévennes never fails to amaze me. For the past three decades I have been bowled over by its spectacular scenery and yet, last year, when I spent another two days there driving over the most obscure roads, I was stunned anew. I was lucky to be there in June as the whole area was a sea of wild flowers, seemingly aflame with burning colours. A strong wind made the air crystal clear – with views stretching a hundred kilometres and more. There was plenty of water in the rivers and the extensive woodlands were at their most entrancing; the new soft summer greens gave the forests a glowing radiance.

You could spend days in the area and still not do it justice. I recommend four drives – three of them requiring a day to complete each one and one of them perhaps two days if you decide to visit both underground caves. Much of Mother Nature's unusual sculpturing is below ground – the caves are amazing places and should not be missed; but don't be worried if you're claustrophobic as much of her best handiwork can be admired above ground – in the shape of numerous gorges and rugged, brutally carved mountain cliffs. Use Michelin map 240. **Drive 1** From Millau head for the world-renowned Gorges du Tarn and don't be put off when I suggest you drive it in both directions – it pays to do this because many scenic aspects are missed if you travel the valley road in one direction only. The drive starts to get interesting at Le Rozier. At Les Vignes turn left and take your car up the snake-like hairpins to the cliffs above the Tarn; at the top use the D46 and continue north to the Point Sublime. The river is far below you; the better vista is to the east, but you also have an eagle's eye view of the ninety degree turn

the green-coloured Tarn completes to then head southwards (the Cirque des Baumes).

Retrace your steps, follow the D907 around that right-angled turn and continue to Ste-Enimie. From there drive south, climbing up the steep D986. In 11 km. turn right and aim for the viewpoint at the Roc des Hourtous. Back again towards the D986 but this time descend down the winding hairpins of the D43 to La Malène. (From the village you can take boat trips to the Cirque des Baumes, returning by taxi.) Return to Le Rozier. If you feel like a walk among the many rock faces, cross the Tarn and, before you enter the town, follow the sign for Capluc. Park your car – there's marvellous walking country above you. **Drive 2** Cross the Tarn at Millau and head north-east up the D110 to the strangely-named Chaos de Montpellier-le-Vieux. The 'Chaos' is a collection of weirdly-shaped rocks that litter the ground over an extensive area – as if a giant had walked this way and left a scene of utter destruction behind him. There's a long, signposted path through them all; most have fanciful names – like the Devil's Chair, Elephant, Arc de Triomphe or even Queen Victoria's Head. Continue north-east on the D110 and the D29. Four km. later turn left on to forestry roads to the viewpoints on the Corniche du Causse Noir.

Retrace your steps and head south-east on the D29 and D28 to Lanuéjols – crossing the Causse Noir in the process. It's one of many limestone *causses* alongside and above the Tarn; the 'plateaux' are always dry as water drains away quickly through numerous fissures. Underground streams abound and have played the major role in shaping Nature's sculptures. Continue east on the D986 through a much changed landscape – dense woods replace the rocky, flat terrain. Visit the Abîme du

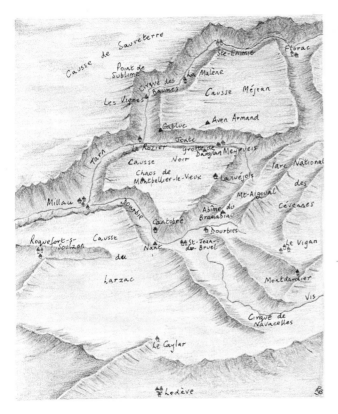

Bramabiau where the River Bonheur has cut a subterranean slice through a rugged rock face.

East again to the summit of Mont Aigoual – the highest point of the Cévennes National Park; from the observatory on its summit (1567 metres) you get staggering views in all directions. Descend to the north and then in a westerly direction to Meyrueis. Here you have the choice of two underground caves: Aven Armand is the most renowned – every imaginable shape of stalagmite and stalactite is to be found there, enhanced superbly by brilliant lighting; the Grotte de Dargilan (the pink cavern) is impressive, too, particularly the huge 'bell-shaped sculpture'. Now head downstream through the Gorges de la Jonte – a direction I prefer as I believe you see more of the many pink and yellow rock faces and, towards the end of the valley, the strange shapes of the Causse Méjean on your right. You also finish with a picturesque view of Peyreleau.

Drive 3 Follow the main N9 south-east from Millau across the flat Causse du Larzac. At Le Caylar turn left and use the D9, D25 and D130 to approach the Cirque de Navacelles from the south. *Cirque* means amphitheatre – in this case one of the most unusual in France. From the cliff top the view is amazing: far below you is a *cirque* – formed by a now dried-up 'meander' of the River Vis; today the same stream provides an additional attraction – a colourful cascade.

At Montdardier the road to Le Vigan seems to 'disappear'; a long descent follows into a valley renowned for its orchards. Climb the Col du Minier; apart from the vast views south it's also the watershed between the Mediterranean and the Atlantic. Six km. later turn left on to the D151. At Dourbies (what a beguiling spot – have a drink on the tiny café terrace) use the D151A and D114 to the south of the river; in late spring wild flowers provide an honour guard alongside the narrow road – endless varieties and countless colours. See the weir at St-Jean-du-Bruel and the 14th-century covered market at Nant. Return to Millau via Cantobre (see drawing on next page) and the Gorges de la Dourbie.

Drive 4 Don't miss Roquefort-sur-Soulzon – the town which gives its name to a legendary cheese. Visit, free of charge, the 'Société' caves where over half the annual production of Roquefort cheeses mature; each year 16,000 tons of Roquefort (or six million 'rounds' – *pains*) are sold throughout the world.

The Roquefort caves are said to be the best natural 'refrigerators' in the world. It's a unique geological site where a mountain top collapsed creating numerous rock faults, fissures and caverns – locally called *fleurines*. The fresh air that blows through them provides the ideal atmosphere for the 'penicillium Roqueforti' – a microscopic mushroom – to mature within the heart of the creamy rounds of ewe's milk. Salt is added to the surface of the cheese to slow down the growth of mould on the outside, while the inside matures.

Your visit to the 'Société' caves will be an eye-opener for the way man has capitalised on this quirk of Nature. Built vertically along the northern face of the cliffs, where the numerous *fleurines* emerge as 'air corridors', man has constructed a series of enclosed 'caves'; it's on these man-made floors, refrigerated by Nature, where the round blue cheeses ripen, emerging eventually into that sharp, exquisite taste.

In your travels across the *causses* you'll see many flocks of sheep – the most important being the Lacaune breed. The ewes provide the milk from which Roquefort cheese is made.

140

MILLAU   La Capelle

Comfortable hotel
Quiet/Terrace/Good value

La Capelle has been a greatly appreciated favourite – for many reasons: its central location – immediately adjacent to the shopping area and all the town's restaurants; the really quiet site – always welcome but especially so in busy Millau; the easy parking in the *place* beside the hotel – there's no need to pay, just show the card provided by the hotel; and, finally, I suspect, because of Jane Rouquet who, with her mother, runs the hotel with such loving care.

Jane's a friendly, attractive lady; her hotel is kept spotless and prices are modest indeed for the comfortable facilities. Two decades ago her parents owned the Mon Hôtel; also in Millau and not too far from La Capelle.

You have a wide choice of eating-out alternatives; remember, too, that you may prefer a cooked lunch elsewhere in the area and just a snack in the evening – Millau has many a pavement café in its tree-lined avenues where you can watch the world go by over a coffee. Many shops are close at hand for picnic purchases if you prefer to eat dinner in the town. Readers have spoken well of the Capion in Millau, the Grand Hôtel at Meyrueis and the Grand Hôtel Muse et Rozier at Le Rozier, a modern building in a glorious position overlooking the Tarn.

category 1 *menus* No rest. *rooms* 46**A-B** *cards* V
closed Oct-mid May. (Open 2/3 wks at Easter).
post 7 pl. Fraternité, 12100 Millau, Aveyron.
phone 65 60 14 72 *Mich* 240 *map* 75

MILLAU   Château de Creissels

Comfortable hotel
Quiet/Gardens/Good value

Hold it – all you disappointed readers! I can hear your loud exclamations: "Where, oh where, is the Buffet de France?" (I always preferred to use its old name – Buffet de Gare.) Well read on – there's a surprise awaiting you. By the time this book is published that much-loved couple, Albert and Janine Négron, will have moved – from their 'home' of over 30 years, the Buffet Gare, to their new *résidence*, the Château de Creissels, two km. outside Millau towards Roquefort.

The Château was a recommendation in both *Hidden France* and *French Leave 3* – but what a mixed response I got about

the standard of cooking of the previous owners. It most certainly was not a favourite. Now it has all the ingredients of a perfect hotel: a comfortable building in a quiet site – with character, an old tower, gardens and an adjacent church (take some earplugs); and, at last, a chef that matches the hotel's bricks and mortar appeal. And let me not forget the friendly welcome of ever-attentive, ever-smiling Janine.

How I like Albert's cooking style. There comes a time when, to be frank, I think I would choose Albert's specialities in preference to many of the great French chefs. It's honest, enjoyable fare – *cuisine Bourgeoise* at its best. And Albert, now a young 72 years, is a chef who doesn't turn his back on regional specialities and local Rouergue produce.

So, on one hand, pleasures such as *trénels maison* and *aligot* (a purée of *pommes de terre* and *Tomme fraîche de Laguiole*) and, on the other, a more conventional *foie de canard chaud* – served with grapes – and *entrecôte de veau au Roquefort* (the sauce works well – it's not overpowering).

With your *apéritif* you'll be offered some small slices of home-made *saucisson* – not served *sec* but in this case they come in a bowl of *arachide* (peanut) oil. Desserts are good, particularly the house specialities which include a *bolet du chef Albert* – vanilla and coffee ice cream, surrounded by lashings of *Chantilly*, a biscuit top covered in chocolate and rum and the whole thing looking like a toadstool; and *île de la passion* – a passion fruit sorbet in champagne and *curaçao*.

category **2(S)** *menus* **A-B** *rooms* 30**A-B** *cards* A AE DC V
closed Feb.Wed(Nov-Mar).Rest:Sat Midday & Wed (not July & Aug).
post rte St-Affrique, 12100 Millau, Aveyron. (SW of Millau)
phone 65 60 16 59 *Mich* 240 *map* 76 Millau 2 km.

Cantobre – see *Captivating Cévennes* map and 'Drive 3'

VIVE LE VERCORS

For the vast majority of motorists speeding along the Rhône Valley autoroute, the Vercors is no more than a motorway sign with an arrow pointing east towards a distant, half-visible mountain range. Half an hour after passing the solitary sign on the A7, the mysterious ridge of peaks fades into the hazy distance. I implore you: please don't make this mistake, because the inspiring Vercors *massif* merits the time of every visitor to France – a natural fortress, full of the majestic handiwork of Mother Nature at her most ferocious and spectacular. Tragically, it was in these high, hidden peaks and gorges that the most emotional saga of the French Resistance unfolded over forty years ago – during the summer of 1944.

The Vercors is a limestone mass of mountains, thirty miles long by twenty miles wide – a triangle of eroded, rampart-like peaks, isolated from the French Alps by three rivers that all but encircle it: the Isère with a ninety degrees loop to the north; the Drac – these days a man-made lake for much of its length – to the east; and the Drôme to the south. Its highest peaks – Grand Veymont and Mont Aiguille – rise to nearly 8000 ft.

Access to the Vercors is unusually difficult: a few, tortuous, narrow lanes climb up in steep zig-zags from the river valleys below – the roads often tunnelled and blasted out of the precipitous mountain sides. Within the *massif* two roaring torrents – the Bourne and the Vernaison – create an even more remote inner sanctuary. This seductive, secret heart of the Vercors wears a vast coat of dense pine forests – cool in summer but an enveloping, dark cover in the winter.

No wonder then that the Vercors became first a citadel of the

Resistance and, later, such a legend; its story is a stirring one, deserving the attention of all those who love France.

Two days after the D-Day landings in June 1944 the tricolour flew on numerous flag-poles in the Vercors. One of the proud flags fluttered above St-Nizier – in full view of Grenoble far below in the Isère Valley. Inevitably the Germans were incensed and, during the weeks that followed, they threw 20,000 troops into the mountains – bent on revenge because the Vercors *maquis* had long been a thorn in their sides.

The Resistance fighters had counted on relief coming from the air and, additionally, from the anticipated Allies' landing in Provence. With hindsight, one can see now that the uprising came too soon after D-Day; help came too late and the Vercors was not relieved in time. Hundreds died defending the citadel that they proudly called the 'Free Republic of the Vercors': an important part of the legend concerns the betrayal of the *maquis* by the Free French and the Allies in Algiers – a tale of tragic procrastination that led to muddle, unnecessary loss of life and bitter resentment that help never came.

By the end of July the overwhelming German force had full control of the Vercors. The *maquis* had stood no chance; their betrayal became a national scandal – even de Gaulle was guilty of cynical, political manoeuvering during those tragic weeks.

As you travel the mountain roads you'll see a great number of monuments in memory of those who gave their lives in 1944: *mort pour la France* say the carved words on the simple, small monuments; no finer words can be used for any epitaph. On the narrow D215 and D221 roads that head west from Villard-de-Lans, through the pine forests towards Valchevrière, are many monuments to those who died in the last critical days

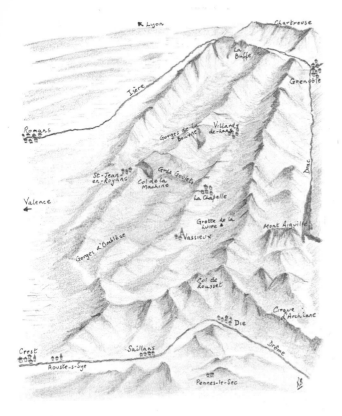

of the 1944 battle. But perhaps the most moving of all is the one at the entrance to the Grotte de la Luire – used by the Resistance as a hospital: its simple words carry an undemanding plea –

Thou that comest here
Bring thy soul with thee

Michael Pearson's *Tears of Glory* tells the story of 'The Betrayal of Vercors 1944'. Borrow one from a library. You'll be enthralled by it; as you explore the area the book will become a series of visual pictures. (The Pan paperback is out of print.)

What scenic sights should you seek out? Use map 244 and enter the *massif* by one of three spectacular roads. The first is the best northern approach. Leave the A48 autoroute at the point it becomes toll-free, at Veurey-Voroize, climb the lane up to La Buffe and, just before the Tunnel du Mortier, admire the sensational view below you. Nearby is a grassy plateau called La Molière (1655 metres) – it provides extensive views to the east towards the Chamrousse. Under your feet are the caves of the Gouffre Berger, the deepest pot-hole in France.

A second exciting access to the Vercors is a southerly one; starting from Die in the Drôme Valley, the fantastic Col de Rousset is a memorable climb of numerous hairpin bends. It's one of the great hillclimbs in the Alps; the view from its summit, at the exit of the old tunnel, is both dramatic and extensive.

The third recommended entrance is via an engineering marvel. From St-Jean-en-Royans – a sleepy peaceful village – climb the Combe Laval, a vast *cirque* (amphitheatre) of rocks that rises sharply above the Cholet stream. The final kilometre or two, before you reach the summit at the Col de la Machine, is a series of tunnels gouged out of the vertical mountain face.

Within the *massif* are further man-made wonders, combining spectacularly with some of Mother Nature's most violent sculptures. One is the amazing Grands Goulets where the tiny, but powerful, River Vernaison punches through a rocky barrier at Les Barraques-en-Vercors. Somehow man has built a leech-like road alongside the torrential stream as it hurtles down the narrow ravine. Equally amazing is the road that hugs the floor of the dark Gorges de la Bourne – west of Villard; steep cliffs, coming so close together that they nearly touch, overhang the claustrophobic, bumpy tarmac ribbon. All these sights played a part in the defence of the Vercors.

The Germans made the inhabitants of the mountain villages pay a cruel price for their defiant stand; retribution was hideous. Villard-de-Lans, La Chapelle and Vassieux were almost totally razed to the ground – even tiny hamlets like Les Barraques and St-Agnan had their unwelcome share of the Nazis' murderous revenge: the new buildings in the villages are a salutary reminder of the sadistic punishment meted out. The National Cemetery, north of Vassieux, is a more emotional reminder of the hundreds of patriots who lost their lives.

Where are some of the other scenic pleasures? Enjoy the huge Forêt de Lente – it helped to hide many Resistance fighters and consequently was an important life-saver; marvel at the sulking, hypnotic slab of mountain called Mont Aiguille – best seen from the east; explore the underground caves at Chorance; relish the isolation of the dead-end road that takes you to the Cirque d'Archiane, and a second that leads you through the Gorges d'Omblèze. Don't miss the inspiring Vercors: your visit will be an important addition to your understanding of geography, modern history and the French.

ELEPHANTS, MAPOHOLICS AND ENTHUSIASMS

What a jumbo-sized jumble for a chapter heading. Let me explain the reasoning behind the strange choice of title.

Of the many books I have read during the last three years, two of the most enjoyable were *Enthusiasms* and *Hannibal's Footsteps* – both written by Bernard Levin. Each book is a joy – with something of interest on every page. *Enthusiasms* is the c.v. of a happy man: if I had to return to the years when I interviewed hundreds of young people, looking for work in the computer industry, I think I would have asked each one of them to write me a 2,000-word essay on their 'Enthusiasms' – a revealing way to discover a 'hidden' personality.

I read *Hannibal's Footsteps* at the end of October 1985. What a courageous undertaking Bernard took on: he retraced Hannibal's stupendous march, made two thousand years ago with 60,000 infantry, 9,000 cavalry and 37 elephants in tow – from the Mediterranean to the mountain border of France and Italy. No modern writer can be quite certain of the exact path Hannibal took but Bernard plumped for his version and then completed the entire trip, walking every inch of the way.

Languages were not my forte at school. I suppose I first heard of Hannibal during two traumatic years of trying to 'master' Latin; but the second time I really took notice of the military genius was at the end of 1955 when I remember reading in *The Geographical Magazine* an article by Sir Gavin de Beer in which he examined the likely route Hannibal took all those centuries ago. My interest in France had by then been aroused and I recall reading de Beer's account with relish. Years passed before I visited parts of Hannibal's march.

Aouste-sur-Sye, alongside the Drôme – see page 145

Denis Parrett

Deris Parrett

Let me tell you of two strange coincidences which took place during 1985 – long before I knew of Bernard's walking 'feat', which he completed in the summer of 1984. The first coincidence concerns the dead-end road in the Jarjatte Valley – see the entry for Serres (Hautes-Alpes). I was there in late spring when the Crête des Aiguilles was covered in deep snow. If a bookie had asked me to bet on Levin crossing those mountains, on foot, the previous summer, I would have wagered a sizeable sum against such a possibility – and lost!

The second coincidence concerned the commission I gave my friend Denis Pannett to paint the watercolours reproduced in this book; he did the work during the spring of 1985. Accompanied by Valerie, his wife, and their daughter, Belinda, the family had great fun following a route which we reckoned would produce artistic dividends. One area I was keen for Denis to look at was the Vercors and the countryside to the immediate south – old favourites of mine. He was only too happy to do so – because, included in that area is the River Drôme, never seen by Denis but apparently a great favourite of his painter 'hero', Russell Flint.

One of the eight watercolours is of a village called Aouste-sur-Sye, alongside the Drôme and east of Crest. A second is of the river near Saillans (another marvellous place to paint – read Levin's rich verbal description). The paintings had been completed when I read Bernard's book – and, much to my delight, he had written some evocative passages about the very same countryside. See the *Vive le Vercors* map.

Readers of my earlier French books will know of my passionate enthusiasm for the Chartreuse and the Vercors. But south of the Drôme is a small area of mountain country which I love equally well. You see it first as you head east from Crest: rows of small, wooded hills, rising in serried ranks, higher and higher, and capped by several mountain-top 'beaks'. To get the best from that magical bit of terrain head south to the Col de la Chaudière (1047 metres) or east and then south-east from Saillans up the Roanne Valley to the Col de Pennes.

For me it has always been heart-stirring countryside – in my motor sport days and when I felt the need to recharge spiritual batteries. But Bernard sparked my interest in a tiny hamlet called Pennes-le-Sec, just west of the col and off the narrow road that leads to it. So, on a glorious Sunday at the end of October 1985, I set off early one morning to look yet again at this enthralling bit of deserted France – to soak in the same vistas that Hannibal and his army must have seen two millenniums ago.

It was a brilliantly clear day – the warm sun was a much appreciated bonus. South of the Drôme, and for the next 100 miles, the landscape was a vivid picture; if I had asked Denis to paint it that day you would say he had exaggerated his colours. Hannibal passed this way in midwinter; a few weeks earlier his path would have been lit by myriad flaming torches – trees of every hue imaginable: dark coppers, stunning russets, glowing golds and burning reds. The poplars were giant beacons of yellow light – their long candle-shaped forms burned with searing, dazzling intensity.

Pennes-le-Sec is a revelation. Restored years ago by Charles Piot (1904–80), a tyre retailer, it is a happy reminder of how many off-the-beaten-track places have been returned to a condition where they provide homes for folk willing to desert city jungles. Bernard went on to describe his climb of the Col de

Pennes and the reward he won as he started the descent to the east. What follows in his book is one of the most revealing bits of travel writing I have ever read: if I could write only one-hundredth as effectively, I would be a happy man.

It is indeed a memorable vista. It comes as a surprise after the ascent on the southern side of the col where you pass through typical Mediterranean scrub. Then, 100 metres over the top, you're in cooler woods where trees are of the northern European variety (little direct sun sees to that) – and, below you, is a stunning view. On that late October day it was even more spellbinding as the trees around me were wearing their autumn coats. What Bernard omitted to include in his description were the vineyards he saw far below him. In future, whenever I drink a Clairette de Die, I'll recall that panorama.

Hannibal's Footsteps is a splendid read – for me especially so, because for every footstep of the way I know the terrain well. At the end of his 'walk' Bernard chose to cross into Italy at Le Pain de Sucre – where there's a 'road' across the frontier. I prefer to think that Hannibal crossed his final barrier in the northern shadow of Mont Viso – climbing one of the best dead-end roads in France, the Guil Valley, in the process.

In his book Bernard praises much of the best of France – but he also has a 'go' at many unhappy aspects of that glorious country: the dirty streets of Avignon (dog excrement in Paris is even worse); the eyesore rubbish 'tips' one finds near many French villages; the numerous French traitors who caused the deaths of so many Resistance patriots; and the hideous Mediterranean coastline are just a few examples.

Why not link together your enthusiasm with your mapoholic instincts and follow in the steps of Hannibal's elephants?

146

PONT-DE-L'ISERE   Chabran

Very comfortable restaurant with rooms
Terrace

At last! The second Michelin star arrived in 1985: Michel Chabran waited a long time for what seemed manifestly his just reward. There are clear signs that the tyre men are getting tougher at the two-star level: the guillotine has fallen numerous times in the last few years and it looks, too, as if they award the second rosette far more grudgingly these days. If only they would bite the bullet and apply the guillotine to some of the three-star 'gods' – like Paul Bocuse for one.

Let's get the negative criticism over and done with at Chabran's. Nothing but praise has filled the letters arriving at Amersham for Michel's cooking skills. But regularly, in perhaps one letter in five, readers moaned about the ultra-modern décor of the interior. True enough, it's not to every client's liking – but perhaps you'll be more understanding when I tell you the background story of Michel and his attractive, hardworking and loyal wife Rose-Marie – her husband's No. 1 supporter.

Michel has just turned 40. He lost his father early in life and was brought up by his grandparents. His grandmother ran a humble café in a tiny corner of the present building. The rest of the property was used by his grandfather as a garage for his company's vehicles! The culinary fire that burns so brightly in Michel today was first kindled, and then flamed, in the kitchens of Jacques Pic – down the road at Valence. Three years there in his teens, followed by compulsory military service, left Michel, approaching 25, with a driving desire to be his own boss. The only place, he concluded, where he could achieve that ambition was by making use of his grandparents' premises.

At the start Michel and Rose-Marie used the café as a restaurant dining room; later they converted part of the garage. Bit by bit, year by year, the couple converted all the original property into an ultra-modern, two-star Michelin restaurant *avec chambres*. To have done that in the most unlikely building, sitting beside the notorious N7, is a mind-boggling marvel. If you study the four black and white photographs in the 'lounge' – taken at the turn of the century – you'll spot how sleepy the N7 was in those bygone days. Not so now; but don't be put off, because the bedrooms have every modern facility and are superbly insulated.

So now you know how the present-day restaurant took shape. Like it or not I cannot help but feel that the modern interior was really the only path the couple could take. But that, after all, has nothing to do with why Michel has been such a success with readers: his skills are in his fingers, in his imaginative brain and in his eye for minute detail.

What a huge talent it is. You see it in creations that match the ultra-modern face of the dining room: *filets de rougets tièdes poêlés, à l'huile d'olive de Nyons légèrement vinaigrée au céleri frit* – an accurate description if ever there was one of a super light dish with no cream, butter or whatever. You taste his creative experiments in specialities like *saumon rôti a très basse temperature à l'émulsion de tomate* – a moist pink fillet of fish cooked for only a few minutes and tasting of just what prime condition salmon should do. And then, as a final example, one is bowled over by a modern interpretation of a classic – *rable de lièvre*. What a stunner: rich, dark meat with a

miraculous *sauce poivrade* – velvety in texture with an intense black colour and aromatic to the point where the 'perfume' is equalled only by the taste!

On my last visit I was lucky enough to spend the evening in the company of Gérard Chave, Michel's great 'mate' and whom I had first met six months earlier (see Valence entry). Both of us spent a happy evening, enjoying our meal and the splendid 'local' wines. We agreed that Michel's *pâtisserie* work is the equal of Pic's: dare we say that it could be better? Not just the splendid desserts, but also the smooth sorbets and ice creams and the *tour de force petits fours*: nine alternatives and each one an example of the very finest work. Shame on some of those wretched *petits fours* served by lazy-bones three-star chefs. You see the 'house' eye for detail and excellence at breakfast time, too, when everything, including the four different breads and cakes, is home-made.

It was fascinating to hear Gérard nattering about some pet topics of his: first he had news of the 1985 harvest – which he reckoned was going to produce some truly remarkable wines in years to come; then he heaped scorn on the French who, so often, choose to drink their wines so young – a 'crime' in his book (the same people no doubt who eat game with literally no hanging at all); he was charitable about the young French of today whom he considers to be far keener to learn about wines; and, finally, he told me how chic it had become to drink Sauternes and Port – the English 'habit' he called it!

Another aspect of the restaurant which will interest you is the considerable number of lithographs gracing the walls of the various rooms – all signed by a mysterious 'Cathelin'. The menu covers – a different one for each of the four seasons –

are signed by the same hand. All the colourful work is done by Bernard Cathelin, an old friend of the family and a cousin of Claude Terrail, the owner of the Tour d'Argent in Paris. Bernard lives in the same building as the world-famous restaurant and, for three months each year, he returns to his *pays* – the village of Montéléger, south-east of Valence.

The Chabran family is a happy one. You'll certainly meet Rose-Marie and possibly you'll also see her two daughters – Delphine, 16, and Carole, aged 14. Michel is a fine tennis player though I doubt whether he will have the time to accept your challenge to a game. He and Michel Bordeau at far away St-Girons in the Pyrénées are the two best *hotelier/cuisinier* players in France; note the racket-designed prize, just inside the entrance, that Michel won a year or two ago. Unusually, most of Michel's dining room staff have stayed with him for years – led by his *maîtrè d'hôtel/sommelier*, Pierre Boucon.

There are two 'trips' for which you must find time. First, the train ride from Tournon to Lamastre on France's best privately-owned railway line, the Chemin de Fer du Vivarais. A metre-gauge run of 33 kilometres, every metre is a real treat – for children and grown-up 'kids'. During the summer there's one 'steamer' train every day – but, even if you miss that, use the alternative 'autorail' service for a memorable ride. And, second, head for Hauterives, to the north-east, and its amazing Palais Idéal – built of pebbles and stones 100 years ago by the town postman, Ferdinand Cheval.

category 3★ *menus* **C-D** *rooms* 12**C-D** *cards* V
closed Sun evg & Mon (out of season). Mon & Tues midday (season).
post Pont-de-l'Isère, 26600 Tain-l'Hermitage, Drôme.
phone 75 84 60 09 *Mich* 244 *map* 77 Valence 9 km. to S
148

A FLY ON THE WALL

You, the reader, wouldn't expect to see many flies in the kitchens of talented French *cuisiniers* but here's one, who at least twenty times during the last two years, has had the great good fortune to be allowed to stand, just like a fly, with his back to the wall and observe talented chefs at work with their energetic, skilful teams of staff. Each kitchen visit where I was a 'spectator' fly lasted some two to three hours. All of them were fascinating and full of interest but perhaps the one that was most revealing was the two hours I spent with Michel Chabran and his five-man, one-girl *équipe* at Pont-de-l'Isère.

I chose a good day to be a fly. November 1st is a national holiday in France, Toussaint (All Saints' Day), an occasion when families remember their departed loved ones; on that day, and during the week beforehand, I must have seen literally thousands of potted chrysanthemums outside florists and cemeteries – awaiting purchasers who would place them on family graves. Lunch at Chabran was therefore an extremely busy time – with nearly 70 clients to be served meals.

A team of seven, cooking for 70 clients, and protecting a Michelin two-star reputation meant that not one of them had a second to spare during the 120 minutes I spent in the kitchen. It was a Friday: on the previous Tuesday Michel had introduced his winter menu; apart from desserts there were 20 dishes listed on *la carte* and there were three fixed-price menus – with many variations to the à la carte specialities. To complicate matters there were many new 'creations'.

Much of the preparation work had been done earlier in the morning: simple things like scores of scallops – fat, chunky things – were sitting in big buckets; sauces were ready; and more complicated dishes, including the new creations, had been partly prepared. One was called *médaillons de sole à la feuille d'épinard au caviar Sevruga Petrossian dans un nage de coquillage*: thin flattened slices of sole and leaves of spinach had been shaped into a sausage – the 'rounds' were cut as required, Swiss-roll fashion, and then quickly cooked with a mixture of *coquillages*, like *huîtres* and *bigorneaux* as examples; the latter were also part of the *nage* – a heavenly tasting, aromatic aroma of the sea.

All of it was done at a sprint speed pace and non-stop at that. Five waiters were looking after the dining room; they were coming in and out like clockwork springs, shouting for their clients' dishes. Fifty per cent of diners ordered à la carte – the remaining clients chose, in equal proportions, the two most expensive menus where three and four courses were served before the cheese trays appeared. One obvious lesson I relearned time after time on my kitchen visits was that organisation is everything. Creativity and imagination are essential prerequisites for any great chef – but organisation and attention to detail are equally as important. Team work, too, is vital: each member of the *équipe* knew exactly what was expected of them. Youngsters or not, they buzzed like worker bees, carrying out Michel's barked instructions to the letter. There were no arguments, no answering back, no panic, no hysterics: it was an efficient display of sheer professionalism – like a well-oiled, well-tuned, high-performance engine.

"Oui chef," was the most common response. Michel kept an eagle eye on everything. Not one plate escaped his attention: he had done his bit in creating the dishes, working out what was prepared beforehand, how the specialities would be presented and which members of the team would prepare the various parts making up the complete *plats*. His whites remained immaculate in the hot, fiery environment – as they needed to because, periodically, Michel would disappear into the dining room to natter with clients for a couple of minutes.

It was the season for *la chasse* so, inevitably, the menus included dishes such as *le rable de lièvre rôti au thym et laurier*, accompanied by the majestic *sauce poivrade* that I had tasted days earlier. Another new dish was a creation called *le rognon, le ris, le foie de veau en feuilleté à la crème de moutarde*. This, one sensed immediately, burnt up the staff's nervous energy as the correct cooking, and critical timing, of the ingredient parts was extremely tricky.

Though there were just 20 specialities on *la carte* nevertheless all of them had complex assemblies: unbelievably huge *langoustines* required last minute skinning, cutting and shaping before they became *langoustines poêlées aux pâtes fraîches et courgettes, à la crème de langoustine*. Two or three dishes required the making of a *feuilleté* – prepared in a very rapid three minutes in a fantastic new oven.

It was a surprise, for once, not to see duck play any part in the menu content: equally amusing, too, to discover that the humble sprout contributed to another tricky dish where the breast and legs of a *pigeonneau* from Gandels (south of Toulouse) had been cooked in different ways. Minute *petites ravioles* from nearby Royans (at the western door of the Vercors) – about one square centimetre in size – fascinated me: later I was able to taste some; stuffed with cheese and herbs, they were cooked in a *bouillon de poule* and served with a *beurre salé aux herbes*.

The remarkable range of desserts had been prepared well beforehand by an extremely capable young *pâtissier*; his skilful talents applied not just to the light, perfectly presented tarts like *citron* and strawberry but also to the light-as-air pear and chocolate concoctions he described as *gâteaux*. But for me his most brilliant touches came with the *petits fours*. Clients were served with a choice of seven or eight different 'mouthfuls' but in fact about 15 alternatives were available in the cool part of the kitchen reserved for the *pâtissier*: tiny choux buns with a caramel topping, minuscule tartlets with six *fraises des bois* somehow balancing on top of them, thimble-sized éclairs – just like their big brothers, chocolate truffles – light and melting; the list goes on and on. The enterprising appetisers, too, had been an eye-opener; when you consider how many pathetic examples of starters and finishers are put before one elsewhere in France and then you see, first hand, such perfect examples of the art at Chabran's restaurant, you know just what it means not to take short cuts in the kitchen.

Finally, well after 2 p.m., I sat down in the dining room to take in the activity there. At 2.20 a couple walked in and asked for a meal. "Of course," was the response – though I suspect the kitchen staff was not that happy about it. Two hours later the couple left, light-hearted and light-headed. It was to be hoped that another couple, real VIPs, left pleased, too: the gentleman was no less than Monsieur Seysses, the President of the renowned Club of 100 – a group of the world's best chefs; membership is by invitation only. On November 1, 1985 Michel was not one of the select 100 – but I, for one, will not be surprised if, in due course, he has been invited to join.

ROYAT   Radio

Very comfortable hotel
Quiet/Gardens/Lift

An artistic touch runs through three generations at the Radio. You see it demonstrated by Michel Mioche in the various specialities the skilful chef creates in his kitchen. His father, 93-year-old Paul, did his bit years ago when he spent much of his spare time painting a huge number of pictures – in watercolours, oils and *en sucre*. The latter may be new to you; one example of an Auvergne winter scene makes particularly clever use of the unusual icing-sugar medium. Viewing Paul's work at the hotel is an easy way to tour the Auvergne – there are dozens of local scenes displayed. And now Michel and Yvette Mioche's son, Jean-François, has put his artistic talent to good use: the thirties-style menu cover and the typographical design of the interior is the work of the young designer.

Yvette has tried hard to brighten up the high-ceilinged, old-fashioned dining room and hall. The rooms now have an art deco style about them; the new decor works well.

Michel is a competent chef. He seems to have found the perfect formula for an intelligently balanced set of menus. The cheapest, really good value at £10 or so, is called a *menu affaire d'aujourd'hui*: a small salad, followed by fingers of chicken, a choice of Auvergne cheeses – more about those later – and any of the full à la carte selection of sweets makes it a budget meal *par excellence*. The next set meal up the price scale is a *menu du terroir*: three courses precede the cheeses and sweets and they make sensible use of local products.

The two most expensive set meals are a *menu de tradition* — classics prepared in a light style — and, amazingly, in the very heart of central France, a *menu de la mer*.

Alas, the latter is expensive but it does allow Michel, now in his mid-forties, to show off his finely-honed talent: typically the menu could include a *petite salade de homard breton* — with herbs and citrus fruit; *langoustines* — the light garnish is described as *gratinées au sabayon de citron*; and, what I thought was a formidable masterpiece, some tiny morsels of sole, sprinkled with shavings of *cèpes* and surrounded by *lentilles vertes du Puy*. Who would have thought such a combination of tastes would result in such a perfect marriage?

The cheese course is described as a *plâteau de fromages d'Auvergne*. How good it is to see the choice restricted entirely to Massif Central varieties — the home of so many superb cheeses. The trolley could well include St-Nectaire, Fourme d'Ambert and some *chèvre* alternatives — but the two highlights are usually a mouthwatering, mature Cantal and, the rival of Roquefort, a salty, sharp-tasting Bleu d'Auvergne. Desserts that follow normally feature feather-light *feuilletés* and *gratins* where hot fruit and cold ice cream combine well together.

The Mioches, in common with all hoteliers who have a short season, have found the going tough during the last few years; the couple know that all their annual income must come from a hectic four month period. The hotel can be hard to find: as you enter Royat from Clermont, pass under the high-arched railway bridge, immediately turn left, left again in 100 metres under the same railway line, and then it's the second road on the right. The spa town is in an elevated site above Clermont-Ferrand; on the doorstep is some wonderful countryside.

CHÂTEAU DE CORDÈS

Why not stay a couple of nights or so and spend a day enjoying the following drive? It's at its most captivating in late May or June when the wild flowers are at their very best. For reasons I do not fully understand they are most profuse on the first half of the drive — alongside the D5 and D36 roads on the eastern heights of the long-extinct volcanic peaks.

Leave Royat to the south and use the N89 until you reach the Col de la Ventouse — about 18 km. from Royat. Turn left and then drive south on the D5 towards Murol; the view of the ruined castle below you as you drop down into Murol is an eerie sight. Detour east to St-Nectaire and admire the grace and beauty of the admirably proportioned Romanesque church — Auvergne's best. Return to Murol and use the D5 again to Besse. Then follow the D36 north-west to the Col de la Croix St-Robert. The route is a majestic one with many fine views.

Descend into Le Mont-Dore, a few kilometres from the source of the River Dordogne, and then head north, using the D983. Immediately after the Lac de Guéry, on your left, there are more spectacular views including two unusual rock faces. Through Orcival, an atmospheric medieval village — see the marvellous church and the nearby château at Cordès, and continue north-east until you reach the foot of the Puy de Dôme. This 1465-metre-high cone is an astonishing viewpoint; the 4 km., 1 in 8 climb, is steep enough for any modern car — but think of those poor Tour de France cyclists who, every year, endure the torture of the same climb.

category **3** *menus* **B-D** *rooms* 27**B-C** *cards* A AE DC V
closed Mid Nov-Feb. Rest only: Sun evg. Mon.
post 43 av. P.-Curie, Royat, 63400 Chamalières, P.-de-D.
phone 73 30 87 83 *Mich* 239 *map* 78 Clermont-Ferrand 4 km.
152

VALENCE   Pic

Luxury restaurant with rooms
Gardens

Before readers visit this fine restaurant they should set aside an hour or so to follow a short, highly instructive 'detour'. Leave Valence, cross the Rhône to St-Péray and then take the D533 towards Lamastre. The road climbs steadily into the wooded Ardèche hills and, eight km. from St-Péray, you pass a small blue sign with the white words 'Le Pin' written on it. Immediately, on your right, stop at the solitary Auberge du Pin. What's the significance of this humble, isolated building?

Le Pin is where the Pic story started — in 1829. From generation to generation, during the last century, it was no more than a very modest *auberge* indeed. Sophie Pic was the first to win a name for the family's culinary skills — serving dishes like *fricassées de volailles* and *les lapins sautés*.

Her son, André, took over the kitchen in 1920. By 1934 — as my oldest edition of Michelin confirms — a small miracle happened in the Ardèche hills: André won his third Michelin star — at Le Pin! A training at places like the Palais d'Orsay in Paris had equipped him to attract an ever-increasing number of motorists up into the hills — to savour specialities like *poularde en vessie*, *homard à la creme* and a *gratin d'écrevisses* (the latter, in those days, came from the Duzon stream, no less, just seven km. away to the west of Le Pin).

André made a speedy decision. In 1935 the family deserted the *auberge* and made their new home in Valence — at the present-day site of the now world-famous restaurant. Jacques, his son, was four years old when they opened their doors for the first time in Valence on January 1st, 1936.

I knew none of this when I made my initial visit to Pic in 1955 – chosen at random from the first Michelin guide I ever bought. In those days it had just one star; I didn't know that André was, by then, very ill and I certainly didn't realise his past success. (Alas, Michelin tells you nothing about chefs.) Within two years, after Jacques had finished a training stint that had taken him to Geneva, Paris and Deauville, and after his marriage to Suzanne, he began to take over from his father. What a proud day it must have been for Jacques, years later, to win his own three stars. Family honour was restored.

In the present-day world of French *haute cuisine* everything is for sale at the three-star chef level: it seems some will sell their souls if needs be. Here is one of the rare exceptions. Jacques Pic is a small, shy man; watch his dark eyes shine with happiness – and his whole personality change – when he starts to enthuse about his *pays*, his family, his wines and his cooking. Happily, his son, Alain, now works alongside him and his daughter-in-law, Marie-Hélène, is often on duty in reception. Her children will ensure the Pic line continues well past the 200-year-mark in the 21st century!

No wonder readers love this happy restaurant – where Jacques is always on duty in the kitchen that means everything to him. I suspect readers like the down-to-earth personalities of the Pic family; none of them wear any airs or graces. I expect that was as true of all the previous generations, too.

The world-renowned Menu Rabelais is still as formidable as ever – changing from season to season as differing fresh produce becomes available. There was nothing outstandingly creative the last time I was there and, if anything, the famous *menu dégustation* seemed harder to cope with because far more was served with each course than ever before. That's worth watching as one highlight of a Pic meal is the desserts: a cascade of delights starting usually with someting like a cold orange soufflé, followed by a hot *crêpe Suzette*, and then an array of numerous alternatives. Leave room for the final course; it may be best to go for the less-expensive menu.

Another guaranteed highlight will be Pic's wine list – a *tour de force* of the best Rhône wines. I don't want to argue here the merits or otherwise of the many excellent Rhône Valley *vignerons*; instead I want to draw your attention to my personal favourite – Gérard Chave. It was a long time ago when I first relished Chave vintages but it was only recently that I discovered the story of his quite remarkable family – and that through the sympathetic work of Robin Yapp who, more than any other wine author I know, writes so much from the heart.

Robin has been the UK supplier of Chave wines for some years (Yapp Bros., Mere, Wiltshire) and during that time he has got to know just what makes the 'ingenious' Gérard tick. The family own various parts of the legendary Hermitage hill; their cellars are at Mauves, downstream and on the opposite bank. The family vineyards have been in Chave hands for more than 500 years – a record probably unique in all France. Bottles are labelled Jean-Louis Chave, Gérard's father.

I have been fortunate enough to spend an hour with Gérard in his cellars. What a happy, passionate man he is – revelling in his work. His red Hermitage wines are superb – available at the restaurants of both Pic and Chabran and in the UK. Equally good are his white wines which I, personally, enjoy even more.

153

What has always amazed me is how a Chave white manages to retain its balance throughout the course of a meal with many varying dishes. If you cannot visit Pic or Chabran at least ask Robin Yapp for his current list; you can then enjoy some Chave magic at home. And for that we must thank the trust and friendship Robin and Gérard have for each other – because there must be many other suppliers throughout the world who would love to get their hands on Gérard's annual harvest.

Set aside a day or two for the hills bordering each side of the Rhône Valley. You'll need a day for the Vercors and only a few hours for the following drive which, on a clear day, is a series of breathtaking views.

From either St-Péray or Châteaubourg climb west to the viewpoint at St-Romain-de-Lerps. The views are vast but what makes it enjoyable are the two semi-circular observation tables. Each one is made up of 19 ceramic tiles – hand painted by Paul Goichot from 1940–43. It's good that they appear to be withstanding the ravages of time and weather as it's a lonely, elevated spot with no protection from winter's frosts and winds.

From St-Romain head south to Le Pin – that gives you a chance to see the old Pic home. Use the D14 towards Vernoux – but at La Justice turn south-east on the D232 and D266 to the Château de Pierre-Gourde. Use the non-metalled track for access to this astonishing mound of now ruined stones; the view west of serried ranks of hills is well worth the drive.

Alternative hotels in Valence: Novotel and Hôtel 2000.
category **3** *menus* **D** *rooms* **5D-D2** *cards* AE DC
closed Feb. Aug. Sun evg. Wed.
post 285 av. Victor-Hugo, 26000 Valence, Drôme.
phone 75 44 15 32 *Mich* 244 *map* 79

SMALL IS BEAUTIFUL Ray Hewinson & Peter Trotter

"If God had intended us to be friendly with them French, he wouldn't have put that big ditch between us," said one of our village characters when the prospect of twinning our little community with a village in Normandy was first discussed.

The parish of Lacey Green is situated in the Chiltern Hills among the lovely beech woods of Buckinghamshire. It consists of three villages with a total population of almost 2,000. Its twin village, Hambye, is of similar size and population but there the similarity stops. Lacey Green has four pubs, two shops and a post office. Hambye is a veritable *bourg* with a fine selection of trades and craftsmen. A large percentage of Lacey Green residents commute to offices in London or to nearby towns, whereas most Hambiots work in, or close to, their own closely-knit community, whose economy relies heavily upon its surrounding small farms.

It is, therefore, quite remarkable how people with such differing life experiences and expectations have grown so closely together in friendship and enjoy each other's life style and company. As one of our older members said, "It's amazing how much twinning has helped us to better understand ourselves as well as our continental cousins."

Twinning between British and European communities is now a well-established tradition. In many larger communities activities are restricted to civic dignitaries and establishments such as schools and Rotary clubs. In little Lacey Green few are unaware of twinning activities, and everyone has an opportunity to become involved; in fact over 100 are!

Our firm resolve in twinning in Lacey Green is to not only

cross the barriers of language and customs between the two countries, but also to embrace the spectrum of social classes and ages within our community. Inevitably, twinning tends to attract the middle-class and the middle-aged, and there are plenty of both in our parish. We have, however, within the five short years of our history, recruited an enthusiastic eighteen-year-old to our committee, supported a pub cycle team riding event between the two villages, arranged exchanges for children from both communities and entered an Anglo-French team in a 'fun run' along a Normandy beach. The village band from Hambye has played at our local fête and the parish church choir has sung in the Hambye church, breaking ecumenical barriers in the process.

Despite a great deal of help from the Joint Twinning Committee, the process of establishing the twinning link was not without its problems and, like many similar ventures, it relied heavily upon the pioneering spirit of the committed few. A visit, at very short notice, from three young men from Hambye was followed by a return trip by our founder chairman and his wife who were taken on a whirlwind tour to view the village and its magnificent abbey ruins. *En route* there were frequent stops to meet local dignitaries, where the inevitable hospitality was dispensed. The whole day seemed like a series of meetings, *apéritifs* and yet more *apéritifs*. Their visit culminated in a meal with 16 guests, lasting well over four hours. A huge gâteau with the inscription 'Hambye and Lacey Green' was then produced! It seemed as though the French had already made their decision: how could we refuse?

The Brussels football tragedy in May 1985 happened days after our friends from Hambye had visited Lacey Green. The consequences of the acts of those mindless hoodlums caused so much suffering and ill-feeling towards our country. Our whole nation experienced a deep sense of shame and horror on that May evening. Many of us in twinning were grateful that we had so recently had a positive opportunity to offer friendship and hospitality to ordinary people from another country. Twinning for us is a sharing of understanding, love and friendship between ordinary, everyday folk. It transcends politics and religion and has created new and lasting friendships, both within and between the two communities.

The spirit of twinning could be recorded in a series of snapshots. The tearful farewells between two love-lorn teenagers, the toothless grin of an old French farmer trying to master the Gay Gordons and, perhaps most poignantly, the sight of two elderly ladies, with hardly a common word between them, walking arm in arm down the village street. For the French lady this was her first visit outside her native country. For our own senior citizen it was the first of a series of exchanges which have kept her active and provided a great interest in her retirement.

Lastly, there is the shot taken with a wide-angle lens. It is a Renoir-like scene of trestle tables, half-filled glasses, crusts of bread and the murmur of relaxed conversation with 'Franglais' as the common language. It is an atmosphere of being at peace with the world which comes from good food, good wine, good conversation and good company. It is a familiar scene but one which does not tarnish with familiarity. Around such a table the world becomes smaller and issues such as milk quotas, lamb production and the price of Golden Delicious apples fade into insignificance!

CABOURG

Host. Moulin du Pré

Comfortable restaurant with rooms
Secluded/Gardens

The Moulin du Pré has proved to be Normandy's number one favourite with readers: I cannot say I'm surprised. The recipe mix for this delectable treat is just about perfect: a pretty, isolated site – yet so close to much of Normandy's historic heritage, and the coast, too; cooking of a standard which all but prompted me to make it a category three entry as a result of my last visit; and, finally, the happy Holtz family who bring the all-important personal touch to bear – the extra ingredient that lifts the otherwise ordinary into something special.

The Moulin was opened as a restaurant in 1970; in the distant past it had been the site of a forge. Today, modern buildings, but built in the traditional style, enjoy the advantage of the old mill's tranquil *étang*; trees and a park-like garden add to the overall pleasure of the natural setting.

It's likely Claude Holtz will welcome you. He's a friendly host and he's proud of his small published book of poems which you'll see on display in the reception area. Unseen by most clients – but readers should ask to meet her 'out-of-hours' – is Claude's wife, Jocelyne, the talented *cuisinière* who, with the help of only two others in the kitchen, does such a first-class, splendid job. One of the two helpers is her father, Roger Hamchin. Her mother, Gisèle, helps Claude in the dining room.

Jocelyne's talents are considerable: she makes her own *foie gras de canard* – exceptional it is too; she smokes her own salmon and duck; she offers a wide range of both fish and meat dishes; and, more than anything else, demonstrates a lightness of touch and inventiveness that is such a welcome change on the normally heavy going Normandy culinary scene. Examples are *pâté chaud de pleurotes au vinaigre de Xérès* and *soupe de langoustines aux bigorneaux, moules et bouquets*. Jocelyne's desserts are excellent, particularly her *tarte aux pommes*.

Claude helps by cooking any orders for grills (mainly beef and lamb) in the dining room – over hot cinders taken from the roaring log fire in the huge fireplace. That fire burns every day; laughingly the couple tell you "even when only one client, out of 40, orders a solitary *côtes d'agneau* from the menu."

category 2 *menus* B *rooms* 10B *cards* AE DC V
closed 1st 2 wks Mar. Oct. Sun evg/Mon (not July/Aug).
post rte de Gonneville, 14860 Ranville, Calvados. (Off D513)
phone 31 78 83 68 *Mich* 231 *map* 37 Caen 16 km.

St-Germain-de-Livet, south of Lisieux

GOUPILLIERES   Aub. du Pont de Brie

Comfortable restaurant with rooms
Secluded/Good value

I would guess there are four reasons for the popularity of the Auberge: an isolated wooded valley setting, a few metres away from the River Orne; a ring of countryside within easy reach – from the D-Day beaches and historical sites to the hills of La Suisse Normande; exceptional value for money (there are 11 bedrooms these days – many are brand new and others have been modernised; in '86 a double with bath cost £11!); and the four ladies who are the heart and soul of the *logis*.

Véronique Dri is the smiling *patronne* – the epitome of helpfulness as many readers have confirmed (there was one exceptional case of trust and service); her attractive sister, Danielle, and their mother, Régine Demonte, are the *cuisinières*; sister-in-law, Chantal, helps in the dining rooms (there's a new one now at the rear). Cooking standards have improved, like the amenities, and cuisine is at a level which puts it just about at category 2; there are lots of nice little touches and an award-winning *terrine de campagne* and light desserts are particularly noteworthy.

To the north-west of Goupillières is terrain known as the Bocage: its numerous primrose-studded high earth banks, topped with trees and hedges, caused great difficulties for the Allied tanks in the summer of 1944. Some of the heaviest fighting of the Normandy campaign took place in the Bocage; it's easy to see why. Towns like Aunay-s-Odon and Villers-Bocage and the village of Tilly-s-Seulles were devastated.

Visit the most poignant of the 18 Commonwealth War Cemeteries in Normandy: the tiny Jerusalem Cemetery, alongside the D6 at Chouain, between Bayeux and Villers-Bocage. It's the last resting place of just 48 souls; the first burial took place on June 10th, four days after the D-Day landing. Of the 48 graves, 47 were soldiers from the British Army and one was a Czech; half of the British dead were members of the 6th and 8th battalions of the Durham Light Infantry.

For me it's a heart-tugging, emotional corner of sacred Normandy; I always shed a quiet tear when I sit on the small bench in front of the Cemetery Register and read the contents of the slim books behind the brass door. The officers and men came from all parts of Britain: Cornwall to Caithness, London to Ludlow. The headstones are etched with both stirring and happy words: 'Cheerful, smiling, always content, loved and respected wherever he went' and 'It is sweet to think of one I've loved' are two of the more joyful memories.

Legend has it that after the war the local villagers staged a 'sit-in' to ensure that the remains of the soldiers stayed where they had been initially buried rather than see them moved to a larger cemetery. Whatever the truth of this story, the little cemetery remained and was officially handed over to the Commonwealth War Graves Commission in February 1946.

Don't miss Jerusalem: stay a while, shed a tear and remember always the treasured lives of the many who died for us in bitter campaigns all over the globe.

category **2** *menus* **A-B** *rooms* 11**A-B** *cards* A V
closed 1st half Feb. 2nd half Aug. Wed (Sept to May).
post Goupillières, 14210 Evrecy, Calvados. (S of Caen–off D562)
phone 31 79 37 84 *Mich* 231 *map* 38 Caen 23 km.

JAVRON   La Terrasse

Comfortable restaurant with simple rooms
Good value

Hidden alongside the busy, and not so busy roads of France, lurks many a culinary surprise. Let me tell you about one of the happiest and most revealing visits I made on my many research trips to France during the last two years. It's an intriguing tale and the subjects of the story, a young couple in their mid-twenties, need your support – as do all youngsters who take the financial gamble of buying their own restaurants.

Jerôme Bansard was born at Lassay-les-Châteaux, a town famous for its noble castle and I suspect, increasingly in years to come, for its annual *spectacle au laser* (June to August) – a *son et lumière* pageant with a 21st-century touch. There's tranquil, wooded hill country to the north and east – but, in culinary terms, the terrain in this part of the world is a desert. For a young man born and bred in Lassay it's a matter of pride that he puts the matter right – and as quickly as he can.

Jerôme has set about the task with a vengeance. The young chef is well equipped: he was trained by Claude Willer and had a rewarding two-year spell with Michel Roux at Bray. But he has an extra advantage which, in my experience, is quite unique in France: a talented wife who is also a professionally trained and qualified *pâtissière* (pastrycook). What is more, the lass is English and, by a quirk of fate, some of her culinary training was done in France: initially as a result of being one of the first Bournemouth students to do a stint with one of the Catering College's top French chefs – a member of a most unusual

network. So impressed was the chef, Albert Parveaux, that he employed Susan for two years – and that's how she came to meet Jerôme.

February 1985 saw the couple make a start by buying their own restaurant, La Terrasse – which is alongside the N12 and west of Alençon (the town is on the main road from Rouen to Le Mans). They put all their savings into the venture but still had to borrow £50,000 from the bank manager at the Crédit Agricole next door to La Terrasse. The French Government, unlike our own, put their money where their mouth is (which seems an appropriate way of explaining it) by giving a grant to anyone setting up their own business; in the Bansards' case the *prime*, as it's called, was the princely sum of £6,000.

What a price the Bansards pay for the £50,000 mortgage. Despite being charged a special low interest rate of 10%, both capital and interest have to be repaid, in monthly instalments, over 7 years. But what brings you down to earth are the 'little' costs: would you believe 40 to 50 francs for each wine glass, and 60 to 80 francs for the high-quality plates? The couple have bought them as and when they could – out of takings.

"We had two customers on our first day," Sue says wistfully. Her slight Birmingham accent reminds you she spent her first 12 years in Quinton and Halesowen. But things picked up when the locals and clients from as far away as Laval, Mayenne and even Le Mans discovered what largesse was lurking on the verges of the N12. Value for money? It's more like charity.

Four menus are set before you: in 1986 they were 50, 85, 115 and 160 francs. The couple's training pedigrees shout forth from every dish: Jerôme prepares, with just an apprentice to do some basic work, all the starters and main courses;

Susan is the artist behind the many desserts on offer.

A *roulade de caille au foie gras sur petites salades* is a super light starter though great skill goes into the preparation of shaping the quail breast around the *foie gras* and forming a sausage-shaped round; this is sliced and is presented with quail legs, a quail egg and a mixed salad. *Mini galettes* (a free adaptation of a Breton regional classic) *de saumon fumé beurre citronelle* is perfect; the thin strips of smoked salmon are served with diced cucumber in a slightly sharpish, light-as-air sauce. The humble *colin* (hake) is used cleverly with local cider vinegar to make an easily-digestible fish course. All are examples of intelligent thinking. And Susan's sweets are delicious: *truffe au chocolat sauce café grillé, charlotte aux pommes et caramel* and silky-smooth sorbets and ice creams are testament to her years of *pâtisserie* work and training.

Supplies are a problem. Take cheese as one example: "Not enough people around here know what quality is – they sell cheeses like bags of sugar," recounts Jerôme with a sad smile. The couple have found one young farmer who makes a magnificent fresh goat's cheese. Served slightly warm, in a dressing of coriander, olive oil and lemon juice, it's a winner. But at this stage Jerôme must watch costs: "As more clients come, Susan and I can progress – using more expensive produce and new ideas of mine." To progress however means potential customers must know of their whereabouts – and that leads one on to the next hurdle.

Susan puts it bluntly: "We must get into the guides." They will – but patience is needed. The latter comes hard as that monthly repayment has to be paid to the Crédit Agricole. The 50-franc menu, when added to half the price of one of their two very simple but clean bedrooms (80 francs), means that a meal and a bed, per person, cost just over £8 in 1986! See what I mean by value for money. But plump for the higher-priced 160-franc 'Le Grand Menu'. With a friendly chortle Jerôme makes a telling point: "We used to call it a Menu Dégustation – but the locals thought we wouldn't serve enough. They must have 180 gm. of fish on their plates, accompanied by plenty of fresh vegetables, for that course alone!" The locals get quantity but more sensible proportions are served to tourists with smaller appetites. "Our objective is to bring local clients, step by step, toward a more modern, lighter style," says Susan.

Susan and Jerôme have all sorts of plans for the future – but, as you can guess, they involve money: the youngsters want to modernise the existing bedrooms and add some more; they would like to convert part of the restaurant into a lounge area for guests to enjoy an *apéritif* before their meals and to put a carpet down over the tiled dining room floor; and one day they would love to have more modern equipment in the kitchen. It's the same headache culinary couples face in both Britain and France. I only hope my readers realise what the difficulties are. I always feel it adds to your pleasure and understanding when you know the personal story behind the bricks and mortar.

Seek these brave youngsters out. Their two bedrooms are simple. If you want something more comfortable use the much-liked Ermitage at Bagnoles-de-l'Orne (*sans restaurant* and quiet) – it's literally just a simple 15-minute drive away.
category 2 *menus* A-B *rooms* 2A *cards* A DC V
closed 2 weeks in Feb. Sun evg. Mon.
post 53250 Javron-les-Chapelles, Mayenne. (On N12–W Alençon)
phone 43 03 41 91 *Mich* 231 *map* 39 Alençon 36 km.

LOUE
Ricordeau-Laurent

Very comfortable hotel
Quiet/Gardens

The Laurent family were great favourites at their previous home, the Host. Renaissance at Rive-de-Gier – an oasis of green in one of France's ugliest valleys. I visited them at Rive in 1985 but, much to my surprise, I heard at the end of that year that the entire family had moved from the Renaissance to the long-established hotel at Loué – made famous over the decades by the late Emile Ricordeau.

In the late spring of '86, I made a flying visit to their new home. Extensive renovation was in progress: the dining rooms looked good – as did one or two of the redecorated bedrooms, though others were somewhat garishly painted. (Readers' reports during the summer of '86 spoke of slow service, few vegetables and other rough edges; let's hope those were just teething problems.) The three Laurent sons are now involved in the business: Jean-François and Gerald work with their father, Gilbert, in the kitchen; Eric, who speaks fluent English, helps his mother, Christiane, in the dining rooms.

Loué has always been famous for its poultry and Gilbert makes fine use of them: one whole section of the menu includes treats like *poulet au curry doux, volaille au Père Natale, pigeon en ballotine aux lentilles* and *pintadeau en aigre doux.*
category **3** *menus* **B-D** *rooms* 22**C-D** *cards* A AE DC V
closed Open all the year.
post 72540 Loué, Sarthe. (W of Le Mans; near junction 1 on A81)
phone 43 88 40 03 *Mich* 232 *map* 40 Le Mans 28 km.
160

VIRONVAY
Les Saisons

Comfortable hotel
Secluded/Gardens/Tennis

Of the dozen or more *FL3* Seine Valley recommendations – from the western edges of Paris to the river's estuary – Les Saisons has been the most complimented. It's hard to put one's finger on just why this should be so. I suspect it's the unobtrusive, natural appeal of the site that wins the votes: the property is in fact eight cottages – a mixture of modern and old; they form a ring enclosing, at its centre, a pretty garden with a number of mature trees, including some shady willows.

Of the many local tourist attractions, don't miss Claude Monet's Water-Lily Garden at nearby Giverny. The artist bought his home and garden there in 1883, long before he became so internationally renowned. He was 42 at the time; during the next 43 years he painted some of his most famous paintings in the inspiring gardens. In the 50 years that followed his death, in 1926, the gardens became derelict but, today, thanks to the French Académie des Beaux Arts and a host of private donors, you can visit the Claude Monet Museum and its eye-catching grounds from April to October.

Back at Les Saisons the owners, Christian and Françoise Bouchinet, will look after you well. The culinary style is classical but is not overpoweringly influenced by cream and butter.
category **2** *menus* **A-C** *rooms* 15**C-D** *cards* A DC V
closed Feb. 3rd wk Aug. Rest only: Sun evg & Mon.
post Vironvay, 27400 Louviers, Eure. (Near A13 Louviers-Sud exit)
phone 32 40 02 56 *Mich* 231 *map* 41 Louviers 5 km.

ARRAS Univers

Comfortable hotel
Quiet

'Who could make truly merry in a town that bore the name Péronne?' Those chilling words were written by my favourite travel writer, the sensitive and sympathetic Elizabeth Nicholas; I first read them over 30 years ago during my school days at Dudley. Péronne, Arras, Bapaume, Cambrai: the same shroud lies ghost-like over all Flanders and Picardy.

Unfold Michelin map 236, spread it out on a table and examine carefully the terrain lying within a circle of 50 km. centred on Arras. Your first comment will be: "What a network of autoroutes, main roads and towns." But, dotted among all the cartographic detail, are the numerous, oh so numerous, reminders of the horrific days of 1914–18. The clues are simple: 'Brit.' is all you need to look for. Each one is a cemetery and carefully looked after all these decades later. Pay your quiet respects at some of them – it requires little map reading effort.

Many Commonwealth cemeteries are in that sacred terrain, too. The Vimy Memorial is the most striking – just north of the A26 Arras autoroute exit. South African, Australian, New Zealand, French, German and American cemeteries – all of them sad reminders of the countless sacrifices that were made in those cold, bleak fields at the beginning of this century.

I cannot make merry in Flanders or Picardy: there's no use pretending otherwise. Arras however is a town with plenty of character – a mixture of old and new. The Grand'Place, the much smaller Place des Héros, the ancient abbey of St-Vaast and the Hôtel de Ville with its high belfry should be seen by everyone passing through the town – all of them happier reminders of man's more creative ability. And that's why I think the Univers, hidden in a quiet corner of Arras, has been such a favourite with readers; it's a reminder of old-fashioned France during the first half of this century.

The building dates from the 18th century and, during its long life, has been put to a mixture of uses: once a monastery, then a college, a hospital during the First World War and now a hotel with lots of solid, likeable character. That applies not only to the fabric of the house – one example is the panelled and beamed dining room with roaring log fire in the winter – but also to the warm welcome of Daniel Gilleron and, more importantly, the culinary ways of yesterday.

Some of you took me to task for suggesting you use the Univers as a base and eat elsewhere. With the cooking standards taking a dive at both the Chanzy and Ambassadeur restaurants there is good reason to stay put and tuck into the likes of *quenelle de brochet Nantua*, *tête de veau Gribiche*, *pintadeau Forestière*, *entrecôte au poivre*, *médaillon de veau Normande* and *sole meunière* – among many classical treats.

But now that the talented Dargent family have moved lock, stock and barrel from their roadside farmhouse at Pommera to a historic new home at 45 Grand'Place you have a decision to make: do you plump for the old or the culinary style of today? As for me – I'm not telling: but I suspect you know the answer!
category 2**(S)** *menus* **A-B** *rooms* 36**B-C** *cards* A AE V
closed Rest only: Sun (Aug).
post 3 pl. Croix-Rouge, 62000 Arras, Pas-de-Calais.
phone 21 71 34 01 *Mich* 236 *map* 42

CAMBRAI

MONTREUIL   Château de Montreuil

Very comfortable hotel
Quiet/Terrace/Gardens

Open the '86 Michelin Red Guide for Montreuil and refer briefly to the first line for the Château de Montreuil entry. It tells you a Michelin star has been awarded (new in 1986 and much overdue incidentally) but no mention in this particular example of even the chef's name! Michelin, alas, explains very little. But the personal story behind a few words on paper is an unusual one – full of interest and an eye-opening example of how fate brings young people together and how married life then takes all sorts of twists and turns in the years that follow.

The heart and soul of the 'hotel' are a young couple: Christian Germain is a 36-year-old *cuisinier*, destined for great things in the culinary world – more of that later; Lindsay, his vivacious wife, is English and I know of no better hostess in France nor of a better ambassadress for Britain. Let me tell you a bit about them because their story will both fascinate you and equip you to appreciate the Château to the full.

Christian was born near Avesnes-sur-Helpe, east of Cambrai. At 16 he failed to get into the famous Strasbourg Hotel School; instead he was offered a job at La Crémaillère in Avesnes. "I was so relieved I celebrated by buying a magnum of Champagne; the only problem was it took me two months' salary to pay for it," he recounts with a chuckle.

Long stints at Avesnes and in a prestigious Parisian restaurant saw him, at 20, join the French Army. He was based, as chef, at the HQ of the French Women's Army in Versailles.

The lady officers were not forced to use the mess restaurant: at the start of his 12-month stay an average of 15 women ate in — at the end 120 were consistently eating Germain meals!

His old boss at La Crémaillère introduced him to the formidable Frenchman Raymond Zarb, who in those days ran his own restaurant at Westerham in Kent. So keen was Raymond to employ Christian he collected him personally from Avesnes in his Jag and took him back to England: the young man was impressed to say the least. In 1974 Christian had a spell in Hong Kong working for SOPEXA; 1975, unsure first whether to work in France or Britain, saw him return to Kent. The reason? Simple: Lindsay!

Who could blame him? French girls are the ones who supposedly are endowed with alluring charm; don't you believe it — find a real English 'rose' and you've found one of the best. Meet Lindsay and you'll realise immediately why Christian headed back to Kent. They had met first prior to his Far East trip — October 1975 saw them married. Sheer chance led him to be introduced to a temporarily hospitalised Albert Roux — who was looking for a chef to assist him at the Waterside Inn (in those days Albert and Michel shared yearly stints at both the Waterside and Le Gavroche); Christian's interview took place at Albert's hospital bedside. He got the job.

In 1976 Christian started his memorable six-year spell working with the Roux brothers. "1976 was a sweltering summer — I never worked, nor sweated, so much in my life. My TR4 hood stayed down all summer," he recalls. Earlier the couple had got to know Peter Herbert (he of Gravetye Manor) and it was that supreme hotelier who one day, in 1981, mentioned that the Montreuil hotel was for sale. The comment

stuck at the back of Christian's mind. Months later he remembered it while sitting in his car at Dover Harbour looking at a map: he and Lindsay headed Montreuil way and there and then they knew that this was where they would start their own hotel and restaurant enterprise.

Within days they returned with Albert Roux who gave the hotel a thorough check over. Albert and Michel 'found' the seven City shareholders who, with the invaluable Roux guarantee, provided the sum needed to buy the property. March 1982 saw the couple make a start: at the time their son, Olivier, was two; Céline arrived that December.

After nearly five years one can say with conviction that the Germains have a success on their hands. Eleven bedrooms have been restyled and three new ones opened in an adjacent annexe. (Plans are also on hand for two *appartements* in a nearby house.) Despite spending huge amounts on renovation work the couple hope soon to be able to pay back the shareholders — with the help of a new mortgage. Their objective is simple: "I'd like to emulate Gravetye Manor," says Christian with quiet pride.

What of the chef's culinary delights? His skills are already at Michelin two-star levels. One dish I relished in '86 was the equal of any of the great chefs' efforts — a *canette de Barbarie en laque de Chine*: 'fantastic' was the one-word note I wrote down. Stay a night or two — or, if that's beyond your means, try a weekday lunch which offers marvellous value for money. *category* 3 *menus* B(lun:Mon-Sat)-C *rooms* 14D-D2 *cards* A AE DC V *closed* Mid Dec-Xmas. Jan-mid Feb. Thurs midday (Sept-June). *post* chaussée Capucins, 62170 Montreuil, Pas-de-Calais. *phone* 21 81 53 04 *Mich* 236 *map* 43 Boulogne 38 km.

ROYE   La Flamiche

Very comfortable restaurant

Read on! Don't be put off by the fact that the line above has the words 'with rooms' missing from it. I've good news to report — but that comes later; let's first celebrate the continuing development of this pleasing restaurant.

Roye itself is a dull place — one of many similar towns in the flat and desolate Picardy countryside. La Flamiche is an unprepossessing building in front of the Hôtel de Ville with its large car park. But inside the restaurant it's a sparkling beacon of pleasure: bubbling, attentive hosts in the shapes of Christine Klopp (her father's name and the one who started the restaurant) and her husband, Gérard Borck; a stylish interior; a formidable wine list of several hundred varieties — ranging in price from 40 to 900 francs (the latter a 1980 Château Yquem); and, hidden in the kitchens, there's Wilfred Travet — celebrating his 25th birthday on the day I visited in 1986.

All the pieces of the jigsaw above fit together snugly. This is one of those rare restaurants where attention to detail is in evidence from start to finish: fresh flowers, a selection of breads, super little hot appetisers — on my last visit two wooden 'spikes', one with a minuscule and spicy boudin noir and the other with a larger boudin blanc; a variety of dishes — with an emphasis on fresh fish; numerous hot and cold sweets; and a carte des cigares is just some of the evidence.

Restaurateurs who want to know just what dedication to high standards means should read and digest the fact that Christine sets off, twice a week, at 1.00 a.m. to the huge Rungis market, south of Paris; she gets back to Roye six hours later. How many British restaurateurs support their young chefs like that?

Wilfred, a local man from nearby Ham, seems particularly happy working with fish and vegetables: a salade de langoustines aux 3 epinards is just one way he shows his unusual culinary thinking — three differently cooked versions of epinard with young vegetables which included the smallest leeks I've ever seen; the latter were grown in Christine's own garden. What's also nice to see is a handful of regional dishes brought right up to date: flamiche aux poireaux of course; anguille de Somme fumée is another; and a talmouse de Maroilles is a lovely way of presenting the famous northern cheese — served hot and hidden within a triangle of puff pastry. Wilfred's only culinary 'debit' is occasional over-elaboration.

Now for that good news I promised you — and how welcome it is. Any of you with my En Route: The French Autoroute Guide will spot a new hotel, the Motel des Lions, clearly shown on the eastern side of the Roye exit on the A1. It's a modern hotel with really good-value, comfortable bedrooms. What's more important is that it's a straightforward, two-minute drive to La Flamiche with easy parking opposite the restaurant.

Finally, back to historical reality — and a grim reminder of the Somme countryside you're enjoying yourself in. Visit the memorial at Thiepval — described by Elisabeth de Stroumillo as 'Lutyens's great pink brick and white stone memorial, rearing like a fugitive bit of New Delhi' above the cemetery.

category 3 menus B-C cards AE DC V
closed 3rd week July. Last 3 wks Dec. Sun. Mon.
post pl. H. de Ville, 80700 Roye, Somme. (N of Compiègne)
phone 22 87 00 56 Mich 236 map 44 Compiègne 40 km.

TETEGHEM   La Meunerie

Very comfortable restaurant with rooms

The good news for readers is that by the spring of 1987 the Delbés should have finished work on seven new bedrooms at their restaurant. Then there will be no excuses for any of you not to visit the smart, stylish home of a thoroughly competent chef, 36-year-old Jean-Pierre Delbé, and his friendly wife, Marie-France – a proud and skilled *sommelière*, incidentally.

The couple are as good an example as any I can think of in France on that favourite hobby horse of mine – they look after the small details and inevitably the overall result is spot on. Add a friendly, unpretentious staff to culinary skills and comfortable amenities and you have an ideal formula.

What are some of the signs you should look for in the area of 'small details'? Well, the first one is when you sit down in the lounge and order an *apéritif*: three perfect appetisers appear – one of them could be a tiny wedge of *quiche Lorraine* and it's as meltingly mouthwatering as any you'll find in France. The next bit of evidence is spotted as you walk into the dining room: a vase of fresh flowers – so often overlooked at far more fancy restaurants with grand pretentions – adorns each and every table. The same can be said for the differing breads served both during the meal and with the cheese course, for the ten dainty *petits fours* and much, much else besides.

Note how the dining room, seating about 40, is divided into open-plan rooms with most tables having a view of the huge internal mill wheels which once ground flour. Prior to renovation La Meunerie was a *moulin*; once steam driven, the old mill engine lies on the grass outside the restaurant.

Why has Jean-Pierre been so liked by readers who've made the effort to find Teteghem? The evidence is plentiful – with all sorts of enterprising touches at each stage of the meal. One course, mysteriously described as *le 'petit déjeuner' aux truffes* is a stunner: a small oval-shaped dish of scrambled eggs with chopped-up truffle, three mouthful-sized hot *croissants* stuffed with 'pin-heads' of truffle, and the most pleasurable of the lot, a cup of truffle *consommé*. Cheeses from Philippe Olivier in Boulogne are numerous in number – about 20 in all: but what is unusual is that the tray includes varieties rarely seen elsewhere. Finally the score of desserts gives you the chance to try Jean-Pierre's marvellous sweets – a green apple jelly was new to me. The only debit is occasional over-elaboration.

How the culinary scene has changed in the north of France during the 80s. If you can't spare a whole week for a French holiday you can do no better than to take a long weekend break – using the rapid Hoverspeed from Dover to Boulogne, staying one night at Montreuil and then moving on to Teteghem, returning on the hovercraft from Calais to Dover. If time is really limited then try a value-for-money weekday lunch.

La Meunerie is lost in the flat, marshy terrain south-east of Dunkerque, just south of the village of Teteghem – at the junction of the D2 and D4. If the bedrooms are not ready, use the Mercure Hôtel – five miles to the west, on the D2 and just off the N225/A25 autoroute that heads south-east to Lille.
category 3 *menus* B-C *rooms* 7D (see text) *cards* AE DC V
closed Xmas-Jan. Sun evg. Mon.
post 59229 Teteghem, Nord. (Site: see text)
phone 28 26 01 80 *Mich* 236 *map* 45 Dunkerque 6 km.

CHAUVIGNY   Lion d'Or

Comfortable hotel
Good value (meals)

There's a sparkling diamond-shaped bit of countryside in Poitou which all readers should try to give some time to. The northern and southern points of the 'diamond' are Châtellerault and Lussac-les-Châteaux; the western and eastern corners are Poitiers and St-Savin. In the centre of it all is Chauvigny – overlooking the River Vienne which flows in a northerly direction, cutting the 'diamond' in two.

What's new at the Lion d'Or? The most significant change has been the addition of a modern block at the rear made up of 16 quiet, comfortable bedrooms. Cooking remains basic *Bourgeoise* with the odd regional speciality; not as good as nearby Vivonne but, nevertheless, still very sound value. Yves and Simone Chartier are friendly, helpful hosts.

The first essential detour is St-Savin. The Romanesque church is the finest example of so many in Poitou. Byzantine in origin, the astonishing interior with its frescoes and decorations is a stunning sight. Chauvigny itself is a picturesque place with several Romanesque churches and ruined castles. To the north, and on the west bank of the Vienne, are two fine châteaux: Touffou (alas, closed, but an enchantment just to look at); and Dissay (open Sundays).

South-east of Poitiers is the village of Nouaillé-Maupertuis where, on September 19, 1356, Edward, the Black Prince, won one of the outstanding English victories of the Middle Ages. There's a simple monument to the men who fell that day – the soldiers of France, Gascony and England. Follow signs on the western D142 exit that say 'Les Bordes' and 'Champ de Bataille'; the memorial was erected in 1956 – 600 years after the battle.

The real hero of the victory was Edward's general, Sir John Chandos; he was the unsung mastermind that won the day. Thirteen years later he was killed in a skirmish at Lussac; seek out the Monument Chandos which commemorates his death – it's on the west side of the Vienne, just 200 metres south of the N147. I suspect not a single Frenchman gives a second glance to the stele under a young chestnut tree; but pay your respects to one of England's greatest soldiers. (The monument was moved some years ago from its previous site nearer the river.)

category 2**(S)** *menus* **A-B** *rooms* 27**B-C** *cards* V
closed Mid Dec-mid Jan. Sat (Nov-Mar).
post 86300 Chauvigny, Vienne. (E of Poitiers)
phone 49 46 30 28 *Mich* 233 *map* 80 Poitiers 23 km.

LE GRAND-PRESSIGNY

Espérance

Simple restaurant with rooms
Good value (meals)

Winter can be a tough time for many restaurateurs. But when you are the owner of a modest, off-the-beaten-track establishment the winter months can be cruelly hard. It's an illuminating experience to talk to Bernard and Paulette Torset about their business problems. They cope – just; but they find it difficult to make sufficiently good profits to enable them to improve their simple bedrooms (no showers or baths) or other facilities. Self-help is a must at a place like the Espérance.

To grasp what that means ask Bernard to show you *le potager du restaurant*. You cross the road, dive through some bushes and then get a surprise at the sight of just how many different vegetables, herbs and soft fruits are grown in a narrow strip of ground less than 100 metres long. Bernard's father, François, looks after the kitchen garden.

Simple, humble – call the restaurant what you like. The dining rooms are small and cosy with tables a touch too close – literally. Bernard is a competent chef and puts to good use his own produce and the harvests from the neighbouring fields and streams. His pride and joy is a super speciality which he calls *œuf Zingara* – served in a small china ramekin; it's a baked egg covered with a finely-chopped mixture of truffles, mushrooms, ham and carrots.

A *sandre frais beurre d'échalote* is excellent – the sauce being a fine example of a masterful, light touch. Portions are generous – so 'weightwatchers' beware; *aiguillettes de canard au fumet rouge* served with *baies de cassis et poire au vin rouge* is too sweet and enough duck is served for three.

Cheeses, inevitably, include fresh examples of the local Ste-Maure, Ligueil, Chabris (near Selles-s-Cher) and Pouligny varieties. Desserts are above average; perhaps you'll be lucky to have some raspberries from *le potager*.

Breakfasts are a bit different from most. The bread is nothing special but Paulette takes great pleasure in telling you that the five jams are home-made: peach, cherry, plum, apricot and a tasty orange and green tomato variety.

Spare time for the numerous river valleys that abound in Poitou to the south: the tiny Claise which runs past Le Grand Pressigny; the Creuse further west – seek out the château at Guerche and the Romanesque abbey at Fontgombault, further upstream; its tributary the Gartempe with the fantastic Romanesque church at St-Savin – a must for all visitors; and the small Anglin, which flows into the Gartempe – there's a ruined castle overlooking the stream at Angles-s-Anglin.

The château at Le Grand Pressigny is a mixture of styles; there's a collection, too, of thousands of prehistoric flints and arrows. North-east of the village is Loches with its renowned Cité Médiévale – an imposing fortress. Further east, beyond the Indre, are two personal favourites: Montrésor with a château and a riverside setting on the Indrois; and the Chartreuse du Liget – a Carthusian monastery built by Henry II as an act of repentance for the murder of Thomas à Becket.

category 2 *menus* A-C *rooms* 10B *cards* AE V
closed Evgs in Jan. Mon.
post 37350 Le Grand-Pressigny, Indre-et-Loire. (SE of Tours)
phone 47 94 90 12 *Mich* 238 *map* 81 Tours 67 km.

167

ST-HILAIRE-LE-CHATEAU   du Thaurion

Comfortable restaurant with rooms

If Gérard Fanton's restaurant had the good fortune to be situated in a popular tourist area, or alternatively, if it sat alongside one of the notorious highways to the Mediterranean – well, by now, he would be considerably richer and undoubtedly he would have won his first Michelin star. But fate has made it difficult for this fourth-generation chef at the family's long-established *Logis de France*. I'll give you a vivid example of his problem: during the evening of my last visit not a single vehicle passed his front door!

Every reader should accept these two simple words of advice: just go. And stay a couple of nights because the area is rich in interest – where Mother Nature weaves a web of delicate magic and where, close at hand, is dramatic evidence of just how skilled human hands can be, too.

Gérard is 38 – born in the very house that you'll be visiting; dark-haired Marie-Christine, his young wife, is from Metz – she speaks English well. During the winter months Gérard heads for some of France's greatest restaurants where he hones his own already talented ability. I rate him as one of my favourite French chefs. He's an artist; his presentation work is an eye opener – brilliantly marrying colours, textures and culinary good taste. In his way, his eye for modern cooking and dazzling presentations matches the present-day tapestry skills you'll discover at Aubusson – more about that later on.

Despite the difficulties he has in getting produce, he cuts no corners. During the course of my meal, he served no less than nine different vegetables – bucking the trend that's so common in France these days. A *bavarois de légumes* illustrates the patience Gérard takes over his work; each of four layers of different vegetable mousse has to set before the next can be added – and the serving of three differently prepared vegetables on the plate was a clever complement. His eye for detail is seen throughout the meal – and bear in mind the only help he has is from two local boys.

A *vinaigrette de rougets aux feuilles tendres à l'huile d'olives* was another illuminating picture – the red-skinned *rouget* set off attractively by spinach, carrots and leeks; the sharpish-tasting tang of the speciality made it a refreshing course.

The couple will go out of their way to help. They own their own *étangs* (pools) nearby where you can fish to your heart's content. They can also organise some riding for you about three kilometres away; you can choose from any of three horses – all of which belong to the Fantons.

Limoges is to the west, 64 kilometres away; I need say little about the porcelain work that makes it a household name throughout the world. Aubusson is to the east – literally just down the road. In 1981 a new Musée de la Tapisserie was opened – dedicated to Jean Lurçat whose work has done so much to restore the proud traditions of the town's weavers.

The museum – with huge, purpose-built halls and superb lighting – is closed on Tuesdays; but if you can manage an hour or two on any other day during the rest of the week you'll not be disappointed. During the summer two special exhibitions are normally held; one where modern work is so spectacularly displayed (Lagrange in 1985) – the other where traditional Aubusson tapestries from earlier centuries are collected from centres all over Europe for proud display in the town's magnificent museum.

Nature, too, has much to offer – but it requires some effort on your part to accept her gift. To the south of St-Hilaire is the strangely-named Plateau de Millevaches – a tableland of countless springs; many of the great rivers that feed the Loire and the Dordogne rise there. Try the following drive – you'll need Michelin yellow map 239; it shows off the tranquil charms of the *département* of Creuse alluringly well.

Use the D34 that heads due south from St-Hilaire, climbing steadily to St-Pierre-Bellevue. The soft hills are covered in mixed woodlands; there are scores of streams; and plenty of rich pastures – where chocolate-skinned Limousin cattle munch away or, inevitably I suppose with Aubusson so close, where sheep nibble the emerald grass non-stop. The lanes will be deserted; you'll be the cause of brown hens scuttling away from the roadside and, if you're lucky, you'll catch the pine-scented aroma of a wood fire or two. Enjoy it all.

Just south of St-Pierre continue on the D58 west to St-Pardoux – then south-west to St-Martin-Château. Stop just before the latter and walk through the trees to the Cascade des Jarreaux. Continue on the D51A to Peyrat-le-Château. If you are heading south make the short detour after Treignac (42 km. south from Peyrat) to the summit of Suc May where the viewpoint called Les Monédières provides amazing views – including, to the east, the Auvergne mountains.

category **3** *menus* **B-C** *rooms* **10C** *cards* AE DC V
closed Nov-Mar. Wed & Thurs midday (not July & Aug).
post St-Hilaire-le-Château, 23250 Pontarion, Creuse. (E Limoges)
phone 55 64 50 12 *Mich* 239 *map* 82 Limoges 63 km.

VIVONNE   La Treille

Very simple restaurant with rooms
Terrace/Gardens/Good value

Vivonne is no more than a small nondescript village, some 19 kilometres south of Poitiers and with the luck of having the N10 bypassing it to the west. There must be thousands of similar villages in France – ignored by tourists hell bent on heading south to other 'attractions'. At Vivonne there are two compelling reasons for stopping a day or two: the first in the shape of an able young chef; the second is local countryside full of historical and architectural interest.

Jacquelin Monteil and his friendly wife, Geneviève, are both in their mid-thirties. Lusignan, thirteen km. to the west is their

THE VONNE at VIVONNE

169

home town and they took over the running of La Treille seven years ago; they don't own the property but hope one day to buy the freehold. If there was a prize for the establishment that presented me with the greatest amount of information on the neighbouring terrain it would undoubtedly go to this dedicated couple. Geneviève has three children – aged 13, 10 and four – but that doesn't stop her from being totally involved in the business. She truly is the most helpful girl – as many of you have pointed out. Ask her about her local *pays*.

The word 'simple' must be emphasised here – the bedrooms and dining room are very basic indeed; but that honest caveat should not stop you enjoying real value-for-money meals. The couple have an enviable regional reputation – witness the 100 or so locals who pack the place every Sunday lunchtime. Jacquelin is proud of his efforts to promote regional specialities – rightly so too; but he also provides several lighter, more modern specialities on his many menus.

So, on one hand, you have alternatives such as *escalope de saumon Angevine* – salmon topped with sorrel; *magret de canard à ma façon* – just a few slices of duck breast in a not too peppery sauce, accompanied by watercress and *pommes dauphines*. On the other hand many regional specialities will make you need *FL3* for translations. Depending on the season there's a whole host of them: *mouclade Vendéenne* – a mussel soup; *huîtres fines de claires* – large dish-shaped oysters from Marennes; *farci Poitevine* – quite magnificent here; an excellent *bouilleture d'anguilles* – an eel stew cooked in the local Haut-Poitou Sauvignon white wine; and *échine de porc à l'embeurré de chou* – the latter is crushed white-heart cabbage.

The VDQS Vins du Haut-Poitou are an example of how well the 'unknown' wines of France are made these days. The area is to the north-west of Poitiers and a host of grape types are used: Sauvignon – the Sancerre grape; Pinot-Chardonnay – popular with the English; a dry Chenin white; and a Gamay red. A recommended *viticulteur* is Robert Champalou at Marigny-Brizay, north of Poitiers and west of the A10.

Jacquelin serves an unusual *apéritif* from Provence; called Rinquinquin, it's made from peaches macerated in white wine. Alternatively, try a Pineau rouge des Charentes. He's proud, too, of his home-made *foie gras frais de canard maison* – served with a glass of Sancerre; expensive but still good value.

La Treille sits near the River Vonne; across the road is a park with walks along the stream's banks – it joins the Clain a couple of hundred metres away (see drawing). To the west of the N10 there's a walk, too, beside the Palais stream.

Within a few kilometres of Vivonne is a series of historical sites: the 500-year-old Abbey of St-Martin at Ligugé – with its double cloisters; another abbey, just east of Ligugé, at Nouaillé-Maupertuis; Lusignan with two ancient treasures – its Eglise Romane and the Maison de Bois, both dating from the 11th century; and, finally, the covered market hall at Couhé. But that list of four towns could be multiplied many times over. Please also read the entries for Chauvigny and Le Grand Pressigny – historical riches come thick and fast just one hour's drive to the east; so many of you have written singing the praises of this lovely part of France – ignored by most tourists.
category 2 *menus* A-B *rooms* 4A-B *cards* A AE V
closed 2nd & 3rd wks Jan. Wed.
post av. Bordeaux, 86370 Vivonne, Vienne. (S of Poitiers)
phone 49 43 41 13 *Mich* 233 *map* 83 Poitiers 19 km.

LES BAUX

LES BAUX-DE-PROVENCE   La Riboto de Taven

Very comfortable restaurant
Terrace/Gardens

It is impossible for me to decide which is the best time of day to visit La Riboto de Taven (the name is derived from *taven* – in Mistral's works a 'fairy' and *la riboto* – a 'feast of the table') in the Val d'Enfer below Les Baux-de-Provence. Perhaps it's at lunchtime, when the attractive garden with its colourful flowers and bushes and shady trees makes it such a pleasant place just to enjoy an *apéritif* for an hour or more. Or is it in the cool of a summer evening when, at the end of your meal, the numerous sodium floodlights are turned on in the valley – lighting up the ghostly shadows of the ruined Renaissance village perched high up on its spiny back, and also revealing the other side of the aptly-named Val d'Enfer (Valley of Hell), immediately above you, where the patchwork of stone colours on the rock faces glow with an eerie, mysterious silence?

Choose whichever time of day suits you best but be sure to beat a path to this highly-appreciated readers' favourite. Opened in 1960, its 25th anniversary in 1985 brought back happy memories for me on my last November visit: 20 years earlier Anne and I, together with our two-year-old son, Andrew, paid our first call on Marino and Louisette Novi. The restaurant had originally been a *mas* (farm) owned by Louisette's mother. In 1965 the couple's two children were just youngsters: today it will be the older of the two, pretty Christine and her husband, Philippe Thème, who will welcome you. Marino and Louisette are supposedly taking it easier now that they've reached

171

retirement age – though Monsieur Novi seems to be as busy as ever, enjoying his new job of tending the super gardens. Both Christine and Philippe speak good English.

The kitchen at the restaurant has been in the capable hands of Jean-Jacques Boissel for 15 years. His repertoire is based on a list of classical specialities – prepared and presented in a modern, light and attractive style. I could give you many examples but let me describe just three: a *minute de loup de mer à l'huile d'olives et au gros sel* is a fabulous way of enjoying some of the finest Mediterranean produce – a quickly poached fillet of sea-bass with tomatoes and courgettes and, added at the last minute at the table, some superb quality Nyons olive oil, chives and grains of sea salt; *medaillons de baudroie aux deux poivrons* – small rounds of firm-fleshed monkfish presented as a 'fan' and accompanied by two attractive sauces – red and mustard coloured (incidentally, small segments of monkfish, cooked in batter, taste just like Dublin Bay prawns); finally, an *eventail* (fan) *de magret de canard au miel et aux airelles* – where, apart from the unusual taste of honey, *airelles* and onions combining well with the duck breast, the accompanying *gratin* of potatoes, using Comté cheese as a topping, is one of the best you'll enjoy anywhere.

Little details appeal: things like the dark, sweet grapes served with the home-made *foie gras de canard* and the conventional glass of Sauternes – cold and dipped in a liqueur de Frigolet (made at the abbey just north of Tarascon) they are an intelligent contrast to the rich, fatty taste of *foie gras*; or the superb olives served with your *apéritif* – a Beaumes de Venise perhaps – where the house treatment is to soak the fruit in olive oil and then to marinate them in fresh Provençal herbs. I'll leave

you to ask what the secret ingredient is – it makes all the difference!

Enjoy the local wines; they're so much improved these days, particularly the Coteaux des Baux en Provence varieties. The Château d'Estoublon *rosé* is excellent – the property is just west of the *FL3* 'base' at Maussane – so are the reds of the Domaine de Trévallon and the Mas du Cellier – the latter owned by James Baring. Trévallon is north of the Val d'Enfer; use the D27 from the village and you'll pass, on your right, the caverns now put to such good use (see *Cathédrale d'Images*). The Mas du Cellier is south of the D99 between St-Rémy and Eygalières. Further afield is the Château de Fonsalette, near Châteauneuf-du-Pape; there, Monsieur Reynaud makes the best Côtes du Rhône white and, from the same estate, he produces a small amount of red – called La Pialade.

All these wines, plus those rather special olives and other Provençal treats can be bought from La Riboto's boutique – built a year or two ago below the overhanging rock face which, in fact, forms one wall of the shop. The Novi family face difficult times these days in France – as all restaurateurs do – and their new enterprise, together with a recently-opened wine bar in Nîmes, should help to keep the wolves from the door.

Of course you'll want to see all the man-made sites of Roman France and some of the more modern ones, too – but can I put in a word for the Camargue, please? Do give it some of your time. Enjoy the wild life: the white horses are the most famous but, in reality, they are not 'wild' at all – they are allowed by their owners to roam free for months on end in the marshes. You'll have chances to ride some of them as you'll pass many stables where the saddled horses are lined up outside ready to go. Look out, too, for the famous black bulls.

Use the 'white' roads that encircle the Etang de Vaccarés – a protected zoological and botanical reserve. For ornithologists it's a paradise: on my last visit, apart from the very common egrets and a host of other birds, I was fortunate enough to see several dozen flamingoes feeding in one of the *étangs*.

Of the dozen or so 'base' hotels recommended in *French Leave 3*, the Soleil at St-Rémy-de-Provence proved to be the most appreciated – see the entry for it. Of the others, the Van Gogh at St-Rémy and the Touret at Maussane-les-Alpilles, both modern hotels, are highly thought of; for my part I find them somewhat soulless places with the owners rather anonymous people. But they both make ideal bases from which you can explore all Provence, Alternatively, Christine and Philippe can arrange for bedrooms to be reserved in a private house just a kilometre or two away from the restaurant. If that suits you ask them to make the necessary arrangements.

Finally, let me tell you about the second of the Novi youngsters I first saw back in 1965 – Jean-Pierre, Christine's younger brother. Now 32, he and his wife, Claire, have established themselves well at their Restaurant Provence in Southbourne, Bournemouth – after a very difficult opening spell. Value-for-money, light classical cooking is Jean-Pierre's forte. If you cannot head all the way south to the real Provence then I can think of no better substitute than paying the couple a call – for a taste of the sunny south in chilly England.

category **3** *menus* **C-D** *cards* AE DC V
closed Jan. Feb. Sun evg (out of season). Mon.
post Les Baux-de-Provence, 13520 Maussane-les-Alpilles, B.-du-R.
phone 90 97 34 23 *Mich* 245 *map* 84 Avignon 30 km. to N

CATHÉDRALE D'IMAGES

CATHEDRALE D'IMAGES

French Leave 3 readers will already know of the great square chambers cut out of solid limestone that lie just north of Les Baux on the D27. John Brown, my old rallying *copain*, described them as 'fantastic stone quarries; you can even drive into some of them – one after another, like the inside of a palace, cool and shadowy!' I copied the drawing (see page 173) from a photograph that Anne and I took in the autumn of 1983; it will give you an idea of the scale of the vast chambers – dozens of them interlinked with each other.

Last year saw the limestone quarries given a new name – 'Cathédrale d'Images'; and what an unusual new use they are now being put to. The brainchild of Albert Plécy, it's an audiovisual spectacle where the giant walls of fine white limestone are the perfect screen for the images flashed on them from 32 Kodak Carousel projectors. The use of mirrors, computers and a cleverly integrated stereo music system adds to the interest. You walk from one chamber to another, and the 'show' of 2,500 transparencies takes 35 minutes to complete; huge images are projected on to walls, ceilings and even floors. During the period the *cathédrale* has been used for its new lease of life, subjects chosen have ranged from 'Egypt' and 'India' to the elements like 'Fire' and 'Water' and themes such as 'The Heavens on Fire'. A reader wrote to say that 'the idea is good but it is poorly presented': perhaps, but give it a try nevertheless. The enterprising project deserves support.

Since long before the time of the Romans, man has used the limestone from the Alpilles' quarries – its dazzling whiteness can be seen in buildings as far apart as Geneva and Marseille.

174

COTIGNAC/FOX-AMPHOUX   Auberge du Vieux Fox

Comfortable restaurant with rooms
Secluded/Terrace/Good value (meals)

This gem has proved to be a much appreciated favourite with readers – despite many personal setbacks which the new Belgian owner, Jean-Charles Martha, had in the years immediately after he took over with his wife in 1983. Alas, she has been seriously ill and is now unable to play any further part in the running of the business. Nevertheless, my visit was one of the real surprises during my travels preparing this new book; the improvements that Jean-Charles has made are to be applauded and all of you should make the effort to share the special pleasures of this endearing hill-top village and its inn.

Perched on a wooded hill, it's easy to understand why the tiny village of Fox-Amphoux was always of strategic importance. The church dates from the 11th century – built by the Templiers who settled in Cotignac, Aups and Fox-Amphoux. The Auberge was once the presbytery of the church; parts of it are 900 years old – the rest was built in the 16th century. Ask to see the cellar of the old building – originally used as a water storage 'tank' by the priests; now it houses a lounge. Until 1955 the building was used as a school – old desks and benches double as tables in some bedrooms.

Between the two wars this century the village fell into serious disrepair; roofs were deliberately taken off buildings when owners left the village so that they could escape rates and taxes – a similar problem these days with factories in the industrial wastelands of Britain. Slowly the houses are now being

restored and Jean-Charles has done as much as anyone to speed that progress on its way; an expensive process it is too.

A magnificent new heating system is one example; the sympathetic addition of a terrace at the rear is another; the modern kitchens married with the intelligent use of old cellars for keeping food fresh and wines at an even temperature are others. The blocking off of most of the eight doors into the dining room is a change for the better – as is the cheerful fire; so, too, is a lot of sensible insulation and the smart new terrace furniture. Most bedrooms, small and modest, have baths or showers – and the German-made heating system keeps them all warm and provides plenty of instant hot water.

Unusually, the Auberge (remember it was once the presbytery) still sits cheek by jowl with the ancient church. Its bell incidentally is reputed to be about the only one that escaped Napoléon's edict that all church bells should be melted down to make cannons. Why? A modest house in the village was the birthplace, in 1755, of Paul de Barras – later to be made a *comte* and the *Directeur* of the Republic; it was he who saved that single Louis XI bell! (Light sleepers should note that the bell tolls the hours through the night.)

Jean-Charles speaks fluent English. No wonder – as, shortly before I left, I discovered he had played a highly significant role in establishing the Ford Motor Company's initial participation in motor sport during the 60s. He was the Competition Manager for Ford International for many years and he has a fund of stories which will interest any reader who shares my passion for both motor rallying and motor sport.

Another major change at the Auberge has been the arrival of 26-year-old Jean-Marc Perochon and his wife, Sylvie; he's a young, English-speaking chef from the Vendée, who worked in Scotland for a spell. Not surprisingly he loves working with fish. It was a revelation for me to examine the newly-arrived insulated cartons of fish; they had travelled overnight from Boulogne and the contents were as fresh as daisies.

His sensible short menus provide a marriage of modern and traditional styles – with an emphasis on fresh fish specialities: *filets de sole à l'étuve de légumes*, a *panaché de mousse de St-Jacques fraîches de carottes*, *lotte aux senteurs Provençales* and an *escalope de saumon* are a few of the possible offerings.

175

Meat alternatives could include a *filet de bœuf aux cèpes, côtes d'agneau aux airelles* or a *magret de canard.*

The entry for Tourtour suggests many places you should see in the neighbourhood of Fox-Amphoux. But one must – wherever you stay in Provence or the Côte d'Azur – is a tour of the Grand Canyon du Verdon. Starting at the western end near Moustiers Ste-Marie, I suggest the circuit is made in a **clockwise** direction – because then the gorge is always on your right-hand side and this makes it easier to park your car at the many viewpoints and it helps passengers to get fine views. The gorge is surprisingly heavily wooded with deciduous trees; in the late autumn it's a luminous, spellbinding sight.

When you reach La Palud be certain to use the 23 km. Route des Crêtes; this circuit brings you practically back to the village. Soon after, immediately after you pass the Point Sublime, turn right down the short dead-end road to the Couloir Samson. At the Pont de Soleils head south, via Trigance, to join the Corniche Sublime: a series of spectacular viewpoints follow – at the Balcons de la Mescla, the Pont de l'Artuby, the Pilon de Fayet, Les Baouchets (walk the latter two sections on foot) and the Col d'Iloire. At many points on the circuit the Verdon River is nearly 2000 ft below you; it requires little imagination to visualise the astonishing views you have from the viewpoints. Serious walkers are well catered for – but I cannot stress enough that the paths are only for those of you who are well equipped and who understand the risks.

category 2 *menus* **A-B** *rooms* 10**B** *cards* AE V
closed Jan-mid Feb. Mon (mid Sept-June).
post Fox-Amphoux, 83670 Barjols, Var. (11 km. N of Cotignac)
phone 94 80 71 69 *Mich* 245 *map* 85 Draguignan 37 km.

COTIGNAC   Lou Calen

Comfortable hotel
Quiet/Terrace/Gardens/Pool/Good value (meals)

Pull the front door open and step inside. To your right, above the foot of the stairs, is an intriguing portrait – painted by a Yugoslav artist. The painting has all the clarity of a photograph – yet it's far more captivating. It's a breathtaking likeness of Huguette Caren, the owner of Lou Calen, as she was some five years ago. Now in her early forties, she continues to capture the hearts of her many appreciative clients.

Cotignac, too, in its own quiet way, also captures the hearts of all visitors to the town; it's one of many in the *département* of Var that retains its Provençal character without commercial intrusions of any sort. It has the good fortune to nestle in a hollow – protected from the harsh northern winds by a sizeable wall of rock behind it and wooded hills to the east and west. To feel the spirit of the place – before you seek out the hotel – drive up to the sanctuary called Notre Dame de Grâces, one km. to the south-west. Shaded by pines – smell their perfume – and encircled by a small, terraced garden, the chapel provides a panoramic view to the south and of the town sitting below you to the east. Then descend to the long shaded *place* in the village where you'll find Lou Calen at its southern end.

The hotel has character and unassuming charm. Many readers have commented on the bedrooms and suites; one of the latter, number six, has its own spiral staircase and a wooden gallery which doubles as a bedroom. The terrace is shaded, faces south and has the advantage of being high above the

A Provençal *mas* on the slopes of the Montagne du Lubéron

Denis Pannett.

Denis Parrett

swimming pool. It's the perfect place for an outdoor summer lunch; but the dining room, with its roaring log fire, is an equally welcome place to be on chilly spring and autumn evenings.

Cooking is of a modest standard with particular efforts being made to promote regional specialities: dishes like *soupe des poissons de roches* and a hearty *soupe pistou*; *pieds et paquets à la Provençale*; *jambon cru d'Aups*; *baudroie à la Raimu*; and a *daube a l'ancienne*. Otherwise choose from conventional *Bourgeoise* alternatives – fare such as *filet de bœuf, faux filet grillé* and *côtes d'agneau*. One super little sweet is apple fritters looking like a bunch of grapes, stalk and all, with a strongly-perfumed spray of acacia flowers as an accompanying touch. Another good idea was bread made with black olives and specially cooked in wood-fired ovens.

Americans will be interested to know that a Palm Springs Lou Calen is now open; designed by Huguette's husband and son – both architects. Provençal in style and concept let's hope it proves to be a great success.

There's so much to see and enjoy in the neighbourhood. Read about it in the entries for Tourtour and Fox-Amphoux; the advice given there applies just as much to Cotignac. Of the local towns Aups is my favourite – famous for its truffles, ham and with a particularly large, shaded *place*; Salernes is renowned for the manufacture of coloured enamel tiles – you can visit factories and showrooms located in and around the town. Give the area a day or two of your time.

category 2**(S)** *menus* **A-B** *rooms* 17**C-D** *cards* A AE V
closed Nov-Feb. Rest only: Thurs.

post Cotignac, 83570 Carcès, Var. (W of Draguignan)
phone 94 04 60 40 *Mich* 245 *map* 86 Draguignan 36 km.

Market day at St-Rémy-de-Provence

ST-REMY-DE-PROVENCE   Soleil

Comfortable hotel
Quiet/Gardens/Swimming pool

Of the 13 Provençal 'base' hotels recommended in *French Leave 3*, this is the one that was most consistently appreciated by readers. And no wonder: an oldish building – tucked well away from the road; a sun-trap swimming pool and shaded terrace; a front gate locked every night – which means cars are well protected; and, best of all, caring owners that take a pride in their craft and in looking after clients from all over Europe.

It's a flourishing family affair. Joseph and Marguerite Denante opened the Soleil in 1965; and, today, those young ladies helping at breakfast time are their grown-up daughters, Françoise and Isabelle – I remember them as young girls when I first met them a dozen or so years ago.

One hundred metres away is a modern Office de Tourisme; pay it a call and leave armed with plenty of literature detailing all the local sights. There's something to occupy you every day – even if you stayed two weeks; this is what a good 'base' should be. But, before brief mention is made of places to visit away from St-Rémy, give an hour or two of your time to walking the town's narrow streets. Two businesses will interest you: the shop called *L'Herbier de Provence* is full of heady aromas (it's about 100 metres to the north of the hotel – round the corner); and the Lilamand 'factory' (it's hardly that) where every possible variation of *fruits confits* is made on site.

Of the more famous Provençal attractions, include on your travels Arles, Nîmes, the Camargue, Les Baux, the Roman excavations at Glanum (half a mile down the road from the hotel), Avignon, Pont du Gard, the hill-top villages on the northern slopes of the Lubéron, Fontaine-de-Vaucluse, Vaison-la-Romaine, Orange and Aix-en-Provence.

French Leave 3 readers will know I had my doubts about including the Oustaù de Baumanière. I revisited it again last year and, to be honest, I would not now recommend it, despite its fame and the top rating it gets from Michelin.

The latter are being unfair to their readers and to Raymond Thuilier's grandson, Jean-André Charial. Thuilier is well into his eighties; Charial less than half that age. Jean-André, who now controls the kitchens, has brought a new look to the list of specialities – the menus are full of modern, lighter dishes. But his high standards deserve no more than a modest second star; if he was establishing himself elsewhere that's all he would win – let's be realistic about it. From start to finish every aspect of the meal is equalled or bettered by the two-star chefs elsewhere in this guide. The wine list is incomparable: the choice is massive – from a Gigondas 50-franc half-bottle to a 5,000-franc magnum of 61 Château Lafite-Rothschild.

The restaurant is always packed; 100 or so guests at one sitting are far too many. It's also now very expensive; unusually, both the offered set meals equal the sum of their parts on the à la carte menu! And I found the cigarette smoke was terribly irritating; it seemed to me that half the diners were puffing away. Go if you must – but ask yourself why are you doing so?

category **1** *menus* No rest. *rooms* 15**B-C** *cards* AE V
closed Mid Nov-Jan. (S of Avignon)
post av. Pasteur, 13210 St-Rémy-de-Provence, B.-du-R.
phone 90 92 00 63 *Mich* 245 *map* 87 Avignon 21 km.

Eygalières, south-east of St-Rémy-de-Provence

SALON-DE-PROVENCE   Robin

Comfortable restaurant

Salon-de-Provence and Nostradamus (famed for his predictions made over 400 years ago) are inextricably linked in all sorts of ways: there's a museum; buildings are named after him – as is a *boulevard*; so is the camping site; and, inevitably, many a dish served in restaurants bears his name. So don't be surprised if lurking somewhere on Francis Robin's menus is a speciality dedicated to the renowned *médecin* (Nostradamus was born in 1503 at nearby St-Rémy-de-Provence and is buried in the church of St-Laurent at Salon).

Francis, now 38, and his gentle wife, Christiane, are a modest, unassuming couple. Like all restaurateurs in France during the last few years they've had a tough time – depending very much on tourists because, during the off-peak months, there's many an evening when perhaps only two French clients turn up. Austerity has hit the French restaurant industry hard. Nevertheless, the couple stick to high standards and, despite many difficulties, they don't cut corners. That's something that cannot be said of all leading French chefs.

You see it in little details. With your *apéritif* come five different tiny hot pastries – together with a home-made *boudin* and some black olives. At the end of the meal you can choose from perhaps 30 or so remarkably fresh cheeses and 20 or more desserts – of all kinds. It would be easy to cut down on those important touches (all of them beat their equivalents at Oustaù de Baumanière); with five staff in the kitchen and two waiters in the dining rooms you could hardly blame the couple if they did.

Francis is lucky to be immediately next door to one of the best cheese shops in France – the *fromagerie* of Gérard Paul. He's a *Maître Fromagier de France* and you can see why when you enter his refrigerator-cool *magasin* – a veritable treasure-chest of all France's great cheeses. Don't miss visiting the cheese *cave* and be sure, too, to try as many of the individual cheeses on offer at the restaurant: ask for a minute *bouchée* of each – treat it as a *dégustation*. Buy your favourites later.

Francis was born in Lesparre-Médoc, north-west of Pauillac, and surrounded by the great Bordeaux red wine country. That will explain why he features Médoc wines so proudly on his list – though in no way does he turn his back on the best Provençal vintages: among them a Château de la Bégude (east of Aix-en-Provence and just off the N7), the inevitable Château Simone (near Aix), and a Château de Vignelaure (near Rians). A new delight for me was a Bandol red – Domain de Terrebrune.

I think Francis is happiest when he's working with fish. You'll be offered all sorts of variations on the three menus and the à la carte list: *saumon cru à l'aneth et les concombres à la crème*, *soupe de crustaces et St-Jacques avec son bouillon de ravioles aux herbes* (the latter – made with herbs and *fromage de chèvre* – are minuscule), a *poisson du jour suivant le marché*, *gâteau de lottes en gelée de vin blanc* and a *civet de homard au Banyuls* (the dark red Roussillon wine) are examples.

Meat dishes are not ignored. The chef makes excellent use of the red Bégude wine in many specialities – it regularly appears in sauces. Lamb is available, too – but, frankly I have never thought much of the local Alpilles' *agneau*; it wasn't that good on my last visit to Salon – but even that was 100 per cent better than the truly awful, stringy meat I was served at the Hiely restaurant in Avignon a year or two earlier.

It pays to ask Francis what specialities are new – his eyes light up as he quietly tells you about his latest experiments. One such case is the lobster stew in the Banyuls red wine sauce. The compulsory bib and finger bowl are absolutely necessary as you tuck in with 'nut grinders' and 'pick'; the dark sauce means it's a messy business – but it's good.

Another new touch during my last meal was a *sorbet* served after the lobster; made from lemons and drenched in a teaspoon of Suze – a *gentian*-based French *apéritif*.

For guests wanting to stay overnight I would recommend the simple Sélect-Hôtel – just 200 metres away. Alternatively, use the Soleil at St-Rémy – allow about 35 minutes to make the drive to Salon. And if any of you are keen to employ, on a daily basis, one of three young ladies as interpreter-guides, then the following are highly recommended by the Robins: Christine Coulomb 42 55 34 34; Christiane Glaize 90 42 15 29 – the wife of one of the waiters; and Myriam Guichard 90 82 34 87. The three speak several languages and know their *pays* well. It could be an interesting way of enjoying the local terrain.

One final tip for those of you looking for excellent quality olive oil – at bargain prices. On the road from St-Rémy to Salon you'll pass through a small village called Mouriès. On the Salon side, just past the Esso garage, turn right for the *Moulin à huile d'olives coopératif* – it's open on Wednesday and Saturday afternoons and Sunday mornings. Take a container!
category 3 *menus* B-C *rooms* See text *cards* A AE DC V
closed Feb. Sun evg & Mon. (NW of Aix-en-Provence)
post 1 bd. G.-Clemenceau, 13300 Salon-de-Provence, B.-du-R.
phone 90 56 06 53 *Mich* 245 *map* 88 Aix-en-Provence 35 km.
180

TAVEL Host. du Seigneur

Simple restaurant with rooms
Terrace/Good value

Mention Tavel to any wine 'buffs' and they will immediately associate what is a very unpretentious Provençal village with the world-renowned *rosé*, reckoned to be the best in France. Ange and Juliette Bodo put the celebrated *rosé* to good use at their 15th-century restaurant: in the house *apéritif* where it's mixed with Campari and a Martini *rouge* and served with morish black olives from Nyons; or at the end of a meal when one of several simple desserts, *pruneaux au vin de Tavel*, is an even more delicious way of showing off the wine's versatility.

And, of course, any meal at the Hostellerie wouldn't be complete without a bottle of the fruity *rosé*; at the Bodo restaurant it will most likely be a Corne Loup, bottled by Jacques Lafond. If it's to your liking then it's a simple matter indeed to buy some bottles as his *cave* is ten yards away on the other side of the place du Seigneur – the latter, the hotel car park, is the smallest *place* you'll encounter in France. The terrace incidentally is only big enough for two tables – though I've seen the same *place* used as an extension to the *terrasse*.

Don't expect miracles of any sort at this modest, homely little place. Juliette will give you a friendly welcome and Ange will prepare the most basic of dishes: fare like *filet de turbot à la crème, saumon froid mayonnaise* or *jambon cuit braisé* as first courses – followed by alternatives such as *cuisse de lapin au vin blanc, agneau grillé aux herbes* and finishing off with cheese and a simple sweet. It's that basic.

My last meal was a starter of *saucisson chaud aux lentilles* – a Cévennes sausage cooked in a *pot-au-feu* and bearing absolutely no resemblance to the 'plastic' variety you often find in French supermarkets these days; the *lentilles* were a *gris* variety from Le Puy, rather than the better-known green lentils for which the Massif Central town is famous. The second course was a *langue de porcelet au poivre vert*: it was a big helping – offered on separate dishes so that you could serve yourself a second big plateful; accompanying vegetables were a modest *ratatouille* and a *gratin Dauphinois*.

Cheeses usually number six or seven alternatives: three *chèvre* varieties – a *frais*, a *demi-sec* and a *sec*; Brie, Camembert, Reblochon and a Bleu de Bresse are typical examples. As with all French cheeses it's best to eat them in the correct order if you try several tiny portions; taking the earlier seven as an example, taste them in the order in which I described them – the 'strongest' must always come last.

Ange and Juliette, both of whom hail from Nice, are proud of their 'exhibition' of paintings in the dining room and bar; painted by local artists, all friends of the couple, every one of the colourful works is naturally for sale.

Within a few minutes drive are many of the most famous Roman Provençal sights: Pont du Gard, Nîmes, Arles and Avignon among them. So for those of you on a tight budget, the Bodo restaurant *avec chambres* (the rooms don't have showers or baths) makes a bargain base.

category 2(S) *menus* A-B *rooms* 7A-B *cards* A
closed Dec-mid Jan. Thurs.
post 30126 Tavel, Gard. (NW of Avignon)
phone 66 50 04 26 *Mich* 245 *map* 89 Avignon 14 km.

TOURTOUR
Chênes Verts

Comfortable restaurant

If nothing else, Paul Bajade is a single-minded individual. In the past I've worried about his financial well-being. I asked myself: would he survive at his isolated site? His restaurant is not exactly on a busy tourist route; four km. from Villecroze, on the D51 towards Tourtour, you are certain to pass Chênes Verts as the sign is barely readable. The small villa has two floors: Paul lives downstairs and the dining room above seats 20 at the most. More than ten years have passed since Paul, then in his early thirties, set up home at Tourtour.

He has survived the gamble. He's a happy, contented man and, I suspect, would absolutely hate the pressures of dealing

AIGUINES

Aiguines – see Grand Canyon du Verdon map

with 50–100 clients at any one sitting. In the evening you're likely to be on your own or, at most, one of eight or so diners. His present-day confidence shows in various ways: he's building a separate house for himself alongside the minute car park; he now employs a first-class young maître d'hôtel and also a smart apprentice waiter; and he has the help of a couple of youngsters in the kitchen. But it's Madeleine, his pretty girlfriend, who has helped him most I suspect. Her light, feminine touch is clear to see; for example each table has its vase of numerous wild and cultivated flowers. Let's hope Paul pops the question soon.

Paul's a talented chef. His two set menus include a fair selection of dishes that show off his skills: *saumon sauvage à l'huile vierge du pays en croqu'au sel*, *rosace de St-Jacques au beurre de crustaces*, *selle d'agneau de Sisteron en noisette à la fleur de thym* and a *parfait glace au miel du pays et la sauce au chocolat* are typical creations. But on my last visit I decided to ignore the menus and, instead, I selected just one à la carte speciality plus one sweet; their prices added up to the cost of a fixed-price menu. Both dishes were superb — two of the

greatest pleasures you could ever enjoy. What were they? First a *millefeuille de foie gras chaud aux truffes d'Aups*; two wafer-thin squares of pastry and, sandwiched between them, a small hot *foie gras de canard* and thinly-sliced rounds of a local, and famed, black truffle from Aups. The aroma and stunning delicacy of the dish is still a mouthwatering memory. (Paul knows his truffles — that's for sure; he's even having a go 'cultivating' his own!) The sweet was a *gratin* of wild strawberries with a perfect *crème Anglaise* — the perfect foil for that opening sensation. It was a classic example of where it paid to ignore the many dishes served on a menu and, instead, spending the same number of francs on just two dishes.

How the Côtes de Provence wines have improved. Try the best of them: Château Vignelaure — from Rians (to the west); Domaine Ott *cuvée speciale* — the map identifies the property north of Taradeau (to the south-east); Château Ste-Roseline — between Draguignan and Les Arcs (to the south-east); and Domaine de la Bernarde — from Le Luc (due south).

Paul, now 42, will take your order and will chat happily with you after the meal; you'll see how contented he is with his lot. Tourtour, the 'village in the sky', suffered terrible forest fires a few years ago and they literally reached the restaurant's doorstep! Seek out the village with its vast panorama — even Mont Ventoux, far to the north-west, can be seen on a clear day. But don't pass this way without paying Paul a visit. Use the modest Le Vieux Moulin (*sans restaurant*) as an overnight 'base': Villecroze, 83690 Salernes, phone 94 70 63 35. Alternatively use one of the Cotignac entries.

The northern corners of Var hide many delights — created both by man and Nature. Like their counterparts to the east of

Draguignan, the villages are a treat: Aups is as nice as any with a glorious shaded *place* and narrow streets; Cotignac has the advantage of no through traffic; Barjols (sorry about the missing 'B' on the map) and Salernes are to the west. But two smaller villages should be on your list: the tiny hill-top hamlet of Fox-Amphoux and Entrecasteaux, 12 km. to the south.

The part 11th/part 17th-century château at Entrecasteaux (dominating the village and best seen from the D50 across the Bresque Valley) is a revelation. Lovingly restored from a derelict state by the late Ian McGarvie-Munn, today his children continue to keep it open and it's an interesting place. All sorts of exhibits are on show. It's also the family home; when you enter you pass through their modern kitchen. You are just as likely to see, as I did, their St-Bernard and Yorkshire terriers sharing a drink from the terrace fountain – a clear idea of the spirit of the château. (Open every day – 10.00 to 18.00.) In August many concerts are organised where artists from all over the world perform. See, too, the Cistercian abbey at Thoronet – a 12th-century creation of simple beauty.

Nature complements the bricks and mortar built by man. Endless vineyards, myriad trees, wild flowers everywhere and the heady perfume of herb-scented air beguile you. On your way to the Verdon make the 15-minute walk from the junction of the D560 and D22 (midway between Cotignac and Salernes) to see the waterfall at Sillans – where the River Bresque cascades over a high, wooded cliff.

category 3 *menus* C *rooms* See text
closed Jan-mid Feb. Sun evg. Mon. (W of Draguignan)
post rte Villecroze, Tourtour, 83690 Salernes, Var.
phone 94 70 55 06 *Mich* 245 *map* 90 Draguignan 20 km.

ARTEMARE   Vieux Tilleul

Simple hotel
Quiet/Terrace/Good value (meals)

"It's all very well," I can hear you say, "but we have to make every penny count, Mr Binns." I understand – much more than you may at first realise.

Are you prepared then to get off the beaten track? If the answer is "Yes" then I can promise you an endless cascade of treats at this unpretentious hotel. Not the least of the benefits is that you'll not break the bank when it comes to settling the bill; you can hardly find better value anywhere.

So where is Artemare – or to be more precise the tiny hamlet of Luthézieu? Both are in the heart of a largely-ignored circle of country called Bugey; enclosed, to the east and south, by the River Rhône, to the west by the River Ain and to the north by the nearly completed A40 autoroute from Bourg-en-Bresse to Geneva. Wooded peaks, roughly-hewn gorges, many waterfalls and, at its very centre, a plateau of unspoiled terrain renowned for the independent-minded folk who inhabit a series of small villages. Not surprisingly the whole area was a major-stronghold of the Resistance during the last war.

Before you book in at the hotel climb the D8 road a couple of kilometres to the west and stop at the handsome monument to the patriots who died fighting the Germans. You'll notice the inscription refers to the *maquis* of Valromey. That's the country you see below you – stretching from north to south. What an inspired choice the site is for an everlasting reminder to the brave fighters of Valromey. (There's a bigger monument to the

Resistance heroes of Bugey on the N84, above Cerdon.)

You'll be warmly welcomed at the hotel by Paul and Charlotte Pras (Paul is the 'President' of the monument). Years ago Charlotte did all the cooking but these days the couple leave the running of the *logis* to their two friendly sons: Michel, who speaks a little English, is the *patron* and his younger brother, Jean Paul, is the competent *cuisinier*.

Guests can choose from four menus and an à la carte list. The highlights for me are usually the *lavaret du lac à l'oseille* and a *poulet fermier aux morilles*. The former is a freshwater fish, the size of a small trout and usually caught in the nearby Lac du Bourget; the accompanying sorrel sauce is a perfect partner for the delicate flesh of the *lavaret*. The *poulet*, inevitably, comes from the Bresse country to the west; local *morilles* combine to make it a classic regional dish.

Choosing your wine is a real pleasure. Ignore the household names and plump for the wines of Bugey; few are made and even fewer travel beyond the boundaries of the nearby towns. They are ridiculously cheap and are of excellent quality. The 'champion' is a *pétillant naturel* Cerdon – a sparkling rosé that cannot fail to please. Alternatives could be a white Chardonnay or a red Mondeuse (both grape types); these are supplied by Camille Crussy from the nearby village of Flaxieu – the great Alain Chapel, at Mionnay, is another contented buyer of the same wines. If you insist on going further afield by trying a Savoie wine then relish the best of them all – a Seyssel Clos de la Peclette white, made from the Roussette grape (the vineyard, on Bugey soil, is on the eastern slopes of the huge Grand Colombier mountain wall you can see to the east from the terrace). The Peclette makes an ideal *apéritif*: why not try it on the very same shaded terrace – finishing it off with your meal?

I promised you a cascade of treats; you could stay two weeks and not exhaust the possibilities. First you may want to try a game of *boules* – the hotel has its own 'green' on the other side of the road. Just west of Artemare is a real cascade at Cerveyrieu and, further afield, south-west of Hauteville-Lompnes, there's a magnificent *chute* where the Albarine falls a considerable distance on its journey towards the Rhône. Three miles east of the hotel is the minute hamlet of Vieu; the legendary Brillat-Savarin (author of *La Physiologie du gout* – a paperback is available in English, *The Philosopher in the Kitchen*) had his summer house there. He was born in Belley where you can see his birthplace in the Grande Rue.

North-east of the hotel is the village of Lochieu where there's an interesting rural folk museum that explains the life of the Valromey people over the centuries. Visit it on your way to the summit of the Grand Colombier – an absolute 'must' for all visitors. A fantastic panorama greets you at the 5000 ft summit: the Alps to the east, the lakes of Geneva, Annecy (the northern end) and Bourget and, far below you, the vitally important River Rhône and its Siamese twin – a man-made canal.

So much more awaits you: the tranquil woods and lakes of the Jura hills to the north and the joys of the Alps to the east. Read the neighbouring entries and, if you have copies, refer to *Hidden France* and *France à la carte* for details of numerous attractions guaranteed to fill every day with pleasure.
category 2(**S**) *menus* A-C *rooms* 11**B**
closed Jan. Tues evg & Wed (not during the summer).
post Luthézieu, Artemare, 01260 Champagne, Ain. (N of Belley)
phone 79 87 64 51 *Mich* 244 *map* 91 Belley 25 km.

CHAMONIX   Auberge du Bois Prin

Very comfortable hotel
Secluded/Terrace/Gardens/Lift

If there is one hotel site in Europe that I would implore you to seek out perhaps more than any other then it must be the Auberge du Bois Prin. Marcel and Andrée Carrier chose the site for their ten-year-old chalet with great care; at least seven generations of Marcel's family have lived in the Chamonix valley and he knew as well as anyone where they should build their second hotel. So, why do I ask you to head for the Auberge – or, more specifically, to its seductive, small terrace?

Across the valley, towering above you, is the snow-covered dome of Mont Blanc – glaciers tumbling down its northern face – and the razor-sharp 'needles' of several *aiguilles*, set in a jagged line across the southern horizon: there's no view in Europe which is more certain to make my neck tingle, my cheeks flame with excitement, and my pulse beat faster. Consider the 'arithmetic' of the setting: the mountain wall looming above you rises nearly four kilometres from the sun-trap terrace; yet it's only five to eight kilometres away. Only in the Himalayas can you better that sort of cold, hard statistic!

For me mountains are most certainly anything but statistics. I lived most of my early life in the high Himalayas; before I was ten I had seen most of the range's mighty peaks – from Kashmir to Darjeeling. Frank Smythe was my first 'hero' – someone I wanted to emulate; I suspect that I have had a chained-up ambition all my life to be a mountaineer. But, in my teens, motor sport took its place – and see where that has led me. Indirectly, without that passionate interest in motoring, not one of my books would have ever seen the light of day.

I pray that you have fine weather when you visit Chamonix. There's nothing better than seeing the early-morning sun awakening the eastern flanks of the mysterious dome; and then, slowly but surely, as midday approaches, the entire mass of Mont Blanc is brightly illuminated – its icy slopes shining with a dazzling intensity. Or is it more alluring in the evening when the setting sun bathes the vertical rock faces and the vast banks of ice and snow with an intense orange and pink light? If you cannot afford to stay in any of the chalet's bedrooms, don't worry; try a lunch (which is not dear) or a simple drink, coffee or tea on the flower-bedecked terrace of the Auberge.

Sit and relax: study the towering mountain curtain above you. To the far left is the sharp pyramid tooth of the legendary Aiguille du Dru (silhouetted by the even higher Aiguille Verte – a *trompe-l'œil*); you may remember seeing live TV coverage of the fearsome climb. Travelling right you'll see a 'molar' formed like a letter 'M'. To its right are two more 'needles': the right-hand one, set further back, is the Aiguille du Grépon. Much of this terrain is linked with Edward Whymper. It was this climber, together with local guides and other British colleagues, men like Wills, Smith, Hudson, Mummery and Forbes, who made most of the first Alpine climbs in the 19th century.

Anne and I were not surprised in the least to hear that the two Carrier hotels proved to be such big successes with readers. I first saw the Chamonix Valley nearly 40 years ago – alas, man has changed it materially during that time span – and Anne has accompanied me there often during the last three decades. Our children, too, have stayed at the Albert 1er many times since they were toddlers. To be with Marcel and Andrée is like being in your own home: you know what I mean – you have that contented feel of being at one with yourself and the world at large. Both Anne and I are always happy to return.

These days the couple are taking it a lot more easily. Denis, the elder of the Carrier's two sons, together with Monique, his wife, look after the Auberge. You will be interested to know it was Denis and Marcel who did much of the wood carving in the chalet: look for example at the pine beam in the dining room where you'll notice that the carving tells you it was 1976 when the building was finished. Denis has little spare time away from his stoves – but you're certain to see him complete more carvings at the Auberge du Bois Prin year by year.

Denis and his brother, Pierre, have given Marcel the job of looking after the vegetable garden; you'll spot it alongside the entrance drive to the chalet. Andrée keeps an eye on her two daughters-in-law and now finds more time to attend to her great interest, flower arranging. Joking apart, I know for sure that both of them will ensure that high standards are maintained at both hotels – and Marcel, particularly, will be on hand to give Denis a lot of help in the Auberge's kitchens. Denis, unlike Pierre, has only recently taken to cooking and has much experience to gain before he can ever match his younger brother's skills. There's an inexpensive set menu served every day – with no choice – and a list of classical specialities for which Marcel was once famous: dishes like *terrine de foie de canard maison*, *omble chevalier*, *tournedos aux morilles* and mouthwatering *pâtisseries*. Try the truly authentic *farçon Savoyard* and then ask Madame for the recipe of the mouthwatering dish; you can enjoy it at home.

Andrée has four children and, at the time of writing this, eight grandchildren – all girls: perhaps by now the first grandson will have arrived? But one thing is guaranteed: the Carrier family will continue to give a great deal of pleasure to everyone who seeks out either of their two Chamonix hotels.

Bois Prin is a small luxurious chalet; the eleven bedrooms face south and nine of them have terraces – all clients can share the eye-boggling view. As all terraces face south, if you are after a tan, you can laze away in your own sun-trap. But then the sun doesn't always shine in high mountain country! There's never a 'dull' day however in Chamonix; read the other entry for suggestions of things to do, but for the keen walkers among you, who don't want to attempt anything too demanding, then try the following walks; take picnic lunches.

Walk south-west from the Auberge to Merlet where, apart from the stunning views, the dividend is the sight of many mountain animals in a small reserve. The second walk starts after you ride the *téléférique* and *télécabine* to the terminus at L'Index; head north-east to Lac Blanc and then descend to the intermediate station at La Flegère. Neither walk is difficult.

Finally, clients staying at the Bois Prin can use the swimming pool and tennis facilities at the Albert 1er – and, of course, there's nothing to stop them trying Pierre's cooking.

(A caveat for those of you who do visit the Val Ferret (see next page): if there's snow on the ground, don't park in it and get stuck; a couple took me to task because they did just that!)
category 2 *menus* B *rooms* 11 D-D2 *cards* AE DC V
closed May. Mid Oct-mid Dec. Rest: Wed (out of season).
post Moussoux, 74400 Chamonix-Mont-Blanc, Haute-Savoie.
phone 50 53 33 51 *Mich* 244 *map* 92

WHYMPER

Edward Whymper, apart from being such a fearless pioneering climber, was also a superb engraver. Thirty years ago I spent more than 150 hours, over 12 months, copying a postcard-sized Whymper engraving of the Grandes Jorasses. I expanded his engraving ten-fold; it was my present to Anne to celebrate her 21st birthday. It took so long because every line was made with a tiny mapping pen and Indian ink: I cheated at the very end because as her birthday approached I had the entire middle section to finish – so the pine trees on the other side of the Doire Torrent (Dora di Ferret) were finished with a paint brush, something I now regret. Whymper's original had appeared, in 1871, in *Scrambles Amongst the Alps*.

About 15 years ago Anne and I located the exact spot in the Val Ferret – eager to see for ourselves the scene that Whymper had engraved. It's a remote site – but we shared an emotional hour looking in real life at a view we can admire every day in our own home. Two whitewashed stones from the stream at our feet today remind us constantly of that precious hour we shared in the Val Ferret. You, too, should seek out the majestic dead-end valley; drive through the Mont Blanc tunnel into Italy and, immediately you exit on the southern side, head north-east into the loveliest of mountain terrain.

The accompanying reproduction of the picture I drew all those years ago is about one-sixteenth of the actual size; much of the detail has of course been lost – but, hopefully, enough remains to encourage you to enjoy the splendid Val Ferret for yourselves. Try to find the exact spot on the stream's left bank (use the bridge); you'll notice the trees have grown!

CHAMONIX   Albert 1er

Very comfortable hotel
Gardens/Swimming pool/Tennis/Lift

The Albert 1er is the older of the two Carrier hotels in Chamonix. A longtime favourite of all my family – in winter and summer – it has been a great success with readers, too. Like us they have enjoyed its many benefits: a warm, comfortable chalet-hotel (bigger than the more intimate Bois Prin); cool gardens with many trees; a swimming pool and tennis court; lounges where you can sit in comfort – with an armchair view of Mont Blanc; and the chance to share in the numerous local attractions – including many engineering marvels created by man and those shaped by Mother Nature.

I expect most readers will want to taste the excitement of the most spectacular of European *téléférique* climbs: the ascent of the 3842-metre-high Aiguille du Midi. It's a thriller for sure – very expensive but a 'must' at least once in your lifetime. Less sensational are the climbs to Le Brévent and to L'Index; both the latter take you well over 2000 metres above sea-level. The train ride to the Mer de Glace is a quieter, more comfortable way of travelling; on arrival you are rewarded by a vast sea of ice snaking upwards to your right – the whole scene dominated by the fearsome teeth of the mighty Aiguille du Dru and the even higher Aiguille Verte towering above it.

For those of you who enjoy sporting activities, you can share in the numerous facilities of the superb Chamonix sports centre – just across the road from the hotel and the most modern of man-made structures. The centre has a huge indoor heated pool, an all-the-year-round ice rink and several tennis courts. The golf course to the north has now been extended to 18 holes: what could be nicer than a round amidst such wonderful mountains? Either they'll inspire you or ruin your game; but it's worth a try. Walks abound – ranging from the most undemanding possible to the most dangerous and severe mountain climbs in Europe.

Another man-made treasure that you most definitely must not miss is the church of Notre-Dame-de-Toute-Grâce at Assy (north of St-Gervais) – full of the works of Léger, Lurçat, Matisse, Chagall, Braque and others.

But I prefer to get away from the surroundings of Chamonix to see some of Nature's handiwork. A must is the easy drive to the summit of the Col des Montets; there you should walk the signposted path that displays the best of the small La Réserve des Aiguilles Rouges. The climb of the col is at its best in June when the rhododendrons are in bloom – but at anytime in the summer the reserve is a fascinating place; you'll be able to identify countless varieties of Alpine flowers and plants.

Continue onwards to the north, cross the Swiss border, and then, almost immediately, turn left towards Finhaut, driving higher and higher until you arrive at the massive Barrage d'Emosson. You reach a spot not far short of 7000 ft above sea-level; the reward is a spellbinding panorama of the entire Chaîne du Mont Blanc. In addition you may be lucky enough to see all the mightiest peaks of the Bernese Oberland and, within 200 metres of descending from the dam, the distant Matterhorn. There are few spots reached by car, if any, where you can revel in such a dazzling array of mountains.

But, as appealing as all the countryside is, you'll relish, too,

CHAINE DU MONT BLANC — from the Barrage d'Emosson

the cosseting material comforts of the Albert 1er. It was Marcel and Andrée Carrier's first Chamonix hotel; now it's in the capable hands of their younger son, Pierre, and his wife, Martine. Pierre's ambition has always been to be a great *cuisinier*; the Michelin star was lost when Marcel handed over the kitchen to his son (the normal Michelin procedure – though not always followed by the tyre men) but I guarantee it will not be long before he wins it back for himself.

Pierre is working enormously hard. On one hand he and his ten-man team have to prepare, twice a day, set meals for clients taking *pension* terms; what delights they are – costing little, any visitor can call in and enjoy them. I have copies of menus covering two weeks (28 meals) and no dish is duplicated; incidentally, all the summer vegetables and herbs are grown in the garden at Bois Prin. On the other hand, Pierre is also

developing a more complex à la carte list and he offers two marvellous 'gastronomic' menus. The 30-year-old chef is a talented *cuisine moderne* master; witness specialities like a courgette flower (from Bois Prin) with a stuffing of minced courgette, egg, basil and a light garlic cream; *foie gras chaud aux airelles à l'aigre-doux* – a clever blend of contrasting tastes; and a superb *filet mignon de veau au foie gras et au jus de truffe* – as good as you'll find anywhere. Desserts are superb.

The wine list is an excellent example of how both great wines and lesser-known ones can be brought together; there are many inexpensive bargains. Try the Savoie varieties.
category 3★ *menus* B-C *rooms* 32C-D *cards* AE DC V
closed Mid April-mid May. Last 3 wks Oct. Nov.
post 74400 Chamonix-Mont-Blanc, Haute-Savoie.
phone 50 53 05 09 *Mich* 244 *map* 93

FAVERGES   Gay Séjour

Simple hotel
Secluded/Terrace/Gardens/Good value (meals)

I would imagine it would be impossible for any visitor to the Gay Séjour to leave feeling unhappy; certainly the enticingly situated hotel has been a great favourite with all those readers who have made the effort to seek it out.

You'll find the Gay Séjour in the hills south of Lake Annecy — a few hundred metres from the road that climbs from Faverges, through emerald-green meadows and extensive, entrancing woods, to the Col de Tamié. It is literally off the beaten track — part of a tiny hamlet of farms and ringed by other equally untourist-like villages and farming communities. Until half a century ago the building was no more than a 17th-century Savoyarde farmhouse; today it's a comfortable, happy place with an interior that has changed materially. (Ask Bernard Gay to show you a watercolour painted all those years ago, shortly before the transformation took place.)

Despite the endless scenic attractions close at hand, nevertheless, it's the human factor that counts as much as anything else at Tertenoz. The family Gay is a remarkable one by any standards. Grandmother Jeanne, now 84, was the one who started the enterprise off five decades ago — one of many *les mères* who set the culinary standards in Savoie for others to follow today. She still helps in the kitchen but now it is her 33-year-old grandson, Bernard, who is the talented *cuisinier* — a chef who is increasingly gaining a fine local reputation; it came as no surprise at all to hear that this amazingly friendly, open-hearted young man won his Michelin 'R' accolade in 1985.

Much of your day-to-day contact will be with Bernard's mother, Andrée, who keeps the hotel spotless. Her husband, Armand, mucks in and does whatever jobs need doing. Bernard started his apprenticeship at the age of eight, working alongside his grandmother. (He can prove it: ask him to show you a treasured photograph.) It's nice to see his 11-year-old son, Pierre, already showing great interest in the kitchen!

Bernard does a splendid job in his modern, gleaming *cuisine*. The range of choice in both cost and quality is very wide. You can choose dishes from the basic menus which cost only a handful of francs, such as an *omelette Savoyarde*, *noisettes d'agneau poêlées* and home-made *pâtisseries*. The menu 'Gay Séjour' is marvellous value for the quality on offer. You could start with a *salade 'petit Pierre' à la truite fumée*, then choose either a fish *pâté* or from no less than six or so fish alternatives, followed by say an *entrecôte*, cheese and dessert.

It's amazing to see the range of fresh fish alternatives offered. Arriving overnight from Brittany they include *poissons* like *rouget*, *sole*, *saumon* and *lotte de mer*; they complement a range of local piscatorial delights from Lake Annecy — perch, *omble chevalier* and pike are just a few. There's an à la carte menu where Bernard can entice you with some Savoie specialities such as *gougère*, *jambon fumé des Aravis* or an *omelette aux truffes noires* with *morilles*, *cèpes* and *chanterelles* (depending on the season). Or he will produce modern-day personal creations like a *salade Landaise* (with *oie fumée*, *gésiers confits* and *foie gras*) or a *pot au feu des pêcheurs* — using whatever fresh fish has arrived from the ports. All in all he does a good job. (Alas, many of you complained about breakfasts; I pointed out your observations and I'm sure they will be heeded.)

Reference to *French Leave 3* or *Bon Voyage* will help you identify the wide range of Savoie wines and cheeses. Don't on any account miss the local Tamié cheese (made at the abbey up the road) or the world-renowned Reblochon (from the hills to the north). You can buy both from the Gays, together with most Savoie wines: you'll see them on display in the reception area – Gamay de Chautagne, Abymes, Crépy, Roussette de Savoie, Apremont and so on.

Don't fail to visit the Cistercian Abbey of Tamié. Better still, try to attend one of the many daily services – Vespers, which starts at 6.15 p.m., is ideal because it only lasts 30 minutes and ensures you get back to the hotel in time for dinner. The abbey is a deeply spiritual place and the inspiring singing will uplift the most depressed of spirits. (You can buy tapes of many of the monks' chants at the abbey shop. I recommend them strongly; they've given me great pleasure back home.)

If any of you stay on a Friday night be sure to leave time on the Saturday morning to share in the weekly village bread baking ritual; the wood-fired oven is adjacent to the hotel. It's a happy feature of most local villages.

If you don't stay at the Gay Séjour, do remember there are many alternatives in the immediate area listed in *FL3*; note, too, that all the suggestions made in the chapter called *Seductive Savoie* apply just as much to those alternative hotels.
category 2 *menus* **A-C** *rooms* 12**B-C** *cards* A AE DC V
closed 3rd wk Oct. Xmas-Jan. Sun evg & Mon (not school hols).
post Tertenoz, 74210 Faverges, Haute-Savoie. (SE of Annecy)
phone 50 44 52 52 *Mich* 244 *map* 94 Annecy 30 km.

SEDUCTIVE SAVOIE

'The more you run the risk of getting lost the more certain you are of seeing the real France.' I first coined that slogan six years ago and I've used it many times since; my 'mapoholic' readers will know exactly what I mean. But let me try to persuade those of you who turn your backs on maps to join the club; this chapter being representative of the sort of exploration I have in mind for members. Navigating is never difficult – providing you have a good, large-scale map available. And remember, the loveliest parts of any country are more often than not found up 'dead-end' roads – roads that, apparently, go nowhere!

I've chosen a ring of country encircling Lake Annecy to demonstrate, in some detail, just what I mean. Buy the right maps, study them carefully, use the minor roads – the narrower the better, get lost – often, and enjoy yourself. Forget the big towns, the tourist 'honeypots' and the choked-up main roads: instead have the countryside to yourself. And take along a good pair of walking shoes, some binoculars and a camera.

Here in the Lake Annecy area you'll need the Michelin yellow map 244 (1 cm. for 2 km.) or, better still, the IGN *série verte* map 53 (1 cm. for 1 km.); both maps cover the *départements* of Savoie and Haute-Savoie. Let's assume you are based at the Gay Séjour in Tertenoz, south of Faverges.

Start by seeing some of the neighbouring terrain – at its best in late May and June when scores of species of wild flowers blanket the pastures. The hills are heavily wooded and there are many streams cascading down from the summits.

Walk to the village of Les Combes – one kilometre or so to the south-east of Tertenoz. After the sharp bends immediately beyond Tertenoz, the fields on your left are a mass of colour in the late spring with dozens of different types of wild flowers. At Les Combes there's a wood carver who has won many national awards and who is only too pleased to show you his work; his is the house with the fine wooden balcony. I hope he's fully recovered from his recent illness.

Further south is the much more strenuous climb up La Belle Etoile. Drive to the summit of the Col de Tamié, turn left and, shortly, left again past La Ramaz and continue north until you reach an obvious place to park. It's a long, steep signposted climb to the 6000 ft summit.

A much different drive and walk is the one up the St-Ruph Valley. Use the road from Le Villaret, pass through Glaise and continue on when it loses its tarmac surface until you cross the stream – then park on the left. The walk up the valley is a delight; dense woods, the rushing St-Ruph torrent and the absence of other visitors make it a real treat.

A similar drive/walk, and not to be missed, is the ascent of the wooded Combe (valley) d'Ire. Drive north-west from Faverges to Doussard and then head due south. Park in the first 'parking' area – just before the 'Sauf Riverains' sign (access forbidden except for residents).

To see the best of Lake Annecy drive to St-Jorioz (the village where Peter Churchill and Odette Sansom were based in 1943); turn right at the traffic lights and park by the lakeside. Walk along the edge of the lake to Duingt. I took the picture on the front cover of *French Leave 3* at Duingt, just a few steps from the Château de Ruphy, facing north.

If you want to visit world-famous Talloires try a 'different' approach route. From Faverges climb the Col de la Forclaz – a

favourite 'hang out' for hang-gliders; continue north and be certain to detour to the Ermitage St-Germain, high above Talloires. The 11th-century Bénédictine Saint returned here after a pilgrimage to the Holy Land; earlier, he had founded the monastery at Talloires – now a luxury hotel, the Abbaye.

Faverges market is on Wednesday. A better version is the Saturday market at Thônes – a splendid town with arcaded shops. You'll hear cowbells clanging away in the pastures around the town – the cows munching away provide the milk for the superb Reblochon cheese (*reblocher* means 'to milk for the second time'). You'll also see many farm signs announcing *'Reblochon vente ici'*. At Thônes you have two options: the first is to return to Faverges via the Col de la Croix Fry, the Col des Aravis, the Gorges de l'Arondine (several waterfalls), Flumet and Ugine – thrilling roads I've driven over countless times.

The second option is to drive 3 km. north-west from Thônes to the roadside cemetery where many hundreds of the patriots who died in the tragic battle with 5,000 Germans and French Vichy *miliciens* on the Plateau des Glières are buried. There's a small museum alongside the cemetery and, acting as sentinels, are two cascades, appropriately bringing water down from the plateau. The SOE did as much as they could to assist the Savoie *maquisards* – led by Lieutenant Tom Morel. Peter Churchill, Odette and 'Arnaud' instigated the first parachute drops of equipment; later Colonel Heslop ('Xavier') of the SOE did as much as he could to help but the battle on the 26th March, 1944, high in the hills to the north, ended in a massacre. From Thorens-Glières climb south-east to the Col des Glières where there's a monument and maps which explain the battle.

Finally two drives which are absolute 'musts'. Both reward

you with superb views: but wait for clear days!

Head for St-Jorioz again and turn left at the lights — aim for St-Eustache and La Chapelle-St-Maurice. Ignore the Semnoz mountain lurking high above you at this stage. Instead, at the Col de Leschaux, head south into the mountain area called Les Bauges. Shortly before Lescheraines, turn north-west and keep to the right bank of the River Chéran. Continue north to Quintat and then make the steep western climb of the Semnoz on the D241. At its junction with the D41 continue climbing south until you reach the Crêt de Châtillon. It's a climb I always revel in; the dome of Mont Blanc seems so close you could almost touch it. Ensure you reach the Crêt in the afternoon when the sun is behind you. (This is where Peter Churchill parachuted down from a Halifax on April 15th, 1943.) Descend to the Col de Leschaux and retrace your route to St-Jorioz. Walks abound on this drive; make your own discoveries.

The second drive is to the east of Faverges. Leave Ugine, on the N212, to the north-east; immediately after the ghastly steel works turn right on to the road signposted Cohennoz and Col de la Forclaz. Soon turn left on the D71 towards Cohennoz; 4.2 km. (2.6 m.) later turn right, climbing a tarmac 'Route Forestière' (sign 'RF Gomberts'). This eventually brings you to a point high above Queige in the Doron Valley. Continue east, keep going left and eventually make the short climb to the Signal de Bissane — just short of 2000 metres above sea-level. The panoramic views are astounding. On my last but one visit, deep snow prevented me from reaching the Signal where I knew one of the best views of Mont Blanc awaited me; alas, I had to make do with the picture printed in *FL3* (opp. page 257), taken from a point well below the summit. Don't miss this trip.

FAVERGES-DE-LA-TOUR   Château de Faverges

Luxury hotel
Secluded/Gardens/Swimming pool/Tennis/Golf/Lift

During 1984 and 1985 I received half a dozen reports from readers suggesting that I visit this admirably situated hotel. So, after the sixth letter arrived, I did just that.

Over a period of 30 years I must have used the N75 scores of times — the link road from Grenoble to Bourg-en-Bresse. Near its junction with the N516 I unfailingly used to admire a handsome tower, part of an otherwise run-down, centuries-old château, high on a hill to the west. Today the property is no longer derelict; in 1979/80 it was restored by a talented couple of hoteliers and, since 1981, has become a luxury hotel.

Because the Château is so ideally situated — just off the A43 autoroute and at the door of the French Alps — and influenced by those many unsolicited letters, I paid it a call. I have no hesitation in including it among the favourites — for the additional reason that it gives readers a luxury alternative to the very simple establishments at St-Pierre-de-Chartreuse, Faverges and Artemare. Access to the Chartreuse, Vercors, Bugey and Savoie (see *Seductive Savoie*) is really very easy.

In extensive grounds, high on a hill and big enough to have a golf 'course' of nine short holes laid out within them, the hotel has a seductive appeal. Jo and Cathérine Tournier — they also own the Lana and Tournier hotels in Courchevel — must have vivid imaginations; ask them to show you the photographs of the place before they started renovation work. What a gamble it must have been to risk so much. I suggested they make a small display of the photographs in the reception area — readers will be fascinated by the changes. (Jo, by the way, is a Chamonix man — his family has lived in the valley for centuries.)

The most striking aspect of the building is the remarkable hall, double staircase and upper landing — where three sides are galleried. The hall and staircase appear to be made entirely of marble — but it's a *tromp-l'œil*, the plaster being superbly painted! Clever use has been made of the old cellars — they house the dining rooms. The tower base forms part of the restaurant and, above, two bedrooms have been fitted into the circular structure. Tennis, swimming, golf, terraces, gardens, extensive views: what else can be added to the 'features'?

As appealing as all those many benefits are, there's yet another good reason for heading Faverges way; the 30-year-old chef, Didier Roque, is an excellent *cuisinier*. Trained by the marvellous Guy Savoy in Paris — both of them are from nearby Bourgoin — he has a light, sure touch and a particular talent for cooking fish. A *nage de pétoncles aux celeris et poireaux* — with a smidgin of fennel and onion — is a treat; even better is a *lotte rôtie au basilic et ravioles de Royans* — the lightly 'roasted' fish complemented perfectly by the minuscule *ravioles* from the area of Royans, at the western door to the Vercors.

The staff are especially helpful and friendly — led by the hotel director, Bertrand Olive. Rooms in the annexe, once a farm, are less expensive. But if pennies count visit the hotel for a bargain lunch — served from Tuesday to Friday.
category **3** *menus* **B**(see text)-**C** *rooms* 41**D-D3** *cards* AE DC V
closed Mid Oct-end 1st wk May. Rest: Mon. (E of Lyon)
post Faverges-de-la-Tour, 38110 La-Tour-du-Pin, Isère.
phone 74 97 42 52 *Mich* 244 *map* 95 Lyon 65 km.

ST-PIERRE-DE-CHARTREUSE

**Chalet H.
du Cucheron**

*Very simple restaurant with rooms
Secluded/Terrace/Good value*

The people of Grenoble are the luckiest in all France. The modern, bustling city is the bull's-eye in a dartboard circle of mountain terrain; no matter where you aim your dart it's bound to score points for scenic attraction. My two favourite mountain areas are the Vercors to the west and the wonderful Chartreuse to the north – which scores 20 points. Despite its proximity to Grenoble the Chartreuse seems to retain, somehow, its mysterious secretiveness – most travellers speed by on the triangle of autoroutes that surround it.

When is the best time to see this seductive part of France? I've seen the *massif* at all times of the year but I think it's most captivating in the spring and autumn. In April and May the roaring streams are full of ice-cold water, the woods are awash with the first hints of green and the pastures are blanketed with wild flowers. In September the same meadows are carpeted with lilac-shaded autumn crocuses and, in October, your eyes feast on the rich shades of dying leaves – a palette of burnished golds, shimmering coppers and flaming reds.

Please don't put aside only one day for your exploration; allow several days so that you can then absorb all the Chartreuse's secrets. I detailed many of those in *Hidden France*; in this new book I'll list some more and remind you, again, of a few of the well-known attractions.

Within a twenty-minute drive of the Chalet is the world-famous Couvent de la Grande Chartreuse – a vast monastery lost in a wooded fold of mountains. No wonder Saint Bruno chose the isolated site over 900 years ago as the first home of the Carthusian Order. You cannot visit the Monastery itself – but La Correrie, at its southern entrance, is a museum which illustrates the way of life of the Carthusian monks in an informative way. Something different, and modern, is the Eglise of Saint Hugues, just south of St-Pierre. The church is a celebration of contemporary sacred art.

Your travels in the *massif* will take you up and down the two strangely-named streams called the Guiers Vif and the Guiers Mort; be sure to see them from their sources to the points where they leave the Chartreuse to the west. Just north of the Guiers Vif 'exit' visit the caves of St-Christophe – where, apart from the splendour of Mother Nature's underground sculptures, there have been some important archaeological finds made recently. In addition, the Voie Sarde and the Pont Romain add extra interest to the immediate neighbourhood.

Walkers are in their element. But serious walker or not, don't fail to climb the slopes of the Charmant Som. Drive your car from the Col de Porte in a north-westerly direction – to the point called 'Bergeries' (sheepfolds) on the map. Then climb as far as you can up the steep slopes – you'll be at a height of about 6000 ft above sea-level whether you reach the summit or not. (Botanists should natter to the lady owner of the sheepfolds – she's an expert on mountain plants.)

Keen drivers should try this new suggestion. Motor enthusiasts will already know the Col du Granier, Col du Cucheron and Col de Porte as famous rally stages; the Col du Coq is as demanding and equally rewarding. Head due south from St-Pierre and, after a dozen kilometres, you reach the

195

edge of the eastern escarpment of the *massif* with extensive views east across the Isère Valley (the road is unsurfaced near the summit). Continue north-east along a plateau to the top terminus of the St-Hilaire funicular. The cliffs fall sharply away to the Isère – no wonder it's a popular rendezvous for hang-gliders. The Château du Touvet is to the north, at Le Touvet.

There's so much to see and do – I have only given details of a few of the long list of possibilities. But there's another good reason for heading into the Chartreuse *massif*. Namely, the simple chalet home of André and Colette Mahaut who, in the dozen years since they returned from West Africa, have charmed many readers at the Col du Cucheron. A new member of the family is on hand to welcome you – a Great Dane called Vicka with a handsome, glowing 'blue' coat.

Enjoy the modest facilities and cooking; there's a terrace and a simple lounge. Menus include basic dishes like mountain ham, home-made terrines, *truites* – cooked in various ways, grills, tarts and sorbets. Be certain to order the local Savoie wines – particularly the Apremont white which comes from the vineyards beneath Mont Granier.

Finish your meal with a Chartreuse liqueur: these days the distillery at Voiron produces not just the green and yellow varieties but others, too, like *myrtille*, *framboise*, *génépi* (made from mountain plants) and a *liqueur du 9e centenaire* (made to celebrate the nine centuries since St-Bruno founded his monastery). The monks have been busy!

category **2(S)** *menus* **A-B** *rooms* 12**A-B** *cards* A AE V
closed Mid Oct-mid Dec(not weekends).Tues(not school hols).
post St-Pierre-de-Chartreuse, 38380 St-Laurent, Isère.
phone 76 88 62 06 *Mich* 244 *map* 96 Chambéry 36 km. to S

CHÂTEAU DU TOUVET

PLAISANCE   La Ripa Alta

Simple hotel
Good value

There was absolutely nothing special about Plaisance a few years ago. You could say with some certainty that it was a somewhat dead-beat town; even the locals wouldn't have quibbled too much about that description. Built 650 years ago as a *bastide* Plaisance's only claim to fame was that it lay on one of the many roads that led to St-Jacques-de-Compostelle. But today the town's pride in itself has changed out of all recognition – for a surprising reason.

It's a super story I have to tell you: a memorable record of determination and faith – one which has done wonders to bring together a dispirited community. The story starts eight years ago when two 22-year-old-friends – Daniel Birouste, an organ builder, and Bertrand Lazerme, an organist – conceived the idea to build an organ for the sadly neglected neo-Gothic Plaisance church. The 'madness' of the idea was the organ would be a huge instrument – big enough for a cathedral!

They considered that the construction of an organ – in a church on a pilgrimage route to Spain – would not be dissimilar to the building of a cathedral itself centuries ago: it would revive flagging community spirit and create opportunities for all sorts of local cultural and social activities. It would be a creative symbol for the entire community.

Initially, the two young men worked on the idea without any financial help – but very quickly they were lucky enough to gain the all-important agreement and support for their extravagant project from the town's mayor. Those were bleak days – but, today, a minor miracle has been worked. The church has been handsomely restored, stained glass windows repaired, the town's streets tidied up, and a cultural centre set up (its membership rose from 10 to over 300 in two years – the population is only 1,500 souls) with a new library and where exhibitions, theatre performances, recitals and music classes are held. The entire population has risen to the challenge – first to raise finance and then to see the project completed.

The superb organ should be finished by 1987. Built entirely locally – in a modest workshop which now employs seven people, all using the skills instilled in them by Daniel – it presented mind-boggling problems of construction and organisation. First let me give you the dimensions: the organ is 33 ft. high, 17 ft. wide and 17 ft. deep. There are no less than 3,135 pipes (Liverpool's Anglican Cathedral organ is reckoned the world's largest with over 9,000); the longest measures 18 ft. and the smallest just fractions of an inch! The instrument has four keyboards, a pedal section and 43 stops. As far as possible only local timber was used in the construction – mainly oak and pine though the keys were made of olive wood from northern Spain. The pipes were constructed from lead, tin and wood from the Pyrénées. The mechanical workings – which I saw being built during 1985 – are complicated and it certainly required an organised mind to assemble the instrument.

The organ has formed the base for a painting by the celebrated Daniel Ogier – in effect it's like a triptych, measuring almost 100 square metres. The instrument fills the top end of the nave – its setting adds regal splendour to the handsomely-restored church interior. In addition two new stained glass windows have been fitted opposite the organ. Daniel and Bertrand, both now 30, have seen their 'seed' grow into a mighty 'tree' – music has revitalised the social and cultural fabric of the community. The economic spin off is that the small factory now employs a number of local people – all engaged in the manufacture of different musical instruments.

So my readers – head for Plaisance and its remarkable organ. My modest contribution to the story is that in 1985 I suggested that cassette tapes be made so that visitors like you and me can see the organ and then hear its glorious sounds back home. If you are fortunate enough to hear the actual instrument being played then count your blessings. I hope the tapes will soon be ready and available for sale at La Ripa Alta – where my old pal, Maurice Coscuella, has a key to the church door which is just about 50 metres away from the hotel.

There's another good reason for seeking out Plaisance – to enjoy the cooking skills of English-speaking Maurice. He's the last person to be put out by the fact that I've put him second this time; not surprisingly he gave as much support as he could – in material terms, like food and drink – to the two young men. Readers who know Maurice will know already of his open-hearted generosity. What they may not realise is that, among Gascony's chefs, he has earned the reputation for being perhaps the most inventive *cuisinier* of them all by his talent for using local produce to create new specialities.

I have highlighted some of them in the past but two new ones I relished on my last visit were a *'misères' de canard aux baies roses* – sharp-tasting thin strips of duck meat, marinated in rosemary vinegar and cooked for only two minutes – and a *poêlée de cœurs de canard aux pleurotes* – the latter fresh as daisies and, accompanying the dish, no less than six excellent vegetables. A third dish was a big surprise – *écrevisses 'mousquetaire'*; small crayfish came served on a 'sword' – they had been cooked for just a minute or so in oil, garlic and salt and pepper. The surprise was that you could eat almost the entire crayfish – except for a small amount of the hardest shell. Use the napkin and the finger bowl; don't make the mistake of only eating the tail – scoff the lot, particularly the main body part! A dozen or so desserts and a selection of nearly 50 Armagnacs, dating from 1900, are the perfect end to any meal.

It's good to see Maurice has recovered from a bout of ill-health and also to be able to tell you that his daughter, Françoise, now helps her mother, Irène, to run the hotel. He appears, too, to be keeping his word processor very busy; each day the machine churns out an ever-changing number of menus – it's nice to report that the idea of using electronic aids for menu creation is spreading fast throughout France.

Don't miss the *donjon* at Bassoues – east of Plaisance and on the road to Auch (a caveat: it has over 200 steps); and navigate yourself to some of the many pilgrimage churches on the St-Jacques road – spot the numerous symbols on the Michelin map to the east of the town. One unmarked chapel – called the Chapelle du Ban – is a 12th-century empty shell surrounded by Armagnac vines and sitting in the shade of two ancient oak trees: you'll find it 400 metres east of Fromentas – itself about 4 cm. north-east of Plaisance on the map.

category **3** *menus* **A-C** *rooms* 14**A-C** *cards* A AE DC V
closed Last 3 wks Nov. Sun evg (out of season). Rest: Mon.
post 32160 Plaisance, Gers. (W of Auch)
phone 62 69 30 43 *Mich* 234 *map* 97 Auch 55 km.

POUDENAS   La Belle Gasconne

Comfortable restaurant with rooms
Terrace

I know of no other chef in France who has such an open-hearted love and intuitive sympathy for her *pays*: I can pay Marie-Claude Gracia no greater compliment. To spend a day, or better still two or three, in the neighbourhood of Poudenas is nothing less than sheer joy; it's in spots like this where the real heart of France beats most strongly and also it's where the interlocking friendships and business relationships that flourish in local communities can best be seen and felt. In Marie-Claude's case I should add the word 'tasted', too.

She's a remarkable woman by any standards. Now 50, she and her loyal husband, Richard, have made a success of their gamble, taken eight years ago, to open their own restaurant, off the beaten track in a hidden corner of Gascony. When you talk to Marie-Claude you can never doubt the certainty of that gamble: her strong brown eyes give the all-important clues — determination and character shine forth brightly. She's a quietly spoken, hardworking *cuisinière* with the most delicate sensitivity for the produce from the surrounding hills.

Why does she have such depths of understanding and passion for her *métier*? That's easy to ascertain: Marie-Claude is the fifth generation of an unbroken line of *cuisinières* who have earned their living from cooking — either in private homes or on their own account. Her great, great grandmother started the chain off in nearby Durance — about 14 km. north of Poudenas. Marie-Claude's culinary training took her to some famous chefs' homes: to Sassenage where she worked for Jo Rostang (his son, Michel, has his own Paris restaurant), and to Les Baux where she spent years with Raymond Thuilier.

What's so nice is that while Marie-Claude has developed and polished her culinary skills year by year she has still managed successfully to bring up five children. Jean-Claude, the eldest, works as the *sommelier* and waiter in the family restaurant; he did much of his training in England at places including Le Gavroche in London; consequently he speaks very good English. His father, Richard, also has a good command of English. So has their second son, Jean-Antoine, who cooks alongside his mother in the tiny kitchen; he worked for a spell in New York and is married to an American girl. So family traditions will continue and I have no doubt that those generations of 'know-how' are instilled in the children, too.

It's fair to say that just about everything Marie-Claude serves comes from one of several smallholdings within a ten-minute drive. I had the good fortune to visit two of them. First, near Mézin, I met the all-important supplier of ducks and the superb duck and goose livers that Marie-Claude uses with such rare skill. Dina Cescatti and her son, Alain, showed me their simple farm with great pride. They explained the three-week cycle during which the birds' livers are fattened with maize and goose fat; twice a day the maize is boiled for just seven minutes so that it expands — mixed with goose fat, which makes it easily digestible, the 'feed' is still warm when the birds are fed. The two different breeds are kept apart, kept quiet and are only fed and handled by the same family members.

It was interesting to ask what the ideal weight of the perfect liver is: 800 or 900 grams was the answer — never one kilogram.

Apparently at that weight they are too heavy and too fatty. Marie-Claude is reckoned to be the 'champion' chef in France for home-made goose and duck *foie gras*. Inherited genes of touch, sense and instinct tell her which liver to put aside, which liver to use. Her preparation of the livers, let alone the accurate choice, is clearly bettered by no other chef – as she has proved. To the family's delight Marie-Claude won a prestigious 'tasting' set up by Gault Millau – knocking into a top hat all the famous chefs' versions of *foie gras*, including Chapel and Senderens. She came top in both categories!

The second family I met supply the restaurant with *chèvre* cheeses. The Chaves family, Spaniards, work prodigiously hard to earn their living: the parents, and their six young sons, live in nearby Sos and keep their herd of 50 goats in the hills overlooking the village. The *frais* variety of cheese, no more than two days old, is used in the magnificent *fromageon de chèvre à l'Armagnac* which Marie-Claude serves; laced with sugar and Armagnac, it's a *fromage blanc* presentation *par excellence*. The driest variety of cheese that the Chaves make is a four-week old *sec*, covered in fine pepper; it's remarkable. That excellence is not surprising as everything is done by hand – including the twice-a-day milking of the goats and all the churning, turning and handling of the cheeses. The family are the salt of the earth; poor, happy and so generous in spirit and in the welcome they give visitors to their humble home.

But there are other *fournisseurs* who supply the rest of the restaurant's needs: Monsieur Lanic, from Lannes (south-east of Mézin), brings them courgettes, tomatoes, strawberries and *'le vrai lait de vaches'* (Marie-Claude's words); bread from Monsieur Manabéra at Mézin and a super *raisins*, *amandes* and

miel loaf baked by a Belgian, Yann Demaître – both use wood-fired ovens; eggs, poultry – including turkeys and *pintades* – and *asperges* come from a friend of Marie-Claude's near Poudenas, Simone Laverny; chickens are reared by Madame Imbert in Poudenas itself; green salad varieties, pears and apples are supplied by Claire Dutertre near Sos; and all the permutations of red fruits, peaches and *groseilles* are cultivated by Monsieur Garrabos at Feugarolles in the Garonne Valley. The list is endless; it's nearly always the local community who supply the restaurant direct.

You, the lucky visitor – willing to seek out a delightful corner of Gascony, on the edge of rolling pastoral countryside that lies to the east and the great pine forests of the Landes to the west – benefit from all this labour in the simple dining room. It may be the tiniest of red tomatoes, served on the branch as an appetiser, or the incomparable duck and goose livers – with smooth, pinky-orange, shining textures, a *civet de canard* – the sauce of Buzet red wine is almost black in colour, the home-made *fromageon* with Armagnac, or a range of desserts – including pear sorbet, a tart made from the legendary Agen prunes and perhaps an extremely tasty *confiture* of green tomatoes and rings of orange peel. I must put a stop to all this tormenting: just go, don't rush, explore the nearby lanes and then relish the happy restaurant and the even happier family.

Before your meal spend a half hour sipping an *apéritif* on the 'terrace': why not a local *floc* (Armagnac and grape juice) which, surprise, surprise, is made by the owners of the château high above Poudenas? The tiny Gélise flows by, over a small weir and through a shady tunnel of trees. By the time you read this you should be able to share in the best news of all: the old *moulin*, alongside the bridge and stream, should be renovated and refitted out by now; so you can book one of the six modern bedrooms. What work — and borrowings — have gone into finishing it off.

Don't stay just one night. Allow time for the nearby architectural gems: the circular *bastide* at Fourcès which I've written about so often — eight km. to the south; the perched *bastide* of Montréal and nearby Séviac — both south of Fourcès; the remarkable two tennis-court sized fortified village of Larressingle — east of Montréal and restored by the Armagnac family. Head north from Poudenas to an unknown treasure at Durance; ask Richard to organise a visit to the ancient priory with its interior murals. Walk the tiny streets of Poudenas; climb the hill to the château and the village church with their backdrop of superb trees. (Don't forget, too, the Gracia's 'shop' where you can buy many of their culinary delights.)

What is especially pleasing is to see the tiny hamlet of Poudenas being improved and restored step by step. This is true of so many country villages which, over the last century, have fallen into disrepair. Head your car up the lanes and seek out the bigger ones — all with a square and shady arcades; the latter are such a pleasant feature of Gascony villages. And the countryside, too, is so alluring — during all seasons.

If by any chance the mill is not complete, then use the 'base' at Agen (Dordogne) — a 45-minute drive to the north-east; or the hotels at Barbotan (see *French Leave 3* for details).
category **3** *menus* **B-C** *rooms* See text *cards* AE DC V
closed 1st half Dec. Sun evg. Mon (not July & Aug).
post Poudenas, 47170 Mézin, Lot-et-Gar. (SW of Agen)
phone 53 65 71 58 *Mich* 234 *map* 98 Agen 47 km.

POUDENAS

BLISS IN BEARN
Selwyn Powell

"What made you come here?" they all ask, Binns included. "And do you like it?" It was, quite clearly, our Guardian Angel who chose the place, and we like it for lots of reasons. Because of the people, the climate, the scenery, the 'browsing and sluicing' as Wodehouse called it. "But in the North . . ." "Oh, they are French; we are Béarnais. Not at all the same thing."

Henri IV (the only good French king. Or, perhaps, not good, but best-loved) thought Paris was worth a Mass when they offered him the Kingdom of France on condition that he became a Roman Catholic. That was, in addition to the King of Navarre. He was born in the Château de Pau which is now a pantheon to his memory. Round here they wonder if he chose right. They are not really fond of 'Paris', meaning the seat of government. They enjoy it as a place to visit, an hour and a quarter away by plane.

So let us examine our reasons for liking it here in this part of non-France. First, the people. At all levels, from the humblest to the grandest, they are kind and friendly and helpful. The day we arrived it was pelting and after Pickfords had unloaded one of their pantechnicons it was parked in a muddy field. It sank up to the axles. "My employers won't be pleased when I go back by train without it," said the disconsolate driver. A couple of hours later a small man in streaming oilskins came up to me. "I've put it back on the hard road," he said. "But how, and how did you know?" "I have the only four-wheel-drive tractor in the district. I farm three kilometres up the road. I heard you were in trouble." He wouldn't take any reward or payment. (About how he knew: they know *everything*!) "I'm your neighbour and you were in trouble." It is true: a neighbour will always help.

Even in the middle of a fearful family feud, your cousin with whom you are daggers drawn will drive your wife ten miles to town to visit you in hospital. Once, when an English family was away at fruit-picking time, they came back to find their trees stripped, and on the kitchen table was a bowl of ten franc notes. The fruit had been taken to market for them without a word.

Now, after ten years, we know dozens of people over a largish area. They are all utterly charming and very hospitable. Of course there is one exception. "Oh, him," they say. "He is *un espèce de salaud*! Don't go near him."

Aquitaine was English for 300 years and the French fought like tigers to get it back, and then in the 19th century the English conquered it, or part of it, again. You will notice in Biarritz the Avenues Reine Victoria and Edouard VII; in Pau there is the Pau Golf Club, founded in 1856 and still a fine example of clubs established by the British all over the world. To this day they possess the gold medal presented by the Duke of Hamilton in 1857; while at the Cercle Anglais (originally the English Club) the chimney-piece in the salon is adorned by a bust of 'Granny Queen', and there are photographs of her descendants Queen Elizabeth and the Duke of Edinburgh, and of the present Prince of Wales and his wife whom they insist on calling 'Lady Dee'. My wife and I may be the only English members now; but at the monthly dinners the silver and table linen are monogrammed EC and menu cards and invitations are printed on the original stationery.

The climate of Pau was described by an English (or was he Scottish) doctor, Sir Alexander Taylor, when he settled there after the Carlist wars in 1836. He considered this the mildest place in Europe and the most beneficial for invalids. We are not invalids, but we, too, enjoy the mild, short winters, and summers that are not too blazingly hot. The countryside is always green and there is hardly any frost or snow. Occasionally there are little slips: the spring of 1985 with intense frosts over a long period ('the coldest for 101 years') and the fearful drought of the same year's summer; an unprecedented tempest in 1976, blowing down thousands of trees and stripping nearly every roof, but these really are exceptions. Usually we are able to drink our Christmas or New Year's Day *apéritifs* in the sunshine in the garden; in the summer we live in the blissfully midge-less out-of-doors.

From our house you can see the Pyrénées like a frieze along the skyline and, as we drive into Pau, they rise dramatically in front of us. There are peaks of up to 10,000 feet or so and the Spanish frontier is only an hour and a half away. They rise sharply on the French side, then fall gently away for a hundred miles to the south. By October the first snows have fallen up there, soon most of the passes will be closed and then the skiing starts. The other day we had an autumn picnic facing this lovely panorama, a mile or two beyond the frontier, each high peak topped with white. It was quite superb, and, as always, we feel 'abroad'. Here, in France, we are at home. In spring and early summer there are wild-flowers that even Alpine enthusiasts have to admit are 'just as good'. Wherever you look, the slopes are splashed in almost vulgar profusion.

As well as mountains, we have the sea. A gleaming white beach stretches the 250 kilometres from the Gironde to Spain, washed by the least polluted sea, and waves that provide the best surfing in Europe, while the beaches, like the mountain slopes, are almost vulgar with a multicoloured profusion of umbrellas and bikinis and stunning bathing beauties.

About the food and drink: I should refer you to Binns, but there is a lot to be said for living within 30 kilometres of one of the world's best restaurants, while our reward for going to church on Sunday at St-Andrew's, Pau, is to be able to stop at one of the roadside stalls on the way home and buy a couple of dozen *fines claires de Marennes* for a fraction of what oysters cost in some other parts of the world.

It is only when you cross the Channel with your car that you remember how narrow and winding and traffic-filled the English main roads are. Here you can drive almost alone on straight country roads, with only the cowslips and the orchids and the enticing scent of cider-apples to distract you. You can wander for days through Les Landes or the Gers, looking at little fortified villages, many of them built by the English 600 years ago, among woods that are growing the oak for wine-casks, and vineyards and châteaux whose names are magic on the labels of bottles far too expensive to drink.

Our *jardin anglais*, made with much toil and almost unaided, though hardly *anglais* at all, is immensely admired by all our French friends. Gardening on this rock-like clay and in this climate make a nonsense of most of what you knew before, but it is very rewarding. There is never a week in the year when some shrub is not in flower. We had a list of over a hundred flowers in a bowl at Christmas. Seasons are utterly different: snowdrops in December, iris stylosa in October.

All in all this is a wonderful place to live, and we haven't had a moment's regret in ten years at that fateful decision made by our Guardian Angel.

SEGOS   Domaine de Bassibé

Very comfortable hotel
Secluded/Terrace/Gardens/Swimming pool

Tony Lord, writing in *Decanter* about Gascony and its incomparable Armagnac, reminded his readers that 'there's even a local joke that the crows fly over the region upside down so they can't see how poor the area is below.' Joke or not, it's an effective way of explaining the dilemma Jean Pierre and Mayi Capelle face at their idyllic Domaine de Bassibé. If their past survival had depended on business from the local population they would have been dead and buried years ago. The season is desperately short and financial success depends completely on visitors arriving from other parts of France and overseas; during the winter months the couple shut up shop totally.

But that doesn't mean that hard work is given a rest during the winter. Not on your life! Jean Pierre heads off to places like Britain and Spain where he annually faces the challenging task of helping to establish restaurants that need the rejuvenating talents of a capable Michelin one-star chef. He's fluent in English and this is a vital aid in assisting him to train others and to demonstrate his culinary talents to kitchen staffs in differing countries. For example, during the last two winters he was a tremendous hit in Britain: first at the White Hart in Sonning two years ago and then at the Old Ship in Brighton last year. The same pattern will continue in years to come.

You can therefore deduce very quickly that life is not easy for Jean Pierre and Mayi. I wish more readers — from both sides of the Atlantic - would head south for this quite unspoilt corner of France. Gascony is a treat: gently curving hills and numerous river valleys; emerald-green pastures and fields of maize and vines; some of the finest woodlands in France; and an amazingly friendly and independent people. The Domaine, once a farm before becoming a small, intimate hotel, is a seductive retreat: secluded but not hard to find; extensive, attractive views to the east from its wooded grounds; a sun-trap pool and terrace; nine bedrooms fitted out with rare taste by Mayi — light, airy and colourful rooms; and, close at hand, many attractions — both man-made and those fashioned by Nature — to suit any visitor to France.

In addition to all these pleasures you have the bonus of a talented chef on hand — able to use the bountiful harvests of the legendary Gascony larder and, what is more, to capitalise on the relative nearness of the great port of La Rochelle for his fresh fish and shellfish specialities. What makes it all particularly pleasing is that, whilst the hotel and restaurant offers every comfort, the prices are not exorbitantly high.

Readers seem to share my enthusiasm for the Domaine; reports regularly confirm that nothing appears to be too much trouble for the Capelles. Many of you have appreciated Jean Pierre's light, *faites simple* cooking — where specialities demonstrate common sense and the best of modern thinking; things taste of what they are and are never unnecessarily complicated. He uses no flour, likes wine for flavouring and prefers stocks based on the meat the sauce is accompanying.

Before I describe some of those dishes it would interest you to know that Jean Pierre is a self-taught cook. Originally he trained as a lawyer in Pau but then joined his father to become a farmer. In 1975, at the age of 32, he and Mayi bought the

Domaine — already established as a hotel. (Mayi's parents were hoteliers; when she became a farmer's wife she had reckoned to have given up hotelkeeping for good!) Jean Pierre had always been a keen cook and, during the first two years, spent much of his time in the kitchens helping the couple's 'employed' *cuisinier*. In 1977 their chef fell ill, Jean Pierre stepped into his shoes and has never looked back. By 1982 he had won a Michelin star — a vivid example of natural talent.

You'll not fail to enjoy any of the many specialities Jean Pierre invents from year to year. In the past they've included his own version of either *saumon grillé* or *truite saumonée grillée* — where in both cases the skin is 'toasted' and the fish is accompanied by a light *beurre de tomates* and *oignons confits*; or a *soupe en croûte aux cèpes* — what an aroma rises from the *consommé* when you break the pastry crust (the piping hot soup contains a more than liberal measure of red wine incidentally); or a clever dish using a relatively inexpensive fish, a *râble de colin rôti en crépinette aux échalotes et au bacon* — the mixture of tastes works wonderfully well; *foie gras frais de canard* — few chefs' versions better the Capelle home-made duck liver; or fillets of sole in a leek sauce — a successful marriage but not apparently with other fish, like turbot, which Jean Pierre has tried.

Jean Pierre has given a tremendous amount of help to students from the Bournemouth College and from elsewhere in Britain. On my last visit no less than five students — three girls and two boys — were working in the restaurant and kitchen. I was fortunate enough to be a 'fly on the wall' in the kitchen for two to three hours during that visit — watching a team of six preparing the orders as they came in from the restaurant. It did my heart good to see how well the British youngsters worked alongside their French chums; all of them were a long way from home but all of them were doing a splendid job.

There's a great deal to see and do locally. To the west are the vast pine forests of the Landes — and, within a two-hour drive, are the long, sandy beaches of the Atlantic coast. With the new A64 autoroute open part of the way from Biarritz to Pau, it's a relatively easy run to the famous resort — a fine idea for a day out by the sea. Nearer at hand are many Gascony villages — some of them *bastides*. Refer to the entries for Poudenas and Plaisance — but also read the additional information set out in *France à la carte* and *Hidden France*. To the south, beyond Pau, are the mighty Pyrénées — studded with some of Nature's finest gems.

If any reader has yet to acquaint themselves with the heady charms of Armagnac, then make the Domaine the place to start. Armagnac ('blazing water' or 'fire water') dates back over five centuries — in fact it's older than Cognac. As long ago as 1462 it could be obtained in the markets of the Chalosse, the area to the immediate north-west of Segos. Any aged Armagnac is a velvety-smooth brandy with a long-lasting aroma which a glass retains well after it's empty. Younger varieties can often come as quite a surprise to Cognac drinkers — these Armagnacs are far more robust and seem to have the dry, earthy taste of the Gascony countryside. Treat yourself to a different variety of Armagnac after each Capelle meal.

category 3 *menus* **C** *rooms* 9**D** *cards* A AE DC V
closed Dec-Easter.
post Segos, 32400 Riscle, Gers. (N of Pau)
phone 62 09 46 71 *Mich* 234 *map* 99 Pau 40 km.

THE CHUNNEL

I wrote these words on January 21, 1986 – the day after Margaret Thatcher and François Mitterrand met at Lille in northern France to announce their 'joint' decision on which of four alternative consortia had been chosen to build the Channel link. Months later, my views remain unchanged.

In my opinion, by agreeing to build the French preferred choice – a rail only link – the British Government capitulated. We will end the second millenium in the same way we started it – by caving in to our neighbours across the Channel. During the days following the signing of the agreement, Margaret Thatcher emphasised that it would be private finance, not taxpayers' money, that would be used to construct the link – yet governments made the decision: the users' preference was completely ignored. The two leaders have suggested a road tunnel should be built in 15 years time.

The road tunnel will never be built: the right time to have constructed it is now. Why am I so sure of this and why will the rail only link become a one-way only benefit for both S.N.C.F. and the economic well-being of France?

Ninety per cent or more of the present-day traffic crossing the Channel is British – whether they be tourists or freight being exported or, worse still, imported from Europe. The joint Government decision should have taken account of that massive British dominance – and the people of Britain, and most MPs, wanted a road tunnel. The French consider their rail system (particularly the TGV) as a national asset and plough heavy subsidies into it; the chemin de fer line with Britain is the cream on top of the S.N.C.F. cake – northern France will become the hub of the European railway network. Any industrialist – European, American or Japanese – wanting to pick a site for a new factory will choose northern France for various reasons: the perfect distribution network is on hand – both rail and road (the French have started already to improve the latter), cheap power, a large unemployed work force and generous Government subsidies among them.

The consortium who will build the link reckon that Channel traffic will double in the next decade: I fail to see how. Will it be exports? Maybe. Imports then? It could be, with our manufacturing industry in disarray. Tourists perhaps?

Therein lies the core of the problem. By the start of the next millenium Britain's oil reserves will be rapidly running dry – and our currently strong rate of exchange will have weakened. Only our high interest rates protected the rate from further collapse during 1986 as oil prices fell. In the year 2004, the 100th anniversary of the signing of the entente cordiale, fewer Britons will be crossing the Channel – a lower sterling exchange rate will see to that. The rail link may take some traffic from the airlines – how just that will be after years of elevated prices; but the huge new ferries, soon to be in service, and the hovercraft – my favourite – will not go down without a fight.

I'm convinced that by the end of the century the builders of the rail tunnel will have a 'white elephant' on their hands; no-one will want to construct a road link. Traffic is not going to double – and within 15 years will have started to fall. Will the French and other Europeans start coming to Britain? Perhaps. For them prices here will be lower; the French turn white when I tell them of hotel costs in Britain today. I'm not convinced the French will come – other than in large numbers, by ferry, to use the hypermarkets yet to be built on the Kent coast. Remember the days of eight francs to the pound?

During the last two years I've talked to dozens of French people about the link, the British, Britain and the *entente cordiale*. I've been amazed by their apathy; so few ever come to Britain and so many of them have grossly cock-eyed views about us, our cooking and our islands. (Explore any provincial French bookshop – you'll see precious few books on Britain.) As for the tunnel they couldn't care less – only the French Government can see the massive economic benefits of northern France becoming the crossroads of Europe.

That leads me to my final sad reflection about the 'EC' business: 'English Channel' or *'entente cordiale'* – choose either. The latter is in a poor state of health because the French do so little to improve it here in Britain – the onus always seems to be on us to work at polishing it up in France! I've done my bit this decade to improve the *entente* but I see no reason for not being totally realistic about its current state of health. To have given the go-ahead for a rail only link now was a deplorable action on the part of the present Government. I, for one, don't expect to see a road tunnel constructed in my lifetime.

Chastellux – see *Maquis Bernard* map

STING IN THE TAIL

Since the publication of *French Leave 3* there has been a sad change at the top of the French culinary tree. Put bluntly, all but a handful of Michelin three-star restaurants have become, for their owners, the culinary equivalents of fruit machine palaces where, when three rosettes come up together, they greedily collect the jackpot that gushes forth. Frankly I've not been surprised in the least to receive so many critical letters about most of the three-star restaurants. 'Selling the soul' has become a way of life now for many great chefs.

A simple story will set the scene for the points I want to make. A Frenchman I met during the spring of 1986 laughingly recounted a visit he had made with a woman companion to one of the three-star temples in Paris. Apparently he was the only French client in the packed dining rooms – the rest a collection of Americans, Japanese, Arabs and Germans. The joke, as he saw it, was that even his Dutch girl friend was a foreigner: it seems entirely appropriate for this final, stinging 'tale' that she was also a call-girl!

Many three-star restaurants have become nauseating, gold-smelting factories for their owners – 'production lines' fuelled by large bands of rich Americans, Arabs, Japanese and Germans; fuelled, too, by the Everest-sized egos of the Jet Set – both men and women who, having invariably amassed their colossal fortunes through the sweat of others, want no more than to be seen and to show off; and fuelled in the 80s by Americans only too eager to return home with the same boring message, repeated at endless cocktail parties, that they, too, ate at Bocuse, Vergé, Chapel, Outhier *et al*.

But that's only the beginning of the swindle. Not content with packing clients into their sardine tin restaurants (one member of the culinary élite is proud of the fact that in the high season he stuffs well over 200 clients into his dining room each day and another seems not to mind one iota that his cheese trolley never gets within 12 feet of some clients' tables), a small band of top chefs waste no opportunity to screw every franc, dollar, yen, mark and pound out of their three-star fame. Their motto has become 'Everything and anything is for sale'.

The system works like this. First find a marauding, high-flyer press agent – because, with his or her help, the opportunities to go gold-digging around the planet are endless: TV, radio and press interviews; franchise operations where the famous culinary names are sure-fire drawing cards; as consultants to the luxury hotel restaurants of this world – only too eager to forge a link with the cooking gods; special banquets for conglomerates or shatteringly expensive weddings where 'Dad' is only too keen to liquidate his fortune for the sake of family pride (the Dynasty/Dallas factor); demonstrations anywhere – even ocean liners will do; opening any sort of new business or even kicking off at a soccer match – as long as enough francs are paid for the effort involved; books, clothes, culinary produce, wines, fast food . . .

It's the world of big, big business. It only works because these entrepreneural cooks pay huge sums to capable chefs to work for them – to 'guard' the reputation of their masters when they are away from their kitchens, which is often, believe me. What other artist or entertainer – and that's what a chef is – can employ stand-ins or locums to 'perform' for them whilst they jet around the world amassing fortunes?

In France the pop-star chefs are household names; their faces appear with monotonous regularity in magazines, papers and on TV. One face, Bocuse, must make an appearance in the media every week: each time I open a magazine in France I seem to see his face – or even his 'body'! One reader actually 'saw' Bocuse in his restaurant – sitting with clients during the entire meal. She said of her awful meal: 'no one could accuse him of being in the kitchen doing the *cooking*'.

The word 'disappointment' is the one that appears most regularly in your letters – but that's only a charitable way of saying how frustrated readers have become with packed dining rooms, irritated by the lack of attention to detail or by the sheer ordinariness of ludicrously expensive no-choice, fixed-price menus and, above all, by the sheer resentment they feel when treated as no more than jangling foreign coins helping to keep the cash registers tinkling away. The restaurants of the almighty have become pretentious vacuums of idotic snobbery. No wonder their staffs have become so contemptuous of their clients.

These days the best culinary talent is to be found elsewhere in France – at restaurants where chefs are to be found grafting away in their kitchens. The French themselves mock the present-day three-star system and, with few exceptions, they turn their backs on the great chefs. I, for one, now intend to do the same. Within these pages only three three-star chefs can be counted as readers' favourites: Boyer, Meneau and Pic.

In 1986 many Americans turned their backs on Europe. The only positive outcome of this insular attitude was that the cash registers didn't tinkle quite so merrily at the three-star shrines. Thank heavens for that!

ST-GERMAIN-
DE-LIVET

RG